EFFECTIVE MANAGEMENT
and the
BEHAVIORAL SCIENCES

EFFECTIVE MANAGEMENT
and the
BEHAVIORAL SCIENCES

Conversations from
ORGANIZATIONAL DYNAMICS
Edited by
WILLIAM DOWLING

A DIVISION OF AMERICAN MANAGEMENT ASSOCIATIONS

Library of Congress Cataloging in Publication Data

Main entry under title:

Effective management and the behavioral sciences.

1. Organizational behavior. 2. Sociologists--
United States--Interviews. 3. Social scientists--
United States--Interviews. I. Dowling, William F.
II. Organizational dynamics.
HD58.7.E36 1978   658.4   78-6695
ISBN 0-8144-5472-0

First Printing

Contents

Introduction to

CONVERSATIONS

As the title suggests, the conversations recorded in this book were with behavioral scientists concerned with behavior in organizations. What makes their contributions significant? What constitutes the credentials for admission to this particular hall of fame?

All twelve men met three criteria. First, their work was intrinsically first class. What they thought and what they wrote was, and remains, a contribution; they originated, not regurgitated. Second, they have all achieved a wide measure of recognition both among their peers and among the book-reading segment of management. Third, there is both pleasure and profit in reading them, whether for the logical precision of their exposition, the breadth and depth of their thought, the elegant simplicity of their language, or the flashes of eloquence or passion that illuminate their presentations. In every one there's the sense of satisfaction derived from being exposed to a first-class mind at work, or perhaps—because thinking is the most exquisite of pleasures—a first-class mind at play.

Alfred North Whitehead once wrote that the justification of a university was "to serve as a connection between knowledge and the zest of life." The thinkers we have chosen personify the bridge between knowledge and the zest for life that Whitehead wrote about. Collectively, their writings display four qualities raised to the highest power: erudition, sophistication, generalization, and conviction—a formidable contribution!

Who are they? What disciplines do they represent?

All twelve have taught at universities. Six of them were formally trained as psychologists, two have degrees in sociology, and a third, George Homans, although he never received a degree in sociology, has taught it for 40 years. Two are economists, although the interests and writings of the first, Kenneth Boulding, transcend the customary boundaries of his specialty, while the second, Peter Drucker, prefers to call himself a journalist. The last, the late Fritz Roethlisberger, was originally trained as an engineer. By his own admission, he floundered for a while studying philosophy and then spent the remaining 40 years of his active life as a practicing sociologist and teacher at the Harvard Business School.

Six taught at Harvard, and a seventh, William F. Whyte, did his graduate work there. Whether this skewness reflects Harvard's preeminence or the bias of the Harvard graduate who did the selecting is left to our readers to decide. Bias or no bias, we are content with our choices. The list might be enlarged somewhat, without diluting its quality, to make room, for example, for Margaret Mead or Herbert Simon, but it's difficult to imagine a list of similar size, selected on similar grounds, that would not include the names we chose.

Now for a question of more consequence than professional discipline or academic affiliations: What, if anything, do their ideas have in common? Presumably, if this galaxy of behavioral scientists has arrived at a consensus on any particular issue or area of common interest, then we could conclude that this represents a consensus among behavioral scientists in general. Behavioral scientists, like the rank-and-file members of most professional groups, are a deferential and imitative lot. In their intellectual commitments they prefer to play it safe and follow the leaders, when and if the leaders are in agreement. The attempt to determine the extent to which a degree of consensus exists among our twelve behavioral scientists will take most of the remaining introduction. Let's start with their basic views on human nature.

What kind of a creature is man?—and we're obviously talking about mankind in general including women. What does he ask out of life? More specifically, what satisfactions does he seek from his work?

We're beginning our search for a consensus here for two reasons: First, we are talking about people who have thought deeply about human behavior in organizations. Inevitably, they have all had to touch bedrock and ask themselves about the basic nature of man, although some have done it more explicitly and in much more detail than others. The psychologists, as we might expect, have concerned themselves much more with the basic nature of man than the economists and the sociologists. Second, and for our analysis more important, the view they hold about what moves and motivates men strongly influences the views they hold about other key issues in organizational behavior, such as the nature of change, the decision-making process, leadership styles, the organization as a system, the right organization design, and so on. Once we know how a behavioral scientist defines human nature, it should be possible to deduce from this definition, with a certain measure of precision, the stances he will assume in other areas of organizational behavior. His views on human motivation are the cornerstone, intellectually speaking, the necessary point of departure, for the remaining propositions that he espouses about human behavior in organizations. Logically, they should complement his views on motivation and be consistent with them.

Because of a persistent gap between logic and reality, we expect to find some inconsistencies. However, because our behavioral scientists are all renowned theorists, we should also expect to see them build bridges between the components in their thinking and to rationalize or explain any apparent inconsistencies.

Human Nature and Motivation

The great divide is between those who take a monolithic view of human nature and those who hew to a pluralistic position. The former group holds that all human beings are fundamentally alike, that they share a common set of needs and satisfactions. Moreover, human needs are seen as immutable—no amount of coercion or persuasion can alter them. The latter group, by contrast, is impressed with the variety of human needs and satisfactions. To quote the old adage, "one man's meat is another man's poison." To change a man's needs and preferences, once set, is not easy, but neither is it hopeless. Given plenty of time, generous doses of persuasion, and appropriate rewards for changed behavior, an individual can learn new attitudes and acquire new values.

The Monolithic View of Human Nature

These two central positions, of course, are sufficiently encompassing to accommodate differentiations—some subtle, others broad. The advocates of a monolithic position among our behavioral scientists—Herzberg, Likert, Argyris, Skinner, Homans, and Whyte—can be divided further into two quite distinct and intellectually opposing camps. The first, in which we would place Fred Herzberg, Rensis Likert, and Chris Argyris, asserts that man is a creature fixated on achievement and self-

3

actualization, goals that span his private and his work life. The second school (to use Homans's term, the "ultimate psychological reductionists") boil down all human behavior to the life-long pursuit of pleasure and avoidance of pain—basically the Benthamite view of human motivation reinforced by 75 years of experimentation by behavioral psychologists, most notably by Skinner's famous experiments with pigeons.

We will leave the details of Herzberg's theory of human motivation to the conversation and its introduction. At this point it suffices to say that Herzberg sees human motivation as ringing changes on one central theme: the human desire for achievement. Management's great fallacy, he believes, is its failure to capitalize on this need.

One singular aspect of Herzberg's thinking is the massive replication of the theory by over 75 different occupational groups and the uniformly favorable results—at least when Herzberg and his colleagues have conducted the experiments. "The theory has held up from the lowest-level job to the highest-level job," he says. "The only differences between workers in various groups is the kind of pathology they normalize." The last phrase deserves comment. Pathology, in the sense in which Herzberg uses the term, refers to the fact that over a long period of time, some people are in effect "brainwashed by their environment." They learn to become motivated by the satisfaction of the lesser and baser security needs.

Argyris, whose view of human needs is similar to those of both Herzberg and Likert, makes a similar distinction. He nails the villain, however, with more precision than Herzberg. "Socialization and formal education processes tend to program human beings with concepts about effective human relationship [that] inevitably lead them to seek, create and reward authoritarian relationships—be they leaders, subordinates or teachers—relationships that subvert and thwart their own basic drive toward achievement and self-actualization." Yet Herzberg and Argyris agree that these basic motives or drives are never extinguished; they're merely suppressed. Under the right circumstances—here Herzberg is more optimistic and simplistic than Argyris in defining the circumstances—these drives will revive and once again determine people's behavior.

The second band of what we think of as the "secular theologians"—because of their dual belief in the indivisibility of the truth and their monopoly of it—are the behaviorists, all of whose theories are related more or less closely to those of B. F. Skinner. His is a dogmatism that permits no exceptions. "Men work to produce pleasant things and to

4

avoid painful things," trumpets Skinner. "The only good things are positive reinforcers, and the only bad things are negative reinforcers." As for values, he states, "The technology of behavior is ethically neutral. It can be used by villain or saint."

Behaviorism denies the validity of John Stuart Mill's classic distinction between "Socrates dissatisfied and a pig satisfied." The behaviorists are concerned with the effects of values on behavior, not with the content of the values themselves. Or to quote George Homans, a self-proclaimed follower of Skinner: "The new psychology tends to emphasize, not that men hold similar values, but that whatever their values, these values have similar effects on their 'behavior.'" Human behavior is a function of its payoff.

Homans has gone further and wrested from research sites as removed from each other in time and place as a primitive Polynesian society, factory floors in 20th-century America, and the English medieval village a few generalizations that seem to stand the test of time and culture as things that habitually have caused men to experience pleasure or pain.

Three prime generalizations emerge. First, people tend to avoid both punishment—an obvious source of pain—and its source. This proposition lies at the bottom of the problems people have with anyone in authority, whether it's the chieftain in a primitive tribe or the forelady in a spinning mill in North Carolina. Second—and this is a principle Homans derives from Skinner and calls the law of success or effect: "If an activity or operation is rewarded, it's likely to be repeated, and the higher the value of the reward, the more likely it is to be repeated." The third and last proposition Homans calls the principle of distributive justice: People feel pain whenever they're convinced that they're being unjustly treated. Furthermore, "people only perceive justice in their relations with other men when each man's profit or reward is directly proportioned to his investments and his costs."

A longer list of general principles, he believes, requires more data and more rigorous techniques of analysis than are presently available. "The propositions of small group research—when we have them—will be found deducible from a general psychology of behavior—when we have it," says Homans, who has made the study of small groups one of his major concerns.

All three of the behavioral scientists we have labeled behaviorists—Skinner, Homans, and Whyte—have a set of personal values; and we suspect, on the basis of their writings, that those values constitute three quite different sets. Skinner's values are ascetic, even nostalgic; they are the virtues and the verities as they were envisioned in small-town middle-class America before World War I. They're remarkably close to the values of the first Henry Ford. Homans's values are more worldly and conservative, as befits the thoroughly urban and sophisticated product of a family with inherited wealth, social position, and, on one side, an overwhelming consciousness of themselves and their past (his mother was born Abigail Adams). Whyte's personal value system is very close to the qualities identified by Herzberg, Argyris, and Likert as the basic human endowment. He strives for a society that facilitates people's search for achievement and self-realization (as he defines these terms). Yet, like Skinner and Homans, he refuses "to impose his own can't-helps on the universe," to use a pet phrase of Justice Holmes.

The Pluralist View of Human Nature

Our pluralists, not surprisingly, don't lend themselves to any division into two camps. Each one is very much his own man. David McClelland, best known for his studies on achievement motivation, divides mankind into three basic types: those who value achievement, those who seek and value power, and those who are content with affiliation (whose purpose in life is to like and be liked). People who seek power are also classified into two main subtypes: those who seek power for its own sake and use it to manipulate others to advance their own selfish ends, and those who use power to help others and to achieve the goals of the group or organization to which they belong. This is McClelland's well-known distinction between personal power and social or institutionalized power.

He also believes in the malleability of human nature. Within limits, people can shift their value patterns and learn new behaviors that make them happier and more effective in their jobs and in their lives. McClelland personally, for example, has participated in a number of programs designed to strengthen the achievement motive in situations in which a strong desire for achievement was likely to result in an economic payoff. The training took, and the achievement motive paid off. McClelland stresses the importance of trying to fit the motive to the situation. Achievement as the dominant motive is appropriate for salesmen, academics, and scientists in research and development laboratories; it is inappropriate, even counterproductive, for the manager in any sizable organization. He needs to cultivate whatever inherent drive he has toward social or institutional power.

Kenneth Boulding's views on human nature bear a resemblance to the ideas of both McClelland and the behaviorists. Like Skinner and the other behaviorists, he believes that behavior is determined almost wholly by past experience, although his terminology is remote from that of the behaviorists. "Human behavior is intended to carry the person into the most highly valued of his images of potential futures." At the same time, the value a person attaches to this image is determined or reinforced by its confirmation through feedback messages.

Like the behaviorists, Boulding takes an ethically neutral stance toward values. However, in his description of the two basic human types his preference is unmistakable. Like McClelland, he talks about basic personality types, only in his case there are not three basic types but two, the authoritarian and the reconciling personality. "The first has a large core of values that he identifies with his person; the existence of differing values he regards as a threat to his person. [. . .] The reconciling personality identifies his person not with any particular set of doctrines, but a learning process, a search for truth, and an interest and concern for the welfare of others."

Boulding has little faith in man's ability to alter his behavior patterns, which he sees as set by his early experiences. In fact, only the reconciling personality is free to heed the promptings he gets from feedback and alter his behavior to fit an altered image; by contrast, the authoritarian personality is fixated on a core of values or set of images that he absorbed early on and only too well.

Roethlisberger eschews first principles; for him, they exist only in science. As he puts it: "On the intrinsic side—in matters of human potential and the potential for its realization—there are no certainties or first principles." He prides himself on being a pragmatist rather than a theorist—not a slight difference. As Bronowski points out: "A fact is discovered, a theory is invented." Roethlisberger, like Homans, however, has searched for what we might call working generalizations at the operating level that seem to be true of the relationships within organizations as they have observed them.

Roethlisberger's second-level principles—or, to use his own term, "syndromes"—are similar to the propositions advanced by Homans, a coincidence at least partially explained by their having worked together for many years. One is what he called the "vicious circle syndrome." In his words: "The breakdown of rules begets more rules to take care of their breakdowns, and this vicious circle leads to a continuous search for new control systems to correct the limitations of previous ones." He also claims authorship of the "distributive justice syndrome," although he concedes readily that Homan stated it more elegantly than he had been able to do.

7

With Drucker, first principles of motivation go begging; we must infer them. As he says: "Whether we will ever know enough about human nature to have any theories about it remains to be seen." He is absorbed with problems at the operating level—with the prescriptions that make organizations work and the things that can be done to make them work better.

We know that he believes different circumstances call for different organizational remedies, that he holds a contingency view on the problems of organization design. We also know that he believes that McGregor was mistaken in thinking that all men possess both the desire to work in and the capacity to contribute to a Theory Y type organization—roughly, the kind of organization that believes in and facilitates the satisfaction of human motivation as defined by Argyris, Herzberg, and Likert. In fact, Drucker attributes the mistake not to McGregor himself, but to a misreading of McGregor by his less discerning followers. Drucker describes Theory Y as a harsh taskmaster that will work only "if you start out with high performance goals and performance standards and don't tolerate anything else." From this, we would infer that Drucker takes a limited view of people's chances of achieving their potential unassisted. They need demanding objectives and demanding counselors to help hold them to these objectives.

At the same time Drucker assumes with Theory Y that there are a substantial number of people in the work force who want to achieve. "Otherwise," says Drucker, "there is little hope." Given the basic predisposition on the part of many people to achieve, it is still the structure of the job, in effect, that determines how people will act and what management they will require. The manager's job is to help individuals to acquire the habit of achievement. How? By subjecting them "to the discipline and demands of management by objectives and self-control—a discipline that substitutes for control from the outside the more exacting and more effective control from inside." And to this approach Drucker applies a term that "I prefer not to use at all [. . .] a philosophy of management, that ensures performance by converting objective needs into personal goals."

Daniel Bell, more explicitly than Drucker, exhibits no concern with man's basic nature. Instead, he focuses his attention on larger issues—governmental, cultural, and economic. His is a cosmic sweep, with civilization as his chosen province. However, we are free to infer something about his view of human nature from his division of modern society into "three realms ruled by contrary axial principles, for the economy efficiency, for the polity equality and for the culture self-realization or self-gratification." Because society is, after all, a collection of individuals, we can assume that individuals are similarly fractionated. In their business lives they are concerned with efficiency, in their political lives—and in Bell's usage this encompasses membership in any form of organization—with equality, and in their cultural lives, which also encompasses the organization side of their existence, with self-actualization and self-gratification. In other words, societies in the more advanced nations, as well as the people who collectively comprise those societies, are at war within themselves. Bell sees no unifying principle or force at work—a generally gloomy assessment of the human condition.

Last is Warren Bennis, whom we feel safe in calling a conflicted pluralist. The time was—and not many years ago—when we would have identified Bennis with those who advance a monolithic theory of human nature, more specifically with Herzberg, Likert, and Argyris and their self-actualizing model of man. But no longer. The Bennis who joyously embraced the future, as exemplified by the title of his article "Democracy Is Inevitable," has given way to the Bennis who ruefully concedes that "bureaucracies are here to stay." Personal experience as a college administrator and college president have chastened, even embittered, his views of human nature as he encountered it in these positions. The new Bennis sees individuals, and organizations too, as facing an uphill fight in any effort to be self-determining. Like Bell, he recognizes the disappearance of any unifying values in our society: "Within the community, we have not only a loss of consensus over basic values, we have as well a polarization. We have not a consensus, but a dissensus." Again, Bennis, like Bell, after surveying the state of society and of the individual, finds more to mourn than to celebrate. While none were Pollyannas, four of our relativists surveyed the state of man in society and organizations and emerged with a qualified optimism about his chances of prospering and fulfilling himself as his likes dictated. By contrast, Bennis and Bell view human beings as conflicted within themselves and at the mercy of forces generated by the external environment that, by and large, they can neither understand nor control.

Human Nature and Changing Human Behavior

At one time it was popular to talk about changing attitudes as a way of changing behavior. In fact, for a whole generation from the early 1940s on, human relations training was widely espoused and widely practiced as a vehicle for changing attitudes and indirectly changing behavior in the desired directions. In the context of the business corporation this meant developing attitudes among employees that were more favorable to corporate goals, and behavior that would result in improved performance.

Not a single one of our behavioral scientists would buy that diagnosis today. Most, if not all, would agree with Herzberg that "behavior leads to attitudes; attitudes are the confirmation of your behavior; attitudes are the rationalization of your behavior." This leads inevitably to the next question: If you can't change behavior by changing attitudes, how do you change behavior? In the context of the business corporation the question becomes: How do you get employees to accept corporate goals and, in turn, to improve their level of performance?

The Monolithic View and Changing Behavior

You would expect our monolithic thinkers—those who espouse a monolithic view of human nature—to have clear, simple, and confident answers to this question. And if you did, you would be only partly wrong. Clear, yes, but for the most part neither simple nor particularly confident. Herzberg blows the loudest trumpet. If you want people to improve their attitudes and performance over the long run, he says, provide your employees with more motivators, restructure the job, provide "tasks that induce growth," that afford more opportunity for self-actualization and achievement. Tasks that induce growth will inevitably lead to heightened motivation and improved performance. It's that simple.

One surprising deviation in Herzberg's thinking: It's necessary in any job enrichment effort to exclude the employees whose jobs are to be enriched from any part in redesigning their own jobs. On the surface this is a paradox; Herzberg explains it by claiming that "their direct involvement contaminates the process with human relations hygiene and, more specifically, gives them only a sense of participation [. . .] that will only result in short movement."

Personally, we find the reasoning unconvincing and the paradox unresolved. It is ironic to embark on a program aimed at increasing people's control over their jobs and at the same time to exclude them from participating in the change process. Apparently, papa knows best. We suspect that the surface argument is dominated by more pragmatic concerns. Herzberg knows his way around the corporate world sufficiently to recognize that the whole concept of job enrichment is foreign to most managers. If it is coupled with the plea to let the rank and file redesign their own jobs, the perceived threat to management prerogatives would severely compromise the chances of having the concept of job enrichment accepted and implemented.

At the core of Likert's theory is what he calls System 4. This system guarantees the best of possible corporate worlds—highly satisfied employees with high performance goals. Yet, as Likert views the industrial world, he concedes that System 4 is the exception: System 2, which he defines as benevolent autocracy, is the rule.

What is the mechanism for changing the behavior of employees in ways that ensure high levels of satisfaction and performance? Group problem solving by consensus—let the group decide—is the mechanism "through which the employees consent to the high-level goals which the satisfaction of their own needs requires." In other words, Likert is more of a democrat than Herzberg, more of a believer in giving the employees the right to decide the what, when, how, and how much of their own jobs. There is a self-righteousness in Likert's writings that is explained and almost justified by his humanism.

Argyris presents the paradox of an uncompromising vision of the destiny to which all men aspire joined to a profoundly pessimistic evaluation of the likelihood that the vision will ever be achieved. Human nature begins with an inherent drive toward self-expression, autonomy, and self-actualization, and as these goals are satisfied, it progresses from the infant state of dependence to the adult state of independence. But the organizations of this world, says Argyris, are engaged in a tacit conspiracy to prevent the unfolding of the human personality, to keep the individual more or less permanently arrested. Argyris wrote a book entitled *Personality and Organization;* a more fitting title would have been *Personality versus Organization,* for this is how he views them: as combatants predestined to clash—individuals striving for relative control over their immediate world, the organization striving to keep them submissive and controlled.

Moreover, Argyris sees change in organizational behavior as a complex, time-consuming, and pain-creating process for all involved. Not only do you have to change the behavior of 99 percent of the chief executive officers; you have to overcome the conservatism of the employees themselves. "They have no interest in seeing their physiological and security needs frustrated or denied because their organization collapsed while trying to increase their chances for self-realization. And the possibility of such a collapse is a very real one." To change organizational behavior, you have to alter four sets of independent but interacting

11

characteristics: "structure and technology, leadership and interpersonal relations, administrative controls and regulations, and human controls." Unless all four are changed, any attempt to bring about substantial change in organizational behavior is doomed.

An obvious question: With so much travail, is the effort worthwhile? Argyris thinks it is, on two counts. "First, on normative grounds we feel that social science research has an obligation to help design a better world. [. . .] I believe with Maslow in taking the behavior that characterizes rare peak experiences and making it the behavior toward which all employees should aspire. [. . .] I agree that the behavior is rare, but go on to plead for systematic research that will tell us how the behavior may be made more frequent."

Things seem simpler for our behaviorists. Because they believe that all behavior is determined by the consequences of previous behavior, changing behavior is simply a matter of changing the contingencies, of altering the conditions in which individuals have experienced pleasure or pain.

A simple formula, and one that B. F. Skinner embraces whenever he talks about behavior modification in organizations, including business corporations—the latter being a subject that engages only his most casual attention. If Homans is right—and few are better qualified to judge—this lack of attention is no loss. Homans is convinced that Skinner is "a great psychologist but not a great social psychologist." Why? Skinner is indifferent to the point of sloppiness about spelling out how contingencies can be altered to produce the desired behavioral changes. Maybe, after so many years of working with predictable pigeons, he is tempted—in fact, although certainly not in his public professions—to write off unpredictable humans.

Skinner, in short, is more concerned with the grand design than with the practical results, with ensuring that the pattern of contingencies produces positive results. But what are such results to Skinner? Positive results are consequences that (1) give people the feeling of pleasure and (2) give them the *illusion*—as Skinner would insist—of feeling free. Says Skinner, "If you act in order to produce positive results—what we call positive reinforcements—then you feel free and I'm for that." It's only when people act to avoid pain that they feel coerced and unfree.

As for Homans, he bears the self-imposed burden of being an ultimate psychological reductionist, but when he gets down to translating concepts of human motivation into strategies for changing behavior in organizations, his sense of complexity takes over. Not for him are Skinner's easy evasions. The following passage encapsulates his approach to behavioral change.

> Our behavior is completely determined but it doesn't make a damn bit of difference to me because I can't predict it. I can't show how the behavior of different men, behavior exemplifying the same general propositions, combines over time to produce particular results. The trouble is that the past behavior that affects—determines, if you will—present behavior is linked together in complex chains, creating the illusion of freedom. I like to quote Justice Holmes, who was also a determinist. He used to say, "The way the inevitable is brought about is through effort."

Another determinist, Karl Marx, used to make the same point.

Whyte would subscribe—in fact, has subscribed—to all of Homans's reservations about Skinner as a social psychologist. But his reason for taking a critical view of Skinner is different: he is much more dedicated to a particular scheme of values than Homans, and to a scheme of values that has much in common with the scheme subscribed to by Herzberg, Likert, and Argyris. He also is far more concerned than Homans with the techniques or strategies of changing behavior. In Homans, skepticism or cynicism breeds indifference; in Whyte, commitment generates concern. However, intellectually they start from the same point: distrust of the simple answers proffered by Skinner. Says Whyte, "Skinner's operant conditioning theory tells us very little about the prediction and control of behavior."

Whyte's basic approach to changing behavior sounds like a rerun of our quote from Argyris—not surprising since Argyris did his doctoral work under Whyte. Whyte is more optimistic than Argyris, however, about changing behavior in the desired directions, in large measure because he is more easily satisfied. Argyris is obsessed with his vision of a rarely-to-be-attained perfection; Whyte will settle for improvement that falls short of perfection. He is a satisfier, not a maximizer.

One quotation captures the essence of Whyte's approach to changing behavior.

> Over the years, the dichotomy of structure versus process has been overplayed. In the group dynamics movement, the thrust has been that process is everything—that you change people and everything else falls in place. [. . .] The biggest payoffs are to be obtained by giving more attention to structure; but one has to move back and forth between structure and process. [. . .] If you change the situation in which the individual is working so that he experiences different rewards and different penalties from before, his behavior will change to some degree.

It's that simple—or, as Whyte would insist, the theory is simple; the application is always complex.

Relativists and Changing Behavior

You would anticipate that the relativists would show greater divergences among themselves about changing behavior than the monoliths, and you would be right. Roethlisberger, along with Elton Mayo one of the principals in the famed Hawthorne experiment, spent half a lifetime pondering the lessons of Hawthorne, its implications for management theory and practice. Specifically, what did he learn from Hawthorne about changing behavior in organizations?

The big lesson of Hawthorne, the real Hawthorne effect, was "the big difference that the little difference of listening to and paying attention to the employees made to them." In an article of his called "Human Relations, Rare, Medium or Well Done," he concluded that Hawthorne taught him to see the worker as a social creature "who has personal and social as well as economic needs, who does not want to be paid for merely doing what he is told, but who also wants to satisfy, through his work, his need for security, independence, participation and growth. We see that work provides him with a way of life as well as a means of livelihood."

In other words, the way you change behavior in order to improve job satisfaction and job performance is by providing opportunities for growth and challenge on the job—the motivators extolled by Argyris, Herzberg, Likert, and Whyte.

What distinguishes Roethlisberger from the first three is the recognition that not all human beings are aspiring beings who cherish challenge and responsibility; some—a minority perhaps, but a significant minority—want the security of an easy job, one that doesn't require them to think. Just as there are natural leaders who crave institutional power, and natural achievers who grab at challenging assignments, so there are natural followers eager to obey orders—at least any orders that don't run contrary to their interests as they perceive them. They may be slobs, but they are not fools.

This was another lesson that Roethlisberger clearly derived from Hawthorne. In this famous experiment involving a telephone relay assembly room and its five female assemblers, three of the women studied responded positively to greater freedom from supervision, increased consultation, more control over working conditions, and so on. The other two resented the changes and were replaced early in the experiment with more autonomous, aspiring personalities. From then on the experiment showed consistent results.

As for Drucker, the deus ex machina for changing behavior in ways that facilitate performance is management by objectives and self-control. "The manager's first task is to make effective the strengths of people, and this he can do only if he starts out with the assumption that people—especially managers and professional contributors—want to achieve." To make this assumption is to ensure a measure of disappointment, but to make the opposite assumption—that people are weak, irresponsible, and lazy—sets in motion a self-fulfilling prophecy. People, for the most part, act as they are expected to act.

What's so miraculous about management by objectives? In the 20 years since Drucker first coined the term, hundreds, even thousands of companies have adopted MBO with decidedly mixed results. The trouble is—at least this is Drucker's argument—that few organizations have realized the full motivation potential of MBO because "only a few have followed through with true self-control." The question inevitably follows: What is true self-control?

Drucker gets rhapsodic when he discusses management by objectives and true self-control. "It makes the commonwealth the aim of every manager. It substitutes for control from the outside the stricter, more exacting and more effective control from inside [. . .] it ensures performance by converting objective needs (i.e., the needs of the organization) into personal goals. And this is genuine freedom."

Discount the dithyrambic language, and the statement reduces itself to a proposition based on an assumption. The proposition is that every manager should participate in developing not only his personal job objectives but also the objectives of the higher unit of which he is a part; the assumption behind it—which Argyris, for example, would not concede—is that there is an underlying harmony of interests between the needs of the individual and the objectives of the organization. Joint consultation almost automatically leads to mutual fulfillment.

McClelland, as we mentioned previously, believes, within limits, in the malleability of human nature. Human behavior can be changed; human goals can be redirected toward more appropriate objectives. But within limits: the desire to achieve can be strengthened; it cannot be implanted where it didn't exist. Where the need does exist, the process of developing the desire requires a combination of providing the right training and creating the opportunities to capitalize on the training.

To provide the training and withhold the opportunities is a formula for frustration and failure—and a combination frequently observed by McClelland.

His other caveat is that the training must be fitted to the task. People frequently, argues McClelland, confuse the need for achievement with the need for power, when they are not the same at all. The achievement-driven individual wants a challenging task for which he alone is responsible. Money and feedback are valued not for themselves, but as confirmation and reinforcement of his own sense of worth. By contrast, the power-seeking personality—at any rate the individual who seeks socialized power—sees self-realization as an exercise in cooperation, as a means to achieve mutual fulfillment by working with and through others.

The Environmental Determinists and Changing Behavior

Earlier we classified Bell, Boulding, and Bennis as relativists, meaning that they had a pluralistic view of human nature—with the caveat that Bennis was a conflicted relativist, only recently weaned from his earlier belief in a self-fulfilling rational model of man.

We stand by our earlier distinction, but we want to add a further differentiation. The distinction is between those who believe that the right structure will enable people to fulfill themselves in various ways and those who believe that the external environment, over which neither individuals acting alone nor the collectivity of individuals acting together in an organization have much control, is what determines whether people live full, happy, and productive lives (or, for that matter, determines whether the organization itself flourishes or fails). That individuals acting collectively over time have shaped the external environment, that the same people again collectively over time can hope to modify some features of that environment, that understanding the environment may increase their chances of controlling the environment—these factors don't alter the central image. Mankind over the long run is in the grip of impersonal forces over which it has little or no control.

Having painted the big picture—and painted it black—let's introduce some qualifiers to do justice to the trio Bell, Boulding, and Bennis. Bell sees social conflict in terms of a conflict between professionals and the populace, with the business corporation as the main arena in which the conflict is waged. Why does the business corporation occupy the center stage in what Bell has labeled the post-industrial society? "To the extent that the traditional sources of social support, the small town, church and family have crumbled, new kinds of organizations, particularly the corporation, have taken their place; and these inevitably become the arena in which the demands for security, esteem and justice are made."

Bell is fixated on the big picture, the forces that are molding society as a whole. And he views the present state of society with mixed emotions. On the one hand, Bell sees a populace that is making more and more demands upon society for the direct allocation of resources through the political rather than the economic system. As a strong believer in the need for greater redistribution of wealth and an automatic increase in the slope of consumption he views with equanimity his prediction that the last quarter of the 20th century will bring state-managed societies.

But his value system is not that simple. He is also a strong believer in economic growth and personal liberty. The former depends on investment that is diminished by the redistribution of wealth and the automatic increase in the slope of consumption; the latter, liberty, is threatened by the dominance of any one institution in society, even a state bureaucracy with benevolent intentions. In short, Bell has seen the future—and his reactions are mixed.

Boulding, although an economist by profession, is concerned more with the human equation than with higher mathematics. In his thinking about behavior in organizations Boulding seems to operate at two levels. At the first, he deals with the larger change processes that occur at the subconscious level and that people comprehend only after the fact. At this level, he sees the problem of society as a problem of finding the right proportions between the coercive system, the market system, and the integrative system. Disproportionate emphasis on any of these systems is likely to result in a "corruption of the moral life and the eventual disintegration of society." Like Bell, he emphasizes the importance of integrative institutions, but unlike Bell, he is optimistic about the efficiency of these institutions, basically because he sees the church and the family as still viable. (By contrast, Bell mourns the eclipse of traditional religions and the absence of any leaders with a transcendent moral purpose. Specifically, what Bell misses is the "common lesson of religion: a community has to have a sense of what is shameful, lest the community itself lose all sense of moral norms.")

As a close student of power, Boulding also concerns himself with the way in which power is first acquired in organizations and subsequently used. He defines an organization as a "structure of roles tied together with lines of communication." Many of our behavioral scientists—we're thinking particularly of Argyris, Likert, Roethlisberger, and Homans—would subscribe to that definition. He then goes on to argue that "the behavior of the organization, however, must be interpreted as the result of the behavior of the image of the executive directed by his value system. [. . .] between the incoming and the outgoing messages lies the great intervening variable of the message."

Boulding, like Bennis, sees bureaucracy and hierarchy as the necessary price to be paid for the benefits of formal organization, and for Boulding, as for Bennis, the price is high: "In a hierarchy there is an inescapable tendency toward pleasing the superior, and hence confirming his own ideas." Hierarchy corrupts communication. "The information-gathering apparatus always tends to confirm the existing apparatus of the top decision makers, no matter what it is." Under these circumstances, change is difficult, because the feedback received by the decision makers reinforces the existing images; communication is thus reduced to a process of self-fulfilling prophecies.

As we implied before, it is difficult to reconcile Boulding's optimism about the progress of society with his deterministic, pessimistic view of the internal functioning of the organization. Let the contradictions stand.

As for Bennis, he is concerned, almost to the point of obsession, with organizations, particularly large-scale organizations. He is overwhelmed by their ubiquity, their impersonality, their indispensability, and their amorality. "Bureaucracies are, by definition, systems of increased differentiation and specialization, and thus the ultimate morality of bureaucracy is the amorality of segmented acts."

He is also overwhelmed by the ineffectuality of the organization. The changes that are made in organizations, the decisions that get implemented are the end result of bargaining between forces in both the internal and external environment. Under such circumstances leaders in organizations are on the way to becoming an "endangered species." The external forces, and the internal constituents themselves with diverse expectations demands and desires, isolate the man at the top as the boundary person trying somehow to negotiate between them. Underneath this concatenation of conflicting claims is a lack of consensus in the organization and the community outside. In fact, Bennis claims that we have not a consensus but a dissensus, a polarization of values. Organizations have almost as much difficulty becoming self-determining as individuals.

Bennis, in his conversation, quoted with approval John De Lorean's observation that Harlow Curtice was the last real president of General Motors; today's chief executives, Bennis elaborates, face a loss of discretionary powers that diminishes their entrepreneurial thrust and zeal. For much the same reason—the withering away of autonomy—he characterized his six years as president of the University of Cincinnati as the "management of decline." We think that Bennis would broaden this designation to encompass large-scale organizations in general. In short, there's plenty of change, but the so-called change agents have lost control.

Human Nature and Organization Design

We have seen that the way our behavioral scientists define human nature strongly influences the way they envision the process of changing behavior in organizations. The relationship is close, but not always determining; the main factor distorting it is each author's estimate of the likelihood of institutional changes in organization that are consistent with his own value system.

The same observations apply when we talk about organization design. The correspondence between the views the individual holds on human nature and his views on organization design depends in large part on his estimate of the relationship between the desirable and the achievable, between institutional arrangements that will benefit human nature, as he understands it, and arrangements that will frustrate it. In the narrower sphere of the business organization, this issue is also relevant for designs that will simultaneously improve performance and job satisfaction.

The Monolithic School and Organization Design

Let's begin with Herzberg. As we have commented before, simplicity accounts for a large part of his appeal. All of us have the same motivators, and a form of organization design that capitalizes on these motivators is the cure-all for the human problems of organization. Job enrichment, at least for rank-and-file workers (Herzberg never applies the concept explicitly to the managerial and professional workforce), is such a panacea.

Even so, he lists a few prerequisites for job enrichment to work. Successful job enrichment can be summed up in four principles: (1) select a job for which the investment in hygiene factors is not too big; (2) select a job in which the existing worker attitudes are poor; (3) select a job in which neglect of hygiene factors is becoming costly; (4) select a job in which motivation will make a difference in performance. If the job is machine-paced, motivation is largely irrelevant and job enrichment is a waste of time and effort.

Next comes Likert with his wonderful sense of certainty: the certainty that the self-actualization model is the universal prototype of the organization in which all individuals will be fulfilled; the certainty that System 4 will produce better results at all times and under all conditions than any of the competing systems; the certainty that the key to effective organization design is consensus decision making in a hierarchy of inter-locking groups tied together at each level by the manager who serves as the bridge or linking pin (Likert's term) between the group that he heads and the next group higher up of which he is a member.

Yet even Likert introduces a few qualifiers into his grand design. While insisting that "the closer the management is to System 4, the better are the results," he concedes that System 4 works better for complex operations in which decision making is of necessity diffused than it does for routine operations that foster centralized decision making. Moreover, as the court of last resort, the supervisor retains his hierarchical authority, even when the decisions affect only the work group that he heads. Group consensus is the preferred mode of decision making, but the supervisor retains the veto power. True decision making by the group awaits the arrival of the nirvana Likert labels System 5, but for which he provides no timetable.

Last, Likert agrees that "if you look at the P&L statement of any firm, or any profit center, it tells you that System 2 is a more productive system on the accounting reports than System 4." Of course, the profit and loss statement is deceptive. Corporations love to assert that "people are our most important asset"; however, the human factor doesn't enter into their accounting. It is possible to produce an impressive bottom line, over the short run, by grinding down employees, neglecting maintenance and the purchase of new equipment, and shortchanging customers by turning out shoddy products that are cheaper to manufacture. Hence the illusion that System 2 is better than System 4.

By and large, Argyris echoes Likert, but with heightened com-plexity and diminished hope. Likert believes that the best-run units of the best-managed corporations currently approximate System 4—although few call it that—and that all organizations eventually will see the light. Time and momentum, he believes, are on his side. Argyris, by contrast, thinks that a few small corporations and a handful of units in larger corporations have made a measure of progress toward achieving his ideal Model II organization. But none has traveled the full distance, and only a few will ever complete the journey.

We have already said something about the sources of his pes-simism. Chief among them is his belief that no major organization change will take unless all the major subsystems in the organization are changed; second is his view that as a body, senior executives resist any movement in the direction of system Model II. "They subconciously encourage conformity among their subordinates and discourage others from taking risks."

This is why Argyris favors beginning any major change in organizational behavior by working on interpersonal competence at the top instead of beginning with structured change. Until you increase the degree of discussion, confrontation, problem solving, and trust at the top, no movement is possible lower down, nor is any structured change that would reinforce the interpersonal changes Argyris advocates. Until then most top managements will permit the apathy, the indifference, the goldbricking to go on and "rationalize it all as human nature." In other words, until top managers learn to trust each other—a situation that Argyris thinks is rare—they will never trust their subordinates.

Through the pessimism Argyris permits a few rays of hope to escape. He describes six entrepreneurs who each began as quintessential Model I managers ("the kind of man I would never work for myself," as one of the entrepreneurs put it) and who after years of pain, travail, and plenty of professional assistance became Model II managers and implemented Model II theories in their organization. Small progress, but, as Argyris concluded, "progress worth recognizing and worth advancing."

Skinner, as we have indicated before, is not particularly interested in the details of organizational design, and even less concerned with the specifics of achieving an organizational design that will simultaneously help ensure high performance and high levels of job satisfaction. To him, it's a matter of providing the right contingencies at the right intervals, which means providing the reinforcers on a random and progressively diminishing schedule. Eventually, the positive reinforcers can be dispensed with entirely. Over time, the individual will become conditioned, habituated to derive pleasure from the activity for its own sake. At some point the intrinsic satisfiers will take over.

In a recent article Skinner expressed a related principle: "Behavior that consists of following rules is inferior to behavior shaped by the contingencies described by the rules. We learn to operate a piece of equipment, for example, by following instructions, but the instructions are soon forgotten, and we operate it skillfully only when our behavior has been shaped by its effect on the equipment."

Until that point is reached, Skinner asserts with surprising confidence, some form of lottery will be sufficient to cure absenteeism or tardiness and generally improve the level of performance. If the organization institutes a lottery—obviously a form of random reinforcement—and ties eligibility to participate to the specific improvement it wishes to achieve (for example, by limiting participation in the Friday drawing to those people who had been on time for work all week), the results are almost certain to be gratifying. Elsewhere, Skinner speculates that "the democratic principle lies in letting the worker tell you what he likes and doesn't like. He may not be the person to decide how to get rid of what he doesn't like or how to produce what he does like." Or again: "If most people are bored with their jobs it's because the system is the product of a battle between opposing forces . . . . Someone should design incentive systems with the dual objectives of getting things done and making work enjoyable." Indeed they should! Unfortunately, Skinner consigns the task to lesser men.

Homans, the disciple, differs substantially from Skinner, his acknowledged master, about matters of organization design. The design principles of Skinner's Walden II utopia, which Skinner took seriously, Homans dismisses because they wouldn't work in practice. Behavior is created by contingencies, all right, but by contingencies that happen by chance, not design. If you tried to apply Walden, he contends, "something like one-half the population would be concerned with closely training kids according to the rules of behavioral psychology." In short, "the illusion of free will is going to be saved by cost considerations."

Another difference between Homans and Skinner is rooted in the elitism of the former, who feels that Skinner glosses over the distinctions of status and power that characterize people everywhere in organizations. People are never equal, nor do they ever receive equal rewards. Inequality is inevitable because a minority in any society has "the ability to provide rewards that are low in supply, but high in demand." At the same time, rewards are socially determined: "An ability that would give a man high status (and power) in one group may not do so in another."

Homans, at another point, attacks Argyris because his Model II system can't be operated by "ordinary damn fools." He quotes the Homans principle that no large-scale system can be successful if it depends on extraordinary ability on the part of the people who run it. With him the preeminent tone is conservative, commonsensical—the very voice of the founding fathers. Take the following words of John Jay in 1796: "I confess that I do not amuse myself with dreams about an age of reason. I am content that little men should be as free as big ones and have and enjoy the same rights, but nothing strikes me as more absurd than projects to stretch little men into big ones, or shrink big men into little ones. We must take men and measures as they are, and act accordingly." There is little or nothing in this passage to which Homans could take exception.

Whyte, as we have mentioned before, is the benevolent behaviorist. Like Homans, he thinks that Skinner is not a great social psychologist, but unlike Homans, he is committed to a vision of the ideal organization that bears a close similarity to the ideas of Argyris. Less immersed in mechanics, less obsessed with the leadership styles of the executive cadre—a group that Whyte, like Argyris, considers largely irredeemable—he contrives to combine complexity with a tempered optimism about the present and the future present.

Take one example—the relationship between participation and productivity. As a rule of thumb, participation increases productivity. But beware of easy conclusions. In one case, the female workers in the paint room of a factory increased their productivity—and their pay—by an incentive system of their own design. This, however, brought their earnings out of line with more skilled workers in other parts of the plant—most of whom were male. Result? The plant manager jettisoned the incentive system in the paint room, and most of the employees in the room quit.

Another case: In an insurance company, employees using participative methods of decision making performed better, over the long haul, than employees who followed orders. However, participation as a mode of operation took hold to the point that the employees decided to take a day off. Result? The program was canceled, and the vice president responsible for it was fired.

Moving organizational behavior in the desired direction is hemmed in with constraints. But within them, Whyte asserts, progress can be made—if only the managers will remember that change takes time; that any organization is a complex of interlocking systems; that the probable impact of any innovation in one part on the whole should be analyzed in advance; and that the changes themselves are of necessity interdependent. "When you institute any structured change, you have to think of the other changes that need to go with it and support it. Changes in the structure of evaluation and monetary rewards are perhaps the most necessary, as well as the most frequently overlooked."

The Relativists and Organization Design

Roethlisberger, despite his identification of the "simple uniformities that reside in human situations," was skeptical to the point of despondency

23

when it came down to stipulating formulas or operational strategies for improving job satisfaction and performance. Some of this skepticism undoubtedly derived from his insistence on the importance of direct observation, for his own observations led him to conclude that the things organizational situations hold in common—the simple uniformities, if you will—were of less consequence than their dissimilarities. Each work group was to him a unique system.

Intellectually, Roethlisberger was an embittered man. He saw the findings of the Hawthorne experiment, with which he was intimately associated, consistently misunderstood and misapplied. His disillusionment over the fruits of Hawthorne led him over the years to a low opinion—quite unjustified, we think—of the significance of the whole experiment. Many years later, in a paper titled "Hawthorne Revisited," he wrote:

> For all our huffing and puffing there is nothing to show. We did not produce anything like the great society or a more democratic society or more humanized bureaucracies or more mature behavior. We did not even produce any sentences or propositions in a scientific sense to verify. We were still just reclassifying things—that is, giving new names to things that had existed in 1936, but which had not been classified this way before.

Perhaps Roethlisberger's was the tragedy of expectations unfulfillable and hence unfulfilled.

Few contrasts could be greater than that between Roethlisberger and Drucker: the one skeptical and hesitant to make any recommendations for action, the other confident that his formulations would result in more effective organizations—if only managers had the wits to implement them properly. To compress Drucker's design formulations into a few paragraphs is an absurdity. Nonetheless, we can deal with some of the highlights.

In any large-scale organization, decentralization is a must; it is "the condition for the conversion of bigness from a social liability into a social asset." Specifically, Drucker hails the advantages of what he calls "federal decentralization"—an approach to design in which each separate unit has the responsibility for its own performance, its own results, and its own contribution to the total organization.

"With respect to communications and decision making, federal organization is the only satisfactory design principle we possess," he asserts. The connection between this principle and Drucker's guiding philosophy of management by objectives and self-control is obvious: by making each unit of the business autonomous and responsible, it promotes by example the diffusion of autonomy and responsibility downward to the lowest feasible levels—a process that is a prerequisite to any meaningful attempt to establish management by objectives and self-control. For objectives to be anything more than empty slogans and sterile exercises, they must have real and significant consequences for the individual and the organization.

But the greatest strength of the federal principle, which makes it preferable to any other, is that "it alone of all known principles of organization prepares and tests people for top management responsibility at an early stage." Of course, the autonomous manager in a decentralized business has neither full responsibility nor complete control. But the federal principle comes closer to meeting the need for a system that will prepare and test tomorrow's leaders than any other known design.

McClelland, as we would anticipate, relates his organization design to the kind of motivation that the situation calls for. Do we want to stimulate the achievement need? The affiliative need? The power need? The measures we take depend on the answers to these questions. Achievers, for example, prefer a moderately challenging task that gives them "a sense of personal responsibility for the outcome" and provides for concrete feedback. In an environment in which the achievement motive should be emphasized, such as an R&D laboratory, the organization should therefore be designed to provide moderately challenging tasks, a sense of personal responsibility for results, and concrete feedback.

Or take the design of incentive systems. "Strongly achievement-oriented individuals work best under odds as slim as one in three or even longer," McClelland says. Thus an incentive plan for a strongly achievement-oriented sales force (McClelland believes that all successful salesmen are strongly achievement-oriented) should obviously offer a different set of odds than a plan designed for a group of chemical workers who score low in achievement need.

What about employees with strong needs for affiliation? Obviously, incentive plans and payments for them should be framed in terms that facilitate working together for the common good; group incentives that emphasize cooperation are needed, not individual incentives that feed the competitive spirit. Small wonder that incentive plans for assembly line workers that traditionally rely on individual incentives don't pan out: "Extra incentives reinforce behavior directly opposed to the affiliation requirements of the task, disrupt normal working patterns and lower average productivity over the long run." The organization designer should determine which one of the trio of job elements—power needs, achievement needs, or affiliation needs—is called for by the task and tailor his design to fulfill the appropriate need.

The Environmental Determinists and Organization Design

The environmental determinists—Bell, Boulding, and Bennis—are only incidentally concerned with problems of organization design. The first two view the problems as secondary, while the third views them as unsolvable, at least in terms of reaching what he would conceive to be a satisfactory solution.

Bell, in his preoccupation with the trend toward state-managed societies in all so-called advanced nations, restricts his discussion of organization design to the federal government. The big question faced by the federal government is, "How do we combine national spending and national funding with decentralized administration?" Organization design involves the solution to two problems: first, the centralization of policy; second the decentralization of administration.

Bell finds cause for optimism in a trend he detects to "retreat from the older visions of centralized public ownership with bureaucratic overload." As Alice Rivlin, staff director of the Joint Congressional Committee on the Budget, put it, the new emphasis is "not on public provision, but on public financing of care." Bell is all for it.

Boulding, by contrast to Bell, devotes some attention to the problems of organization design. Like Bell, he is concerned with preserving the integrity and dignity of the individual against the very organizations with which he is involved. At the same time, he believes that the organization has its legitimate claims on the individual too.

One device for reconciling the conflicting claims of the individual and the organization is something akin to Drucker's management by objectives, but without the emphasis on joint formulation and self-control. Boulding observes that "it is difficult to keep large purposes before the minds of small people." Hence the need arises for organizations to devise a system of minor goals that collectively fit into the larger purpose yet are sufficiently close to the individual and his level of aspiration to be powerful motivators.

However, Boulding doesn't see this system of minor goals as being an adequate substitute for a system of formal controls. For every organization there is an optimum degree of trust for its employees. Maintaining that optimum degree involves every organization in a dilemma. "If its control system is too tight, so that the lower members of the hierarchy with little trust placed in them are in constant fear of being spied on, the identification of those members with the organization will be low, the apathetic reaction, if not actual sabotage, is likely to prevail, and productivity will be adversely affected. At the other extreme, a control system that is too loose destroys the sense of integrity and purpose of the organization itself."

A related problem is that the larger the organization, the more controls take the form of reports that pass up the hierarchy and do not always reflect reality. Therefore, Boulding hypothesizes, "the tighter and more rigid the control system, the less reality will be reflected in the information flow as it passes up the channels of the hierarchy."

Is there a way out of this dilemma? Perhaps—that is about as definite as Boulding gets. He sees grounds for hope in the emergence of what he calls "the society of the skilled," which would seem of necessity to be based on extensive discussion, accurate feedback, a network of information channels, and the absence of coercion. Similarly, Drucker bases much of his optimism for realizing management by objectives and self-control on the preponderance of what he calls knowledge workers in our society. Boulding is more cautious; what should be may not come to pass. "The images which are useful in gaining power are seldom useful in exercising it wisely or in keeping it."

What about Bennis? As we have seen already, his basic intellectual posture after surveying the current organization scene is to throw up his hands. He seems almost as convinced as Bell of the inevitable growth of public-sector institutions and laments their handmaiden—"a cat's cradle of regulations which tend to restrict or reduce the institutions' autonomy in decision making."

As an individual long identified with organization development he laments the eclipse of OD: "Consensus is the end of OD, a consensus based on trust, openness, confrontation and feedback. With the problems of today's institutions consensus is chimerical, as appropriate to today's organizations as buggy whips are to G.M." Or again: "We're at the end of the consensus period—if we were ever in one at all."

The sense of gloom that permeates Bennis's recent writing contrasts strongly with the euphoria that characterized his writings in the past. As he states in an article with the ironic title "A Funny Thing Happened on the Way to the Future" (we say ironic because what happened was, to Bennis, clearly a tragedy): "The organizations of the future I envisioned would most certainly be, along with a Bach chorale and Chartres cathedral, the epitome of Western civilization." Instead, we have a world in which "the sun will never set on bureaucracies," a world populated by "the shallow gnomes who are calling the shots because we don't know enough about management to challenge their narrow and shallow concerns."

At this point, Warren Bennis is the Henry Adams of behavioral science, but with an obvious difference: Adams despaired of the present out of mourning for an irretrievable past; Bennis despairs of the present out of mourning for an aborted future.

Lest we do him an injustice, a few more observations on Bennis are in order. He achieved fame as perhaps the most prolific—and certainly the most eloquent and unswerving—proponent of the view that because of the increasing nonroutineness of organizations, decentralization, participative management, and democracy were inevitable. The democratic imperative as envisioned by Bennis rested on three stools. First, management was increasingly staffed by professionals to whom participation was the sine qua non of cooperation. Second, the increasingly turbulent environment required that, to be effective, more decisions had to be made at lower levels. Third, as Charles Perrow put it: "Rapid technological change by itself is supposed to produce new-style democratic organizations," because under the conditions induced by rapid technological change, progressively larger increments of power would accrue to professionals such as scientists or engineers.

Perrow dismisses Bennis as the arch exemplar of "the science-fiction wing of organizational theory"—which is a witty half-truth. The problem is that the conditions that Bennis anticipated would characterize the overwhelming percentage of organizations in fact apply to only a minority—organizations such as research and development laboratories or relatively small firms operating on the frontiers of knowledge with a heavy complement of professional personnel. Such organizations or organizational units have moved in the directions predicted by Bennis— and where they haven't, the price paid, in morale, productivity, and profits, has been high.

Bennis is now engaged in writing two new books. We hope that he has recovered from environmental shock, that his undoubted qualities of imagination, insight, and eloquence will eventuate in a new synthesis combining the former idealism with the new realism that he so painfully acquired.

How Much Consensus?

Let's begin the conclusion of our introduction by trying to answer a question that we raised in the beginning: Is there a logical connection between the views our behavioral scientists hold about human nature on the one hand and, on the other hand, their views on changing behavior in organizations to improve both employee satisfaction and performance and on an organization design that would further the same ends? In other words, do their views on human nature constitute the foundation upon which the rest of their thinking on behavior in organizations rests? The connection is present in all twelve thinkers, although it is more difficult to detect and document with some than with others.

To answer our question, we need to divide our thinkers into four categories: the universalists or secular theologians (Herzberg, Likert, and Argyris); the behaviorists (Skinner, Homans, and Whyte); the pluralists (Roethlisberger, McClelland, and Drucker); and the environmental determinists (Bell, Boulding, and Bennis).

With the universalists, what strikes us most is the extraordinary degree of certainty that inspires their thinking: certainty that human nature is uniform and unalterable; certainty that there is one right direction and one right way to change organizational behavior; certainty that there is one right organization design that will enable men to fulfill their basic needs and aspirations.

Of course, there are cracks even in the sense of certainty that envelops their thinking. Herzberg says very little about changing behavior above the level of the rank and file and nothing about how organization design can be changed to enrich the jobs and the lives of people above the lowest rung on the organization ladder. Presumably, because their intrinsic needs are already satisfied and their jobs are already enriched, they don't constitute a problem. Likert admits that even his System 4 contains one serious flaw: True consensus decision making by the group awaits the arrival of System 5. And Argyris perceives so many roadblocks to the realization of his Model II organization that he seems to have expended his energies in describing an edifice that, for the most part, is doomed never to be built.

The behaviorists begin with a theory of human nature every bit as certain as that advanced by Herzberg, Likert, and Argyris. All men seek pleasure and avoid pain. But from there on the certainty diminishes and their paths diverge.

Skinner, by and large, simply begs the question of behavioral change and organization design in business corporations. It's all a matter of tailoring the contingencies to the demands of the situation. Skinner's notable lack of specificity—leaving the utopian Walden II aside—invites a couple of interesting speculations. Either he forgoes specificity because the contingencies he favors are rooted in a past that cannot be reclaimed, or he eschews specificity because he tacitly concedes the point made by Homans: that contingencies can be planned only in tightly controlled environments, such as research laboratories or academic institutions, but not in the relatively freewheeling corporate environment. Maybe the truth lies in a combination of these factors.

Homans is in basic agreement with Skinner that man is controlled by the environment and that freedom is an illusion that arises whenever a man feels free, not coerced. But he goes further than Skinner in trying to spell out the contingencies, the conditions in which people feel free, the circumstances under which they enjoy the liberty that Homans identifies as a "beloved discipline." But a combination of skepticism and conservatism inhibits Homans from going very far in spelling out the contingencies. He divined several operating principles that stood the test of times and cultures but shows scant interest in pinning down the implications of his principles for the management of people in organizations. In the end, he has nothing much to say about organization design. He suspects, for example, that participation and giving people close attention provide continuing rewards. But these suspicions remain untainted by conviction.

Whyte is different. Starting with the same psychological assumptions as Skinner and Homans, he goes much further than either in spelling out the conditions for successful behavioral change and effective organization design. More than they, he is deeply committed to a value system that his approaches to changing behavior and organization design are calculated to advance.

Of our three pluralists, Drucker and Roethlisberger are closer to each other than either is to McClelland. Their value systems are similar; where they differ is in their estimate of whether behavior and organizations can be changed in ways that lead to the fulfillment of these values. To put it differently, both men began with a similar theory of human nature that appeared to be reasonably true and capable of generating useful rules of thumb for practical implementation; but whereas Drucker went busily about the task of implementing, Roethlisberger ultimately ran out of confidence—although not before making some important contributions.

McClelland stands by himself. The bridges that he builds between his tripartite theory of human needs and satisfactions and of behavioral change and organization design are logical, explicit, and internally convincing. To tell whether men in fact correspond to McClelland's models requires a lot more research and evidence than we currently possess. He has richly documented his theories on achievement need, but given only passing attention to the needs of affiliation and power.

That mankind collectively, over extended periods of time, has determined the environment doesn't rule out the proposition that the individual, or even people assembled in groups as large as the great corporation or the national state, are controlled by the environment. This is the core position of the environmental determinists. Within this central position, however, the trio Bell–Boulding–Bennis displays differences.

Bell is preoccupied with the preeminence of the state and with finding the formula that will preserve the balance between equality, growth, and liberty. Within the constraints set by the environment, purposeful human activity can accomplish something—although how much depends largely on a transcendent sense of moral purpose, which he feels is largely lacking.

Boulding, as we have observed, operates on two levels. At the first, where he deals with cosmic patterns, he envisions a basic psychological conflict between the authoritarian and the reconciling personality; about the outcome of this conflict he is neither too certain nor too hopeful. At the second level, where his focus is on the management of power within the organization, his stance is one of qualified optimism based on his assumptions about the emergence of the skilled as the dominant factor in the workforce and about the design conditions that will foster the full utilization of their skills.

As for Bennis, seeing his vision of the future contradicted by reality has caused him to give up on the present. The polarization of values that characterizes our society as Bennis conceives of it necessitates bureaucratic control, but that control is enfeebled by the very necessity of constant arbitration between sharply conflicting special interests. The paradox is that the same forces that perpetuate bureaucracy also undermine it and keep it from being effective. No wonder that Bennis is gloomy. Sometimes reality justifies despair.

So far, we have looked at the forest; now let's shift our attention to the trees and look for points of agreement rather than differences. Are there any important areas of consensus among our twelve behavioral scientists?

That they differ over the universality of human nature, over the details of what most consider to be the prevailing needs, and, even mord strongly, over the likelihood of changing behavior and designing structures to fulfill these needs should not obscure a basic core of agreement. Economic man is dead; self-fulfilling man is very much alive. The central purpose of any organization is to fulfill human needs, variously defined, of which economic need is but one, and not the strongest need in any of our thinkers' hierarchy. There is not one of them who would dissent from the following, generally forgotten words of Adam Smith:

> The man whose whole life is spent in performing a few operations, of which the effects, too, are perhaps always very nearly the same, has no occasion to exert his understanding or to exercise his invention in finding out expedients for removing difficulties which never occur. He naturally loses, therefore, the habit of such exertion, and gradually becomes as stupid and ignorant as is possible for a human creature to become. The torpor of his mind renders him not only incapable of relishing or becoming a part in any rational conversation but of conceiving any generous, noble, or tender sentiment and consequently of forming any just judgement concerning many even of the ordinary duties of life.

All of them would agree that it is the purpose of the organization to prevent that "torpor of mind" described by Smith from developing, and that effective organization design should promote the exercise of understanding and invention, qualities shared by most human beings.

All our thinkers conceive of the organization as a system, a network of connecting, logically complementary but mutually interdependent parts. The one exception might be Herzberg; his concentration on job enrichment that can be applied successfully in one subsystem and ignored in others tends to blind him to the realities of interdependence. The late Joan Woodward, when in 1970 attempting the task of describing the areas of agreement between behavioral scientists, concluded: "Whether the approach is basically mathematical, psychological, sociological or economic the starting point is the identification of a system and the questions subsequently asked are very much the same: What are the objectives and strategic parts of the system under review and how are these parts interrelated and interdependent?"

Our sample was larger and included people such as Herzberg who neglected the systems factor. But our basic conclusion is the same: the behavioral science view of organization is *the* systems view of organization. As Whyte wrote:

Relations among persons tend to be structured through organizations, and within these organizational contexts behavior is linked to reinforcements in structural ways [. . .] unless we change the pattern, we can do little to change the behavior. If we are to devise new organizational systems that maximize both performance and positive reinforcement for organizational members we need to come down from the sphere of political ideology and undertake detailed analyses of the sociotechnical systems: the system of interpersonal relations that is linked with the structure of technology, work-flow, and task organization.

From the systems view of organization follows a corollary sub-scribed to by all but one, Argyris—and even he is a partial exception. This is what is commonly identified as the contingency approach to organization change and organization design.

In talking about change, this means the recognition that motivation never exists in a vacuum but is surrounded and conditioned by a wealth of factors in the external and the internal environment; of these the structure of rewards and recognitions is always important and sometimes predominant. The conclusion is becoming widespread that changing the structure of the organization may be the most effective as well as the quickest and cheapest way of altering behavior and improving performance.

Charles Perrow has provided us with an excellent example of the contingency approach at work. As he observed:

If too many defective products are going out the front door, don't subject inspectors to sensitivity training or issue a ukase to do a better job. Study the inspection procedures themselves. Are there any defects in information? Are there any interdepartmental conflicts that make for poor communications and maybe defects? Look at the reward structure, manipulate the variables and wait a few months for changes to take hold.

We could almost say that structure is in and motivation is out. The right structure will generate the right behavior patterns. We will say that the emphasis has shifted, that structure has come into its own, and that no leading behavioral scientist would argue that you can ignore structure in changing behavior. Even those who—like Bell, Boulding, and Bennis—downgrade the impact of internally generated change would concede the impact of structure within their circumscribed view of the discretion available to the internal change agents.

On the design side, Jay Lorsh, head of the division of organizational behavior at the Harvard Business School and one of the most articulate advocates of the contingency approach (which he prefers to call the situational approach), stresses the importance of achieving the right fit between tasks, people, and organizations. We must "make sure that the formal structure, rewards, standards, and measurements in any organization are consistent each with the other, [. . .] make sure, moreover, that these elements of internal design are compatible with the external environment, corporate strategy, job tasks, the prevailing preferences of the organization's members, and top management's preferred style of managing." Clearly, the undertaking required to operate an organization at anything close to maximum efficiency is formidable, and few organizations make it. Most are content with muddling through.

The contingency approach is dominant almost everywhere we look. Take leadership. Few would contradict the contention of Professor Fred Fiedler, another chief guru of the contingency school:

> There are a limited number of ways in which one person can influence others to work together toward a common goal. He can coerce them or he can coax them. He can tell people what to do and how to do it, or he can share the decision making and concentrate on his relationship with his men rather than on the execution of the job. [. . .] No one has been able to show that one kind of leader is always superior or more effective.

Even Likert, Argyris, and Herzberg would subscribe to the last statement. Of course, if you substituted "usually" for "always," the battle would be on.

Roethlisberger, in writing about the Hawthorne experiment, observes: "I wasn't preaching any model of the way an organization should be. The conceptual scheme of a social system was primarily an investigatory, diagnostic tool." In a real sense, behavioral science in organizations has come full circle from the first significant experiment at Hawthorne and the contingency approach advocated by Roethlisberger (obviously, he didn't call it that) through the various normative models to the contingency model that pretty much monopolizes the field today.

Behavioral scientists are beginning to heed the warning Whitehead issued many years ago about falling into the error of thinking that the facts are simple because simplicity, or at least the simplest explanation of complex facts, was the object of their quest. Instead, said Whitehead, "the guiding motto in the life of every natural philosopher should be: Seek simplicity and distrust it."

Organizational problems are inherently complex. No rationalization, however ingenious, seems likely to wring universal propositions from recalcitrant data. At this point we probably know more about what won't work than what does work. But with the new sophistication comes the search for uniformities that are true for at least some situations. The key words in behavioral science today are complexity and selectivity. There are no broad-spectrum nostrums beyond the truisms previously cited that themselves limit the potential range of application for any formula. Perhaps there is a third key word: realism. The best hope for the future viability of behavioral science lies in the fact that it has largely put behind it the search for universals that in the past absorbed the time and energies of so many of the best behavioral scientists.

Conversation with
FREDERICK HERZBERG

In a survey conducted some years ago by The Conference Board, Frederick Herzberg was ranked by its members as one of the five best-known behavioral scientists—just after Peter Drucker in the pecking order. The reasons for his celebrity are clear. He has developed a theory of human motivation that is simple and all-encompassing. The theory reflects the intuitive judgment of many managers who are incapable of articulating it formally. It has been replicated empirically in over 75 studies conducted by Herzberg and his associates. Last, and definitely not least, it has been merchandised with remarkable zeal by Herzberg and his associates. Edmund Wilson in *To the Finland Station* dubbed Karl Marx "a great secular rabbi"; Herzberg deserves the same designation.

What is the theory? We will keep our explanation simple—Herzberg obviously will go into much more detail in the conversation. He divides human needs and goals into five job dissatisfiers and five job satisfiers. Under dissatisfiers he lists company policy and administration, supervision, salary, interpersonal relations, and working conditions. The satisfiers are achievement, recognition of achievement, work itself, responsibility, and advancement.

Herzberg is clear on two points. First, motivation is monolithic—like "the colonel's lady and Judy O'Grady." All humans—male or female, housewife or scientist or bank president—are sisters and brothers under the skin. They share the same basic job needs and goals. Second, there is a sharp distinction between job motivators and what Herzberg, taking a leaf from preventive medicine, calls job dissatisfiers or, prefera-

Reprinted from Management Review, *July 1971*

bly, "hygiene factors." He asserts, for example, that "a good hygienic environment can prevent job dissatisfaction but cannot create true job satisfaction."

Is the theory true? Does it work in practice? Given Herzberg's claims, these are indispensable questions. Our answers have to be qualified. All of Herzberg's studies have replicated his theories. Studies conducted by outsiders, presumably more objective, have yielded mixed results. Some have confirmed his findings, even more have found them faulty.

At AT&T a variety of attempts at job enrichment based on Herzberg's principles were largely successful. Other efforts based on the same principles didn't turn out as well.

Why? What is the problem with Herzberg's theory? Scientifically we await a definitive finding, but intuitively we have our suspicions. At one level the distinction between job satisfiers and dissatisfiers seems more semantic than real—what Porter, Lawler, and Hackman called a "methodological artifact." Herzberg himself, in discussing the distinction between money as a mover and as a motivator, came close, in our opinion, to giving the game away: "The promise of money can move a man to work, but it cannot motivate him. Motivation means an innate desire to make an effort." In other words—strictly our own interpretation—it is possible to obtain the same results from decreasing the sources of job dissatisfaction as from increasing the sources of job satisfaction.

Another problem lies in Herzberg's monolithic view of human nature. John Stuart Mill thundered that it "would be better to be Socrates dissatisfied than a pig satisfied." He had a point. Herzberg ignores the diversity of human nature—the fact that different employees have different needs and goals. Not all will respond equally to the motivators that Herzberg is convinced are the sole bases of true job satisfaction.

Herzberg has answers to those objections, as the conversation will reveal. And he could be right. In any case, it is a theory worth considering, and a theory that, in many applications, has achieved impressive results. To be significant, a theory doesn't have to be universally applicable. By that criterion, few theories work.

Dowling: Maybe the best place to start is with the title of one of your *Harvard Business Review* articles, "One More Time: How Do You Motivate Employees?"

Herzberg: Historically, we have to begin with a grant I received to investigate the whole area of job attitudes when I was at Psychological Services in Pittsburgh. This particular interest originated during my days in the Graduate School of Public Health. After I got my Ph.D., I went to Public Health School and received an M.P.H. in what's called Industrial Mental Health—it's never been properly defined. When I went to Psychological Services as research director, I was interested in aspects of mental health, which certainly included job attitudes. The first stage of this research program, obviously, was to review the literature in the field, and my staff and I did a very comprehensive review of that literature. We had a bibliography of 3,000 books and articles. The result was a book called *Job Attitudes: Review of Research and Opinion,* a scholarly review of what was known on attitudes from 1900 to 1955.

However, when we had finished *Job Attitudes: Review of Research and Opinion* we could make no sense out of it. It seemed that the human being was forever debarred from rational understanding as to why he worked.

We looked again at some of the data describing what people wanted from their jobs and noticed that there was a hint that the things people said positively about their job experiences were not the opposite of what they said negatively about their job experiences; the reverse of the factors that seemed to make people happy in jobs did not make them unhappy. So what happens in science, when your research leads to ambiguity? You begin to suspect your premises. In my Public Health School days I had conceived the concept that mental health was not the opposite of mental illness; that mentally healthy people were just not the obverse of mentally sick people. So I took a stab on the basis of mental health not being the opposite of mental illness and came up with a new concept.

Dowling: That was your core insight?

Herzberg: That was the core insight. I said, perhaps we're talking about two different modalities. Job satisfaction, let's use that term, and job dissatisfaction are not opposites; they are completely separate continua, like hearing and vision. If this is true, if we recognize that they are separate continua, then they must be produced by different factors and have their own dynamics. That was the stab I made.

Then I said, O.K., let's test this idea. Obviously, what had to be done was to find out what made people happy separately from finding out what made people unhappy. And you couldn't just ask people, "What do you like about your job?" That's like asking, "How do you feel?"—a nonsensical question. In fact, two questions must be asked: What makes you happy on the job? And, equally important, What makes you unhappy on the job?

Dowling: Your methodology was different, too, as I recall.

Herzberg: Yes, people respond for the sake of responding. And they tend to give the answers that will win the approval of the people asking the questions. You ask people a lot of questions in a public opinion poll and you get a lot of answers without any real feelings about them. Instead of asking people what makes them happy or unhappy, I thought it would be better to get at the kinds of experiences that produced satisfaction or dissatisfaction with a job. By doing these two things—by asking two questions where one was usually asked and by obtaining my data from analysis of the kinds of experiences people had rather than what they say makes them happy and unhappy—I found that the two systems existed.

With the appearance of the two systems, my thinking that what makes people happy and what makes people unhappy were not the same things was verified. In analyzing the commonalities among the factors that make people definitely unhappy or definitely happy, I found that the factors which make people happy all are related to what people did: the job content. Contrariwise, I found that what made people unhappy was related to the situation in which they did their job: job environment, job context—what I called hygiene factors. So now you have a finding that makes much more sense. What makes people happy is what they do or the way they're utilized, and what makes people unhappy is the way they're treated. That pretty much summarizes my second book, *The Motivation to Work*.

Dowling: Then in your third book, *Work and the Nature of Man*, you searched for the psychological underpinnings for your theory.

Herzberg: Why does job content make people happy? Yes. I had to ask that question. Further research and experience suggested what makes people unhappy is pain from the environment. We have this in common with all animals. We're all trying to adjust to the environment—to avoid pain. On the other hand, man is also different from an animal and what makes him different is that he is a determiner, whereas the animal is always determined. What man does determines his human characteristics—I cannot become psychologically taller unless I do things.

So I developed the Adam and Abraham concept, the two natures of man. As Adam, he's an animal, and as an animal he tries to avoid pain from the environment as all animals do. As Abraham, he's a human being, and as a human being he's not the opposite of an animal, he's qualitatively different. His dynamic is to manifest his talents, and the only way he can manifest his talents is by doing things that allow him to develop his potential. In short, *Work and the Nature of Man* provided the rationale for the findings of what motivated men to work.

In summary, you had a three-step sequence. First, what we knew about job attitudes from the past made no sense, so we had to look at the problem differently. Second, when the problem was redefined, a very different research result was obtained. Third, I had to explain the research results. Now I have a theory, documented with research and supported by an understanding of why the theory worked. You ask, how do you apply it? Now we come to "One More Time."

Dowling: How do you apply the theory? That was also the subject of the last chapter in *Work and the Nature of Man*.

Herzberg: "One More Time" does two things. First, it suggests that you can get people to do things as Adam, and you can get people to do things as human beings—but the ways you get them to do things are very different. To get people to do things as animals, you move them. When I respond as an animal because I want to avoid being hurt, that's movement. I called it KITA, for "kick in the ass." When a human being does something, he's motivated. The initiative comes from within. Further, I showed how the various techniques of human relations are just different forms of positive and negative KITA.

Second, I went on to demonstrate the difference between management by movement and management by motivation or job enrichment. How, by changing what people, do you motivate them to do better work? I described how job enrichment paid off handsomely in one company—AT&T, although it wasn't identified as such in the article. Since then, many other companies have applied job enrichment with equal success. That's what happened in the past.

Most of my work now consists of looking at the total problem of mankind living in society through motivation-hygiene theory. Not only must we reorient our management thinking in terms of how you motivate people for better P&L statements, but how we apply the same theory to develop a sane society. AT&T faces not only problems with dial tones and profits, but the central and more crucial problem of whether or not it can survive as a social institution in our society. Of course, the problem is not unique to AT&T. It faces every institution.

That pretty much summarizes motivation-hygiene theory, what it is, how it came to be, and where it is going.

Dowling: It certainly does. But let's dwell a bit longer on some features of the theory. One fact that I found very significant was that your motivators had a much more positive and long-term impact on performance than did your hygiene factors, and this was true even in the relatively rare instances in which the hygiene factors had a positive influence.

Herzberg: We have just completed a study replicating that perfectly. The hygiene factors are always short term, like the length of time you're not dissatisfied with your salary. It takes about two weeks for the effects of a raise to wear off.

Dowling: I think I've had experiences where I've been happier a little longer than that. But I buy your general point.

Herzberg: Also, the hygiene factors go back to zero. No matter how many times you have told your wife you love her, if you fail to tell her you love her, she says, "You never tell me you love me." The hygiene factors are all subject to the "what have you done for me lately" syndrome. A colonel bucking for general in the Army feels as deprived status-wise as a private bucking for corporal. A colonel is the zero point. If you get a $4,000 increase in salary and the next year they give you a $2,000 increase in salary, psychologically you have taken a $2,000 cut. By contrast, the motivators are long term and don't go back to zero. I write a book and I achieve some growth. If I don't write another book, I don't get back to where I was before. When I achieve, that achievement never disappears. Of course, if I write a book and then write an article, I haven't developed as much as I did with the book, but it's still an addition. You see, with the hygiene factors, you've got to have as much as, or more than, you had before to notice any difference, but with the motivators, you do not have to have as much as before to know the difference and feel the growth.

Dowling: Another point that struck me was the fact that your dissatisfiers or hygiene factors very seldom appear as satisfiers. One exception I recall were the lower-level supervisors in the Midwest utility who felt happy about getting along with their employees.

Herzberg: That's what in motivation-hygiene theory we call a pathology. The pathology can be either in the individuals or in the company. Let's take one in the company. I have people tell me what made them happy and unhappy, their experiences, and then draw a profile and tell you what's going on in that company. Take, for example, the lower-level supervisors in the utility industry. The hygiene factors became so important that relief from them gave people the false feeling of being happy. For example, if you hit yourself over the head, you say you feel good when you stop doing it. Actually, it is not that you feel good, but that you don't feel as bad. There's nothing positive about the way you feel. If this were true, then the mechanism for feeling good would be to hit yourself over the head so that you could stop. Do you see the idiocy of it? However, because many people say, "I feel better" or "I feel good" when hygiene factors improve, they get the mistaken notion that they're feeling good; sometimes the relief from pain can be so great that you mistake it for a satisfaction feeling.

Now in any company where hygiene factors are so important for individuals that their relief gives people the mistaken report that they feel good, what they're really saying is, "I stopped hitting myself over the head with a hammer and I felt good." If this happens in a company, you know that the company's so damn hygiene-oriented that people find their only happiness in relief from pain.

Dowling: You at least hinted that this probably was true of this utility company.

Herzberg: Oh, it was. And we have other examples where utility companies were hung up on hygiene factors.

Dowling: In your first study, the one "swing factor" was the factor of money. At least, it appeared with almost equal frequency as a satisfier and a dissatisfier.

Herzberg: Let me explain money to you. Money is a hygiene factor. However, because it is associated with so many other factors, it's included with them. For example, advancement is a motivator, but correlated with advancement is usually a salary increase, so money gets pulled along. Increased responsibility is a motivator, right, but more money is frequently associated with increased responsibility. So money hides in different concepts and becomes a ubiquitous factor. But dynamically, the fact is that money isn't what you do, it's what you get for what you do or how you're treated for what you do. By definition that is a hygiene factor.

Another reason for the confusion is that money is the biggest KITA available, and what many people do is to mistake movement for motivation. I say money is not a motivator; it's a good mover.

Dowling: In talking about one electric utility and its extraordinarily large bonuses, you made the distinction between ordinary wages and money earned as recognition for extraordinary performance, and you said that the latter could be called a true motivator.

Herzberg: I've changed my mind, because at that time I hadn't clarified the concept of movement in relation to motivation. At that time I had to explain why the company got such impressive production, and the easiest explanation was that money was recognition for achievement. Now I recognize that it's the biggest KITA they have. What they're getting is not motivation, but movement.

Dowling: Considering that their workers out-produce workers in competing companies by two to one—or at least they used to—you certainly got a lot of movement.

Herzberg: If you can afford to move people, move them. But don't forget that KITA costs more and more to move people less and less. In many cases, we're getting a negative return on our investment with such things as profit sharing and fringe benefits.

Dowling: You had a very striking analogy between heroin and hygiene: You need to provide more and more of both to get less and less effect. In other words, your suggestion is that most managements are not using their resources properly when they concentrate on the hygiene factors, in many instances almost to the exclusion of the motivators.

Herzberg: There are two ways of getting people to do things. One way is to play on their pains. It's no great effort to find out what makes people hurt; play a tune on it and they will tell you where the gold is buried—

right? The trick may be money, fringe benefits, security, or human relations, which is the most vicious form of KITA.

Dowling: Why do you call human relations "vicious"?

Herzberg: Because it says, "I will be decent to you if you work harder." I say, "You be decent to me to be decent to me." You say, "You know, I'll be a nice guy if you work harder." That's like saying "I took the old lady across the street, give me my reward!" This is why I'm so critical of sensitivity training and of human relations programs. They prostitute human relations and prostitute human decency.

Now, there's another way of getting me to do things—not because you want me to do it or because I just want the reward. Remember, a reward is something I get for doing something I wouldn't ordinarily do if it weren't for the reward. Motivation is another way of getting me to do something. Motivation says do this because it's very meaningful *for me* to do it. This is where management has missed out.

Dowling: The reward is intrinsic?

Herzberg: The reward is the personal satisfaction in what you do. What management has failed to do—incredibly failed to do—is capitalize on the human desire for achievement. Managements have always looked at man as an animal to be manipulated with a carrot and a stick. They found that when man hurts, he will move to avoid pain—and they say, "We're motivating the employees." Hell, you're not motivating them, you're moving them. What I've been advocating is, for God's sake, only to give hygiene to solve hygiene problems or because people hurt. Another and far more efficient way of getting people to do a good job is to give them the opportunity to get satisfaction out of doing a good job. That's the area management misses. I love the term "delegation." That's the most bastard technique I know—that's letting someone borrow your job for a while.

Dowling: Why has management been so derelict in using motivators?

Herzberg: Because of the obviousness of man's pain. Man's achievement motivation is not as visible as man's pain—it has to be discovered. Second, it's easier to manage with hygiene factors. You can have lousier managers. It doesn't take many brains to hold up a jellybean and get a guy to do something. Every dog trainer knows the trick. But it takes a lot of talent to manage people through their abilities, and because this is so, we don't have managers; what we have, by and large, are animal trainers. All you have to do is go into the typical corporation and see the managers at work with their bags of jellybeans and their whips.

Dowling: You had another suggestion. A lot of managers are afraid to encourage employees to actualize themselves because in the process they might buck the organization, challenge authority and infringe on what managers regard as their prerogatives.

Herzberg: Let me give you another reason. Most organizations are manager-proof. What I mean by manager-proof is that in most organizations you don't need creative managements. What you need are good policemen. And I could paraphrase Lincoln on this: You can fool all the people some of the time, and that's enough to make a profit. What most organizations ask about their people is "How well housebroken are they?" rather than, "How creative are they?" Most organizations are very unimaginative. The only substantial use of imagination in organizations takes place in marketing. There's some in R&D, but it's pretty much suppressed. For the rest, top management wants the housebroken guy.

Dowling: What about jobs that allow no real room for creativity or growth?

Herzberg: Mickey Mouse jobs.

Dowling: Ideally, maybe you ought to automate them and get rid of them. But that may be too expensive in many instances.

Herzberg: There are a lot of Mickey Mouse people. So put the Mickey Mouse people in Mickey Mouse jobs, okay?

Dowling: It's as simple as that?

Herzberg: No, unfortunately, it's not that simple. Intrinsically, very few people are Mickey Mouse people. They're made that way. However, you live with reality, and there are a lot of people who will not be unhappy in Mickey Mouse jobs, and who can be moved into them.

Dowling: In other words, it's a matter of selection, of fitting the Mickey Mouse jobs to the Mickey Mouse people.

Herzberg: In a sense. I don't approve of it, but until you get rid of the Mickey Mouse jobs, I see the logic of it.

Dowling: I'm thinking of people who are really only suited for the simplest, most monotonous tasks, performing outstandingly on them, like the example you cite from Argyris where people who were actually mentally defective turned in outstanding performance on routine tasks.

Herzberg: I'm more concerned not with biological morons but the more frequent cases where industry has psychologically extirpated the brain. It's a very sad thing when you have a college graduate performing like a moron in a Mickey Mouse job.

Dowling: That's quite different. What do you do about the college graduate in a Mickey Mouse job? Presumably you enrich the job. However, the term enrichment in itself is a kind of slogan. What does it mean when you apply it within an organization?

Herzberg: It would take me two hours just to go through the hygiene factors and describe how you manage them.

Dowling: I would be more interested in how you manage the motivators.

Herzberg: You can't manage one without considering the other. I come into a company and I ask two basic questions: What kind of talent do they have? If they have low talent, but are well-housebroken, the company can't go anyplace because you can't be motivated if there is no know-how. All you can do is fall back on a lot of slogans. This is why all demagogues substitute slogans for talent.

The other thing I ask is how they use the talent they have. If they haven't used the talent, then the talent is considered to be scrap in that company. To the degree that you consider talent "scrap" in your company, it spills over into many of the hygiene factors and your people become psychological amputees.

Now, when a man has a leg amputated, you fit him with a prosthetic device and you say he's made a good adjustment. But despite the adjustment he is sick, because he's still only got one leg—normal is two legs. Psychologically, the same thing is true on the job. The attitude that these people have on the job is as normal an attitude as that of the amputee or as normal an attitude as that of a guy who's been kicked in the ass all his life. They simply adjust. You have the attitude of seduced people, of a woman who lost her virginity but doesn't want to admit it.

Dowling: You talk about jobs where lower-level supervisors have spent their time checking on performance. You would enrich the supervisors' jobs by assigning these jobs to someone else and releasing them for higher-level jobs of training and managing.

Herzberg: When you have a supervisor checking a man on a job, he's not a supervisor, he's a checker. You have a manager checking the supervisor. He's not a manager, he's a checker. What happens in the typical company is that people are overchecked and undermanaged. When this has happened, two people are doing the same job and neither takes responsibility. What we get is the ludicrous situation of bawling out the supervisor for the mistake of a subordinate.

Dowling: Job enrichment, in other words, doesn't come by giving the guy a human relations course or any kind of training. It comes about only through redesigning his job and making it more meaningful to him.

Herzberg: When a production supervisor is told to stop hanging over an employee, that usually accomplishes nothing. The approach that works is to make it impossible for him to hang over the guy. If two guys don't get along with one another, you can send them to five years of psychotherapy or you can separate them. You see the point.

Management has this God-awful belief that you can change attitudes in people, and that attitudes lead to behavior. Nonsense! Behavior leads to attitudes. Attitudes are the confirmation of your behavior; attitudes are the rationalizations of your behavior. If you were forced to behave as if you believed in segregation, you would have attitudes that conform to that kind of behavior. The attitudes enable you to read the environment. Then you choose arenas or ball parks where your behavior is again acceptable. This then leads you to go to a school that practices discrimination, and that behavior therefore is acceptable. There you develop other behaviors that lead to other attitudes that correlate with them. You build up a whole system of attitudes that confirm the various behaviors that you manifest, and this constellation of attitudes becomes your value system. Your value system, then, is a confirmation or rationalization for your behavior. What determines your behavior on the job is primarily two things: What kind of talent you have, and what you're permitted to do—the degree of job initiative.

Dowling: The degree of initiative allowed by the organization.

Herzberg: That's right. What really tells me whether or not I'll play the piano are two things: Do I have a piano, and can I play the piano? If I can play the piano and have a piano, then I'll have an attitude that's favorable to piano playing. If I can dance and get an opportunity to dance, then I'll have an opportunity to develop an attitude favorable to dancing: If I can't dance, I'll say, "Who wants to dance?" Do you see the point?

Dowling: Yes.

Herzberg: Many of my colleagues are saying, "Let's change the attitudes of people" and I say you cannot—you're getting things backwards. These colleagues have the best of all possible worlds—they have a value system substituting for science. That is, they're trying to change people's attitudes to proper attitudes. The proper attitude for a man in a Mickey Mouse job is a Mickey Mouse attitude. Second, because the attempt never works, they never have to face up to the reality of accomplishing anything and being held responsible for the results.

Dowling: I can see that job enrichment leads to increased growth and self-actualization, but the connection between job enrichment and improved performance isn't nearly as clear. Isn't job enrichment more likely to take the form of an improved interest in quality instead of productivity?

Herzberg: Yes, much more of an interest in quality, for two reasons. One is an industrial engineering reason: Productivity is more determined by the technology than by the individual. The productivity of many factory workers, salesmen, telephone operators is determined by so many different factors. Quality, however, is much more determined by the individual. Therefore, the employee who is motivated to do a better job improves the quality of his work.

Another reason for the emphasis on quality is that quality has more nuances to it than productivity. Productivity is on a single continuum. Quality is on many continua. There's more possibility for a man to actualize his talents by emphasizing one of the many facets quality has.

You can always improve productivity at the expense of quality. The Russians are masters at this. If you were a Russian manager and were given a quota for turning out so many tons of sewing machines, what would you do? You'd make them out of the heaviest cast iron, wouldn't you? We laugh at the Russians because they get productivity at the expense of quality this way, but so do we. How many companies over here are more concerned with indexes than with total performance? In more than one company the productivity indexes are all high, but the quality stinks.

Dowling: You mentioned in *Work and the Nature of Man* that the motivation-hygiene theory had been confirmed by 10 studies in 17 populations.

Herzberg: Now it's over 50 studies.

Dowling: How many of the additional studies deal with lower-level employees—where you logically would expect to find the most exceptions to the theory?

Herzberg: We've got a lot of lower-level ones. I will give you this flat statement: The theory has held up from the lowest-level job to the highest-level job. The only differences between workers in various groups is the kind of pathology they normalize. It doesn't change the basic nature of man. My colleagues, you know, say that lower-level workers don't want achievement. Well, lower-level workers don't want achievement because they never have been allowed to experience it. My colleagues are following a kind of circular, self-confirming hypothesis: You don't give the Negro a good education, so he doesn't show up bright, so you say he's stupid and make it unnecessary for him to get a good education. Similarly, your lower-level workers have no chance to do anything, and since they can't do anything, my colleagues say—see, they don't want to do anything. Of course, they have attitudes appropriate to people who don't do anything—they have adapted.

Dowling: In light of their adapting, it's surprising to find that they still express a preference for motivators as things that make them feel happy on the job. Apparently they treasured these opportunities, no matter how rare they were.

Herzberg: My book points out what the basic needs of these people are, not what they checked off in opinion surveys. You see, the difference is that I get the kinds of experiences that affect people, not the kinds of rationalizations dealt with in rating scales.

Go out and interview the hard hats. So many Mickey Mouse behavioral "scientists" would talk to them to get them to confirm their sociological concepts of stratification. I'd want to talk to these people like human beings. Many psychologists don't know people. They know what happens to people, they know the cultures of people, but they don't know people.

Dowling: Have you ever gone into an organization that you felt recognized the true potential of motivators and was doing something about realizing them?

Herzberg: There is no organization that I would say was a perfectly motivated organization. Take the Bell System. Some parts are marvelous; other parts are bad. I can characterize the leadership of an organization in terms of KITA's as opposed to motivation. But a company that makes a good use of motivators—there isn't any. I can talk in terms of a division at best, but usually about a section, a group, or a man.

I believe in organizations based on mutual respect through mutual distrust in the hygiene area and mutual trust in the motivator area. That's more real and sane. When two people trust each other in the hygiene area, the guy who trusts most loses. I don't want to sound cynical, but I didn't make this world, I just report on it.

Dowling: You talked a while back about applying motivation-hygiene theory to the larger problems of society. Where do you begin?

Herzberg: The major problem in our society is that we don't know how to manage success. Throughout history, the great tragedies of cultures or organizations have not been in the failure to produce success but in the failure to manage it once it's been achieved. Managing success needs a different managerial style than producing success. We can produce success with KITA's, but once people have success they no longer are moved by KITA's. They begin to ask the question consciously and in ever-increasing numbers, "How do we spend our lives?"

In producing success, you treat people as animals, hoping that the end result will be a human being—this just doesn't work. We have to start treating people as human beings and not as KITA objects if we're going to be able to manage our society successfully. If you fail to produce success, you don't get something, but if you fail to manage success you produce catastrophe. Personally, I've abandoned the possibility of developing a sane society through hygiene. You're only going to develop a sane society through giving more satisfaction to people, not less dissatisfaction.

Dowling: How does this relate to a specific problem like the blacks in our society and giving them more satisfaction?

Herzberg: There are so many problems related to the blacks, and so little time in which to solve them. If any nation could have solved this problem, I think this nation could have. Look at the three problems facing the United States today—nation building, in Viet Nam; people building here, the blacks and other minorities; and earth building, the ecological problem. That's just too much. We can't nation build, earth build, and people build simultaneously. We don't have much ingenuity or time.

Let me add that I think you can only solve the race problem in terms of whites behaving toward blacks as their equals and developing attitudes to accompany their behavior.

What really bothers me, and where I get pessimistic, is the competence problem. You can't motivate anybody to do a job if he can't do it. We can set up all kinds of job corps programs, but that's a drop in the bucket—there are 22 million blacks and the overwhelming majority are incompetent to do a job in which it's realistic to talk about motivation and satisfaction.

People say, "Why don't the blacks begin to pull themselves up by the bootstraps?" The answer to this question lies in the recognition that it is an inappropriate question to ask. The background and initial experience of the black in the United States cannot be equated to those of *any* other ethnic group. As such, it is only within recent memory that the legal and extralegal barriers to entry into the institutions of our society have been lowered to permit the opportunities to gain competence. In other words, the black has had further to go than other nonracial ethnic groups to develop competence.

Competence and the opportunity to use that competence are prerequisites to motivation. If I'm motivated, I'll achieve, but if I've never achieved, I can't be motivated. It will necessitate the spending of a lot of expensive KITA before the black will develop the intrinsic achievement to feel equal on the motivation-happiness continuum as well as minimizing the "less than" feelings on the hygiene-unhappiness continuum. I don't think we're going to lick the competence problem immediately—certainly not in our lifetime, and maybe not in the lifetime of our children.

Conversation with
RENSIS LIKERT

In 25 years as the director of the Institute for Social Research at the University of Michigan Likert was certainly responsible for more research on the human organization, and probably influenced more people's thinking about the workings of the human organization, than any of his contemporaries—Drucker, McGregor, and Herzberg being his only peers. Now that he is in very active semiretirement the research continues—and the influence.

Likert's theory is both descriptive and normative: He combines a method for measuring the characteristics of an organization with a prescription for the ideal state of the organization, and a formula for moving the organization from its actual state to the ideal state.

First, how do you measure an organization? Likert, together with his colleagues, developed a questionnaire—typically it ranges from 50 to 100 items that graphically portray what he calls the management system—a cluster of factors that includes structures, controls, and leadership behavior, plus the attitudes, motivations, and perceptions of the employees. Everyone in the organization or unit of the organization being studied completes the questionnaire.

From this data, it's possible to prepare a profile of organizational characteristics and to identify the organization as being System 1, System 2, System 3, System 4—or somewhere in between (a streamlined version is given on pages 54–55).

Likert labels System 1 Exploitative-Authoritative; System 2, Benevolent-Authoritative; System 3, Consultative; and System 4, Participative Group.

Reprinted from Organizational Dynamics, *Summer 1973*

The ideal state of the organization Likert identifies as System 4—at least, it's the most ideal of the four. And by ideal Likert means organizational performance or effectiveness defined in both humanistic terms—maximum employee satisfaction and morale—and the traditional business criteria of performance—maximum output and earnings. Specifically, System 4 appears to be consistently associated—in every type of organization Likert studied—with the most effective performance, and System 1 with the least effective performance. System 2 was more effective than System 1, but less effective than System 3, and so forth.

How do you move an organization? Likert identifies three sets of variables: (1) casual variables, factors controlled by managers—such as organizational structure, controls, policies, and leadership behavior; (2) intervening variables—the attitudes, motivations, and perceptions of all the members; (3) the end-result variables, factors such as productivity, costs, and profits. Likert's break with traditional organization theory came first in his insistence that there was no direct linear relationship between managerial actions and organizational end results, and second in his insistence that the only way to affect either employee attitudes or organizational success was to work on managerial behavior. It is a waste of effort to attack either the intervening or end-result variables directly. Until management behavior changes, nothing changes.

We have left the $64 question to the last—and to Likert himself. How do you motivate managers to change their behavior and move toward System 4? Not for nothing has he been called "The Picasso of Organizational Research." We'll conclude by commenting that he is his own most eloquent and convincing spokesman.

Dowling: Could you begin by briefly summarizing the key principles of System 4?

Likert: One underlying concept is that you use quantitative measurements as the basis for arriving at conclusions as to what kind of management system works best. The emphasis in System 4 is less on judgmental conclusions and more on what can be demonstrated in terms of scientific method.

System 4 is an organization concept that ought to be looked at in a comparative social evolutionary manner. I'm going to start with System 0. System 0 is an organization that has no structure. A good example was the Jewish nation prior to the time that Jethro gave Moses advice on what

	ORGANIZATIONAL VARIABLES	SYSTEM 1	SYSTEM 2	SYSTEM 3 Substantial amount	SYSTEM 4	Item no.
LEADERSHIP	How much confidence and trust is shown in subordinates?	Virtually none	Some	Substantial amount	A great deal	1
	How free do they feel to talk to superiors about job?	Not very free	Somewhat free	Quite free	Very free	2
	How often are subordinate's ideas sought and used constructively?	Seldom	Sometimes	Often	Very frequently	3
MOTIVATION	Is predominant use made of 1 fear, 2 threats, 3 punishment, 4 rewards, 5 involvement?	1, 2, 3, occasionally 4	4, some 3	4, some 3 and 5	5, 4, based on group	4
	Where is responsibility felt for achieving organization's goals?	Mostly at top	Top and middle	Fairly general	At all levels	5
COMMUNICATION	How much cooperative teamwork exists?	Very little	Relatively little	Moderate amount	Great deal	6
	What is the usual direction of information flow?	Downward	Mostly downward	Down and up	Down, up, and sideways	7
	How is downward communication accepted?	With suspicion	Possibly with suspicion	With caution	With a receptive mind	8
	How accurate is upward communication?	Usually inaccurate	Often inaccurate	Often accurate	Almost always accurate	9
	How well do superiors know problems faced by subordinates?	Not very well	Rather well	Quite well	Very well	10

54

DECISIONS		At what level are decisions made?	Mostly at top	Policy at top, some delegation	Broad policy at top, more delegation	Throughout but well integrated	11
		Are subordinates involved in decisions related to their work?	Almost never	Occasionally consulted	Generally consulted	Fully involved	12
		What does decision-making process contribution to motivation?	Not very much	Relatively little	Some contribution	Substantial contribution	13
GOALS		How are organizational goals established?	Orders issued	Orders, some comments invited	After discussion, by orders	By group action (except in crisis)	14
		How much covert resistance to goals is present?	Strong resistance	Moderate resistance	Some resistance at times	Little or none	15
CONTROL		How concentrated are review and control functions?	Very highly at top	Quite highly at top	Moderate delegation to lower levels	Widely shared	16
		Is there an informal organization resisting the formal one?	Yes	Usually	Sometimes	No----same goals as formal	17
		What are cost, productivity, and other control data used for?	Policing, punishment	Reward and punishment	Reward, some self-guidance	Self-guidance, problem-solving	18

he needed to get to the promised land. After spending 39½ years and going half the distance to the promised land, Moses was advised by Jethro that what he was trying to do was too much for him to undertake; he needed a set of captains of 1,000, captains of 100, captains of 50, and captains of 10—in other words, he had to apply the span of control and basic concepts of organization—and he also needed to set up staff. Ernest Dale has an organization chart that shows the way Moses ran things for the last half of the distance from Egypt to the promised land—and he went the last half in six months instead of 39½ years.

Dowling: Was Moses the first System 1 manager?

Likert: As far as I know. Under Moses, System 1 was a pretty brutal system, a punitive system—an eye for an eye, a tooth for a tooth—and so were many of the feudal systems. Over time, people found that benevolent authoritarianism resulted in better performance, so there was a trend to move toward System 2. Then, as people became better educated and workers became more competent, System 3, consultative management, began to appear. Finally, many of the more able managers in American business and government found that if they involved people in decisions affecting them they got still better results—and we moved to System 4.

Dowling: What are the central concepts of System 4?

Likert: Well, the principle of supportive relationships, multiple overlapping group structure, group problem-solving by consensus, high performance goals and adequate levels of technical competence. System 4 harnesses human motivation in ways that yield positive cooperation rather than fearful antagonism on the part of the people in the organization; by contrast, Systems 1 and 2 tend to develop less favorable attitudes, more hostile attitudes, or more submissive attitudes. System 4 doesn't use economic motivation alone to accomplish goals; it also uses what Maslow calls the higher needs of self-actualization and sense of personal worth and importance, and it combines those kinds of motivational forces to help achieve high productivity, high levels of satisfaction, high levels of sense of personal worth, which in turn yield high levels of physical and mental health.

System 4 emphasizes that the structure of the organization ought to be looked at as a series of face-to-face groups, each of which is effective in having the capacity for highly productive problem-solving in the face of difficulty. Each group consists of a superior and his subordinates. The groups work toward finding solutions that are going to yield results favorable to all the different parties and interests represented, so it's not a zero-sum game as the problem-solving tends to be in Systems 1, 2, and even 3. It is much more a win-win rather than a win-lose kind of problem-solving.

The System 4 organization is held together by people who hold overlapping memberships—who are what I call linking pins. This kind of linking occurs both vertically and, when necessary, laterally, in order to achieve effective coordination in large, complex organizations. These are some of the central concepts.

Dowling: You've stressed the necessity of moving gradually into System 4, especially if you have an organization that is, to begin with, a System 1 or possibly even a System 2 organization. How do you explain the need for gradualism?

Likert: I'd like to underline that we learned gradualism the hard way, the way we've learned so many things. In one company with a few hundred clerical employees, management was trying to jump the organization from about System 2 to System 4, and the people in the organization couldn't adapt that fast. The process of learning problem-solving, accepting responsibility for the decisions that you're a party to making, was too much of a challenge, particularly for the girls who had come from authoritarian schools and had lived in homes where father was the boss, where they weren't supposed to make decisions. They said, "Look, the supervisor is paid to make the decisions, and if he makes mistakes it's his fault. If we're involved in it, then we could be held responsible, and if we make mistakes then papa spanks, so . . ."

Membership in System 4 groups—the problem-solving kind of relationships, interdependent, cooperative relationships—requires a set of complex learned skills. Moreover, the members have to have the feeling that this is the appropriate way to behave. French, for example, in the famous study he did at the Harwood Manufacturing Company, showed that if you involved people in decisions, you'd get higher productivity. When he repeated the experiment with rubber footwear workers in Norway, the workers did not expect to be involved in decisions. It violated what they felt was the proper way for a manager to behave. As a consequence, he did not find the expected increase in productivity. Harwood had the same experience in Puerto Rico. When they asked the girls for their suggestions about how to organize their jobs to make them easier, the girls got frightened. They began to talk about it after work, and they began to quit. They reasoned that if management didn't know any more about how to run a company than this, they had better look around for another job before the company went out of business. Harwood found that you've got to move gradually so that people's expectations and skills can grow progressively and keep step with the changes you're instituting. You find that as you move from System 2 to System 3 you begin to build cooperative relationships, confidence, trust and commitment to the organization.

Dowling: The key point, then, is to move toward System 4 gradually, rather than attempting a giant leap forward.

Likert: That's right.

Dowling: You've made the point somewhere that authoritarian organizations breed dependent people. If you are going to change an organization that's been authoritarian from the beginning, you face a formidable problem.

Likert: You're putting your finger on a very important point of confusion today in research about management and leadership. There are a number of people who emphasize the contingency concept. . .

Dowling: Fred Fiedler, for instance.

Likert: Fred Fiedler, and Woodward, and Lawrence and Lorsch, and others, all of whom argue that you have to adapt your leadership to fit the circumstances—the culture, the environment, the industry, or the particular employees. That's right, you've got to—but the idea that neither leadership nor followership can change is fundamentally unsound. The fact is that we can take a System 2 organization and progressively move it from a System 2 to System 2½, to System 3 and eventually to System 4 and consistently get improvement as we move. This means that you start out at the beginning with a leader who behaves in an authoritarian System 2 manner in dealing with the rank and file because this is what they're adjusted to and what they expect. You get better results with a System 2 manager supervising System 2 people than with a System 4 manager managing System 2 people. But progressively, you can move that System

2 organization. The leadership, of course, moves ahead of the follower-ship, toward System 4. I don't know of a single study that has been made in which, if you have congruence, System 4 isn't significantly more productive than System 2.

Dowling: How are you defining congruence?

Likert: If the rank and file expect System 2, a System 4 leader would deliberately back down toward about a System 2½ model. He's more toward four than their actual expectations, but not so far that they can't adapt successfully. Gradually he moves toward System 4, always keeping a little ahead of the rank and file. We've moved from a static concept of leadership-followership to a dynamic concept that recognizes that both leader and the people being led can move progressively toward a much more sophisticated model of leadership and organization.

Dowling: I think you estimated that it would take, depending on the size of the firm and where you started, from three to five years to teach System 4.

Likert: Yes, depending on the size of the organization and where it starts from. With very large corporations, for example, I'm not sure you could teach System 4 within five years.

Dowling: Yes, I think you did say longer.

Likert: You don't change people's basic habit of relating to people and leadership style and decision-making and these kinds of things rapidly. We've discovered that we can take a component unit—that is, we can take top management or a top of the division or an operating profit center of a few hundred people—and move that organization from System 2½ well over toward System 4 in a year or a year and a half. It's also true that if you have a large corporation and you run into a recession such as the recent one, you can use a System 4 approach to cost-cutting; you don't change the whole organization to System 4, but you begin the movement toward it, and you can achieve significant cost reductions in ways that strengthen rather than weaken the human organization. The president of Continental Oil, for example, recognized several years ago that we were heading for a recession that could require substantial cost-cutting. He shared this in-formation with his top-management group in their regular meetings, and he did it on a problem-solving basis. He said, in effect, "Well, fellows, it seems to me that we better start planning now where and how we're going to cut back to meet the decreased income that's going to come as a result of this recession." He problem-solved around the facts with his group, and his group said, "Okay, you're right, but now let's do exactly the same thing with our subordinates that you're doing with us. You gave us the facts, presented the problem, gave us the chance to think through what ought to be done and how it ought to be done. We ought to do the same thing with our own subordinates rather than going out and issuing orders where and how they're going to cut. We ought to get them to problem-solve about how they can do it in ways that will strengthen rather than weaken their organization over the next five years."

They decided that the best way to insure that the problem-solving would really be a group effort would be to send a top manager who knew nothing about the technical details of a function to launch the planning in that function. That way, he couldn't tell them what to do if he wanted to. So they sent the vice-president of sales to tell this story to the R&D department and the R&D vice-president to sales, and so on. They took their cuts early enough so they didn't have to make any drastic cuts in personnel, and they did it in ways that enabled them to wind up with a stronger organization than they had before. Now, this illustrates what can be done with innovative problem-solving that reduces costs and yet does it in ways that don't seriously undermine your human organization.

Dowling: One area that puzzles me is the area of group decision-making. You say that decision-making in the group should be by consensus, and yet, at the same time, the leader of the group, at whatever level of the organization he is, is completely responsible for that decision. It seems to me that that puts an unreasonable burden on the leader if he is responsible for a decision that is imposed on him by consensus. Or is this a correct understanding of the decision-making process as you view it?

Likert: It's not quite that the decision is the leader's. Let's look at that more carefully. What I'm saying is that it's the leader's responsibility to build his subordinates into a highly effcient problem-solving group that can take any problem and work through it in light of all available facts to the most constructive solution. Now, if he's built his subordinates into that kind of a problem-solving group, they can do a better job of problem-solving than he can alone. Then he's accepting responsibility for two things: first, accepting responsibility for having built his subordinates into a highly effective problem-solving group, and second, accepting responsibility for the decisions that they reach.

Take the situation of a president in one of today's high technology companies. He can't possibly have the technical background and competence to make the best decisions in all areas. His only hope is to build his subordinates into a group of people who share information fully, accurately, and honestly, and work together in a cooperative way to reach a decision that's going to be in the best interest of the entire company, and not just in terms of what's best for R&D, accounting, or some subunit.

A System 4 operation is needed to develop this teamwork. When a superior deals with his subordinates on a man-to-man basis, as in Systems 1, 2, and 3, he often, deliberately or unconsciously, pits his subordinates against each other. They respond by competing with each other instead of cooperating. The superior in a System 4 organization stimulates cooperation and teamwork among his subordinates by using group problem-solving with consensus. The problems always are those at his hierarchical level. A company president, for example, would use group problem-solving with his vice-presidents to deal with company-wide problems. When this problem-solving is done with consensus, each vice-president is encouraged to think about problems and solve them in terms of what is best for the entire organization and not to focus narrowly on doing what benefits his own department no matter what effect it has on the rest of the company.

Dowling: Let's take it down to the lowest level of organization, the first-level supervisor, whether he's a sales supervisor or a supervisor of a group of clerks, or the foreman in charge of a machine shop. Am I correct in assuming that at this first level, decision-making still should be done by consensus? Am I also correct in assuming that decisions that are made at that level are restricted to decisions that affect only the group itself?

Likert: Well, you're right in a sense that they should make decisions by consensus. Now, time and again, a rank-and-file man at the bottom of the organization will see things that have impact far beyond his work group and may raise a question in his own work group. Maybe he'll complain that "We talk about saftey, but our basic safety problem is in the raw materials." The work group can't lick that problem; the foreman has to raise it with his general foreman, or it has to go to the plant superintendent.

Dowling: The foreman is the linking pin.

Likert: Right. He takes the problem up and it's dealt with at that level where all the people who are going to be affected by the decision are represented.

Dowling: You recognized the fact that you will have problem-solving groups that are ineffective, and, as I recall, you said that the answer then is not for the superior group to take over. What does the superior group do?

Likert: It's the responsibility of the superior group to ask themselves what needs to be done. In some instances, it will become clear that the person in charge just doesn't have the intellectual capability or the technical competence to do the job. In fairness to him, fairness to the people under him, and fairness to the entire organization, that person ought to be moved into something that he can do successfully.

Dowling: In other words, one answer is to replace the leader.

Likert: That's right, replace the leader. Now, that ought to be done only after the evidence is clear, and the evidence won't become clear until you've really tried to help that man become an effective leader through coaching, training, and supervision. One of the best coaches is his own boss. And another very good bunch of coaches are his own peers. If these people will work with him on his problem-solving, you can begin to help that man become a more productive supervisor, and help him build his subordinates into a highly effective group.

 The supervisor can be assisted in this process by collecting objective measurements of his leadership behavior and the kinds of response he gets as a consequence of that leadership, and by giving him information about what he's doing and how it compares with what he ought to be doing to get the best results.

Dowling: To continue with this primary group: In your System 1 and 2 organization, and I suppose, to a lesser degree, in your System 3 organization, performance standards and goals are set at the top, and are filtered down. It is the job of the primary group to accomplish these given goals.

In your System 4, you seem to start off with two premises. The first is that it is desirable for the group themselves to set their own performance goals, and your second is that these goals should be high. Could you describe the goal-setting process in a primary group under System 4?

Likert: Well, first it's well to recognize that when these goals come down from above, they are issued as orders. Evidence is quite clear that whenever you develop pressure from above, you get resistance from below. You get restriction of output on the part of the rank-and-file work groups. And the evidence is also quite clear that the more cohesive the work group, the more they enforce the goals they set, whether they're high or low.

If you're going to use the System 4 model, there are several relevant considerations. The first is that everybody's got the need for a sense of personal worth and importance. We're all proud to belong to and to work for a highly productive, hard-hitting organization that has prestige, and we're embarrassed about working for an organization that everybody recognizes as ineffective, incompetent, and unable to accomplish its goals.

Second, people want a chance to set goals for themselves. There are two or three ways of helping them to do this. One is a historical base: Let people know how much they're producing. You can use the historical base and look at progress against it and make periodic adjustments in it. Another way is to say, "Look, would you like to know what's par for the course?" There are established ways of measuring work and setting standards, so you can say, "Here's an approach, this is the way it's arrived at, and if you'd like to have it applied, and get information as to what's par for the course for this kind of job, we can get it, but you're going to decide whether that's a reasonable goal. We're not going to impose it on you. If you want to set it at 80 percent of par for awhile and see how well we do, okay, let's do it."

A third relevant consideration is that people are interested in job security, good pay, and promotions. If we can't compete in the world market, we lose jobs—we export jobs overseas. The American worker's being hurt because his productivity isn't up to what it can and should be.

Dowling: Relative, particularly, to, say, Japan.

Likert: Japan and Germany both. Now it's very interesting, what they're doing in Japan. They're using this kind of problem-solving and goal-setting. The American worker ought to have the chance to do the same thing. In a hardheaded way, let's say, "Let's look around here for inefficiency." I don't mean are you going to work harder. To use Mogensen's slogan, let's "Work smarter, not harder." Let's look around for inefficiencies and unnecessary costs. Then let's set goals for ourselves, based on where and how we can eliminate the waste, and see how well we can achieve them. People get a kick out of it when they set their own goals and have the satisfaction of accomplishing them. They don't feel that they're working under pressure, they don't have the emotional stress of working under pressure, and their physical and mental health is better.

Dowling: You gave an example of the possibility of a group setting a goal of only 80 percent of standard. I gather that, from your own experience and observations, that would be an atypical situation—one that didn't happen very often.

Likert: For the first round, management could live with 80 percent, especially if they've been running at 65. That much of an improvement isn't bad.

Dowling: Again, you're advocating the gradual approach to improvement.

Likert: Yes, certainly.

Dowling: A question that I think would occur to almost everyone is that System 4, wherever it's been tried, has consistently proved more effective than System 1, 2, and 3, yet System 4 still is used by relatively few companies. You have estimated that the average company in the United States is probably in the median range of System 2. Presumably, all organizations are interested in maximum effectiveness. Why aren't more of them System 4?

Likert: There's a very good reason for that. If you look at the P&L statement of any firm, or any profit center, it tells you that System 2 is a more productive system on the accounting reports than System 4. Put the heat on, introduce standards if you don't have them, tighten them up if you do, cut the personnel budget 10 percent, your earnings go up, productivity goes up, therefore, it's perfectly clear that System 2 is more productive than System 4, according to the P&L statement.

To illustrate that it's an illusion, let me tell you about a man who was made vice-president in charge of a division of a very large corporation. His bosses said, "We're going to put you in charge of a division that is in a superb shape. This division has an extraordinary earnings record, one of the best in the corporation. So all you've got to do is sit there and study it and you'll learn a lot."

He begins meeting with the people in the division headquarters, and he notices that there is an appalling amount of in-fighting going on among them. It doesn't quite fit with what he thinks a highly productive division ought to be. Then, he goes out to one of the major plants, and he finds a lot of equipment sitting out in the rain, rusting. "How come?" he asks. "Well," the people showing him around reply, "we've been trying to get a warehouse built to protect this equipment from the weather, but the division vice-president wanted to maintain earnings, and wouldn't build one." In the plant, he noticed that relations between the foremen and the men aren't very good. At the far end of the plant, there's an area filled with units they can't deliver because they're not up to quality.

Dowling: They're defective.

Likert: They're defective, they need rework. He goes up to the second level of the plant, and while he's talking to a foreman, a piece of heavy equipment moves across the floor, and the floor goes down a few inches and he says, "That's going to go through one of these days," and the foreman says, "Yeah, that's what we've been telling them, but they won't do anything about it." He gets back into the office and looks up the facts about foreman compensation, and he finds there's a big surplus in the merit award budget for foreman and that his foremen are the lowest-paid foremen of any division of the company.

Okay, there you are. A highly profitable plant, according to the P&L statement, but a very sick organization. So he says to himself, "What should I do? Here I am, a newly promoted vice-president. Shall I let it go for another two years, get a reputation as being a hot-shot manager because of highly profitable operations, and get nice fat bonuses?"

Well, he told me later, "I decided I had to be an honest man." One of the first things he did was to increase foreman pay in two or three steps; when he was through, in about two years' time, his foremen were among the highest paid of any division in the company, rather than the lowest. He built a warehouse, he repaired the plant so that the floors didn't sag, he did all kinds of things.

What happened to his P&L statement? You know very well what happened—it went to pot. He went in the red the first year, the second year, he was just breaking even. What happened to his bonuses? He didn't get any. In fact, his reputation was on the line. But, after two years' time, he had rebuilt that plant to the point where it began to be a productive organization, and from that time on it became a really sweet operation. But it took three years for the P&L statement to start showing it.

Dowling: What about the situation where the P&L statement looks lousy and the man in charge improves things by consciously but gradually moving toward System 4?

Likert: I can give you an example of a large plant with 5,000 employees, the worst-producing plant of several comparable, almost identical operations in this corporation. For the first year and a half that a new man was in charge, costs went up still more, quality got worse, there were sitdowns and wildcat strikes. But he was convinced that in moving toward System 4 he was moving in the right direction. One thing he faced was a traditional practice of swapping grievances for discipline cases. Any time a foreman slapped discipline on a worker, the union would throw a bunch of grievances into the hopper against the foreman. The union then would come in and offer to drop the grievances if the discipline case were dropped. The new man refused, saying to the union, "You know it is wrong and I know it is wrong and we aren't going to do it." There was a strike, but he made his decision stick, and people began to recognize that he did mean to be fair and honest. After a year and a half, production and quality leveled off and labor relations got a little better, but it was still the poorest-producing plant in a large corporation. After three years, he had trouble with corporate headquarters. He sent his personnel officer up to say, "Look, we're convinced we're doing the right thing, we're convinced we're making progress, but we can't show it yet."

Dowling: Give us more time.

Likert: Give us more time. And his corporate management had sense enough to give him some more time. Within four and a half years from the time he took over that organization, it was moving up. In eight years, it was the highest-producing plant of comparable units in the corporation. So it took eight years to go from the bottom to the top.

In another large comparable plant we can show from our human organization scores that a new System 4 manager had made impressive progress in less than a year in building a more productive organization. It took three years for the P&L to show it fully. The reason that top management today concludes that System 2 is more productive is simply that the P&L statement ignores the investment in the human organization, in customer loyalty, in supplier loyalty. When you engage in activity that shows short-range increase in cash flow as profits, but that liquidates these other assets, you draw erroneous conclusions as to what kind of management works best. The reason I'm pushing human resources accounting isn't that I'm interested in accounting, but that management will never recognize the greater productivity of System 4 compared with System 2 until they have accurate information as to what is happening to customer loyalty, the productive capability of the human organization, supplier loyalty, and so forth.

Dowling: In other words, the most important reason that System 2 is still preferred is a defective, an imperfect measuring system that concentrates only on P&L.

Likert: The P&L statement ought to show the impact of management decisions on the productive capability of the human organization. It ought to show the impact of management decisions on customer loyalty. If I substitute shoddy merchandise for superb merchandise, I can show a beautiful increase in profit, but I'm writing off a very valuable asset.

Dowling: You can show increases in profit over the short run.

Likert: For three, four, five years.

Dowling: In turn, the defects in the measurement system are reflected in defects in the reward system.

Likert: Yes, what you do is promote the manager who's exploiting your organization. The compensation system, the managerial bonus system, the promotion system are all defective for the same fundamental reason. What we do is promote the System 2 s.o.b.s and consider that this is smart management.

Dowling: You made the intriguing comment that the average management was probably somewhere in the median range of System 2, yet if you looked at top management circles, it was closer to System 4, and if you looked at the rank-and-file employee, the same organization looked like System 1. What's the explanation of this?

Likert: The bottom doesn't get quite as far over as System 1, but it gets down below System 2 sometimes, high System 1. There are two explanations. One is that the better corporations are managed much more in a System 4 model or System 3 model at the top. In other words, your finance committees, your executive committees, and so on work very well as productive problem-solving groups and frequently work using consensus as the basic mode of decision-making. Then they put earning requirements on divisions, and where they introduce a decentralized operation the manager's compensation and promotion is based on performance of the division, as reported by the P&L statement. Okay, the manager's going to say, "I'm going to get fast returns, and I'm going to move in the direction that's required." So, he shifts over from a System 4 model to the model he knows will yield fast returns, which is, "I'm going to plan, organize, direct, and control, and I'm going to set performance, production, and earning requirements for the subordinate levels, and I'm going to put the pressure on them to perform." This goes right on down the organization. As you go down, the controls become tighter and tighter, and there is less and less opportunity for problem-solving and decision-making.

The second explanation is that if you ask managers at several hierarchical levels the kind of management system they use, and you ask their subordinates to describe the system their bosses use, you'll find a rather consistent pattern: The manager sees himself more toward System 4 than his subordinates report him as being.

Dowling: I wonder if another explanation isn't the feeling in some managerial circles that System 4 is not the respectable or most approved method of management. Drucker has just reissued his *Concept of the Corporation*, and he comments in an epilogue that Alfred P. Sloan described himself in his own book as if he were, in the terms we're talking about, a System 1 or at best a System 2 manager, whereas Drucker's observation of Sloan and the way that he managed in relation to his close associates was that he was much closer to System 4.

Likert: When you analyze Sloan's book, *My Years at General Motors,* you find that Sloan used problem-solving approaches. Look at what he did with the dealers. He brought them in, he got them to problem-solve around the kind of relation they ought to have with the corporation, then he was guided by that problem-solving. He used a similar approach in several places. While at times I suspect that he may have been fairly System 1-ish in the way he made decisions, I was impressed with the extent to which he used problem-solving and encouraged problem-solving in a way that I would call a System 4 model.

Dowling: Though in the book itself, he emphasizes structure.

Likert: Yes, Sloan emphasizes structure but his structure parallels the System 4 overlapping group model. This comes out clearly in his chapter on "Coordination by Committee." He also emphasized measurement and obtaining objective, accurate facts to guide group decisions and he made a point that he issued few flat orders. There's another thing. A top G.M. executive said to me a few years ago, "Sure, we use group problem-solving, but that doesn't mean that everyone has equal weight in the decisions." Fred Donner exercised more influence than most because he always did his homework and came to meetings well prepared. I think that's a profound observation: The man who does his homework—who has studied what the facts are, who knows what the situational requirements are, and on the basis of that is able to say, "Gentlemen, if these are our objectives, these are the hard facts, and here are the realistic choices we have"—is the one who has a real impact on the problem-solving. Will you state your question again? There was something I wanted to come back to.

Dowling: Yes. Do you agree that one factor holding back the acceptance of System 4 is that it's not considered an acceptable or even respectable system of management?

Likert: That's a very important point. One of the things that's happened where we've started working in corporations at the vice-president level or department head level is that management levels above that first give their approval, then they begin to think, "If that manager and his subordinates learn how to manage in a way that is 20 to 40 percent more productive than I know how to manage, then I'm headed for early retirement, and I think I better cut this out." And they do cut it out. In one situation, a manager we had trained had a highly productive sales organization—the most productive out of fifty similar ones in the United States. He was promoted, and the vice-president in charge of that operation disbanded it.

Dowling: That's not really a case of feeling that System 4 isn't respectable, but of fearing it, paradoxically, because it may be *too* effective.

Likert: Most executives feel the pressures of managing according to the way their boss wants them to manage. If the top manager wants you to be a System 2 manager you don't have a whale of a lot of latitude unless you want to look for another job or are willing to gamble that you can build a System 4 organization fast enough to have your outstanding record protect you.

Dowling: I wonder if part of the problem is that most managers start with a very low opinion of the leadership skills and problem-solving abilities of the employees low down on the totem pole. I remember the survey that Mason Haire did a number of years ago. He surveyed 3,000 managers in about 40 countries and he came up with the conclusion that, although there were differences between the countries, by and large most of the managers viewed rank-and-file employees as preferring to be directed, wishing to avoid responsibility, and possessing little talent for leadership. To the extent that this kind of feeling is widespread among managers, it obviously inhibits the development of System 4.

Likert: Well, it does if you hold it as a steady concept, and it's probably correct that this is true for the bulk of these managers. However, this doesn't mean that they can't learn to be more effective.

Dowling: Yes, but it means that you start out on the part of many managers with a predisposition to be suspicious of the abilities of their subordinates.

Likert: Effective group problem-solving is a highly sophisticated skill that calls for a lot of learning. System 4 calls for learning more complex skills of leadership, more complex skills of interacting, more complex skills of problem-solving than you use in a System 2 model. So any suspicion managers have that people aren't prepared is true; it's true of managers, and it's true of the rank-and-file. Part of the problem we have is helping people to learn these skills. Now, the converse of this is also true. At an American Management Association meeting this morning, Jack Riley, vice-president of Equitable, pointed to the fact that there are significant cultural changes going on in the United States and the rest of the world. People are expecting, to a much greater extent, to be involved in decisions affecting them. They're learning, in school and in their extra-curricular activities, more effective models of leadership and of problem-solving. If they come into business with a System 4 expectation and run into a System 2 organization, our data are clear and unequivocal, they're going to be very frustrated and very dissatisfied. This applies not only to rank-and-file employees, but also to lower levels of supervision and even to technical specialists.

Dowling: It might apply especially to your young man getting out of college and his expectations.

Likert: High school or college. They're coming out of high school with some of these same orientations and expectations.

Dowling: Are there differences in types of organization as regards their suitability for System 4? I'm thinking of the distinction you made between jobs involving varied work—I think you used research, engineering, and selling life insurance as examples—and jobs that are machine-paced, highly functionalized, and repetitive jobs. I got the impression that, with varied types of work, you have no doubt that System 4 would work best, but with the repetitive type it might not make much difference. Or, to put it another way, the pay-off from System 4 in a varied operation would be considerably greater than the pay-off in a repetitive operation.

Likert: I have enough evidence now to know that System 4 pays off well with both kinds of work. In any fairly routine kind of manufacturing operation, for example, you'd get 20 to 40 percent higher productivity with System 4 than you do with System 2 or 2½.

Dowling: On the basis of observable data, then, the pay-off may be greater from System 4 in a varied type of operation, but you're stressing that the pay-off is substantial irrespective of the kind of work.

Likert: Yes, it's sizable. The other point is that the employees are more satisfied, they're healthier, labor relations are a lot better—it's just a sweeter, better operation.

Dowling: You referred in one of your articles to System 5. What's System 5 going to look like?

Likert: Well, the essential difference between System 4 and System 5, I think, is going to be that System 4 still carries a fair amount of emphasis on the importance of the authority of the superior. You recall that in *New Patterns of Management* and *The Human Organization* I state that if a supervisor cannot get consensus, and there's need for action, it's up to him to see that action's taken; it's his responsibility. So the superior still has hierarchical authority. System 5 will do away with that. It won't be hierarchical authority, but it will be an authority of relationships. So that, if a group can't reach consensus, the next higher group, through the linking pin, could very well say to this group, "If you can't make up your mind, we're going to make it up for you." And they problem-solve and do it. So the manager does it, not by authority of his hierarchical position, but by the authority of that group and his responsibility to the entire organization. The next higher group will also take responsibility for rebuilding the group as an effective component unit in the operation.

Dowling: Won't you still have a leader with larger responsibilities, higher status and title?

Likert: Yes, but he'd be a linking pin. There will be a leveling of status. The person who performs the linking-pin function has higher status than the other members of the group. But he won't say, "You do this because I tell you." He won't have that authority. The linking process from above would come down through him and he would say, "Look, in terms of the total enterprise, we can't let this matter go undecided. There are time constraints, there are financial constraints—it's got to be settled. So we've dealt with that problem and our decision is as follows. This is what's going to prevail if you can't decide."

Dowling: Do you look on this as an evolutionary process? Will System 4 naturally or inevitably develop into System 5, or is it going to be necessary to develop it as a formal system?

Likert: I look on the whole development as social evolutionary. System 4 in comparison to System 2 more fully satisfies the fundamental needs of the human being. System 4 is a more socially evolved way of harnessing the innate motivations, the innate capabilities of the human organization. System 5 will just be a more sophisticated, evolved model but it will be a formal system just as System 2 and System 4 are formal systems.

Dowling: To get an idea of the frequency of System 4, would you say that any of the companies in *Fortune*'s 500 are System 4?

Likert: Not to my knowledge. In 1965, at the Institute for Social Research, we started an intercompany longitudinal study. We designed it so that we would use the same basic measurement instrument in each of the studies we did. A series of studies has been done, largely in companies on the *Fortune* 500 list. Taylor and Bowers have analyzed these data and they find that there is a consistent pattern. Those divisions, plants, profit centers, and sales regions whose management is closer to System 4 achieve higher productivity, lower costs, better quality and less scrap loss than do the divisions, plants, etc. that are closer to System 1. This relationship holds also for employee satisfaction, physical and mental health and labor relations: the closer the management is to System 4, the better are the results. These same relationships exist, of course, in smaller companies.

Share of market also is related. Small companies and divisions in large corporations whose management is System 4 or close to it typically have from 50 to 90 percent of the market for their product. One System 4 life insurance agency, for example, sells 50 percent of all ordinary life insurance sold in its state.

Dowling: What do you feel is the likelihood of many of *Fortune*'s 500 being convinced by the weight of the internal evidence and, in the foreseeable future, moving their total organization to System 4? Or are the forces of institutional inertia and top management's autocratic bent too powerful to make this a real possibility?

Likert: Competition within the U.S., and internationally, will force *Fortune*'s 500 and all other firms to move toward System 4. No firm can long survive when its competition is using a system of management 20 percent to 40 percent more productive than its own style of management. But I believe that human resources accounting will bring this shift toward System 4 faster than will competition alone.

Every one of *Fortune*'s 500 is interested in obtaining and using accurate financial data to enable them to make sound plans and decisions. There is great interest in human resources accounting and its use is spreading rapidly on a trial basis for estimating the investment a firm has in its human resources. Bowers and I have just published, in the *Michigan Business Review*, a new method for estimating in dollars the change in value of the productive capability of a firm, profit center, or department from one time period to the next. Well-managed firms, I am sure, will start using this change in value method of human resources accounting along with the investment method. In using the change in value method of human resources accounting, firms will discover that System 4 is appreciably more profitable than their present inaccurate P&L statement tells them. As this takes place, there will be a much more rapid shift to System 4 than is now occurring. In fact, the top corporate management of some of the largest and most successful corporations have decided to move closer to System 4 and have started efforts to do this. And as their plants or departments shift toward System 4, they experience a sizable improvement in performance.

Conversation with
CHRIS ARGYRIS

Chris Argyris has formidable credentials: James Bryant Conant Professor of Education and Organizational Behavior, Graduate Schools of Education and Business Administration, Harvard University; author of 16 books and over 125 articles; consultant to the top management of over 50 public and private organizations, including the U.S. Department of State and some of America's largest and most prestigious corporations.

Florence Nightingale earned the designation "governess of the governors of India." It might be equally appropriate to dub Argyris "teacher of American presidents." A more important question than what to call Argyris is what he teaches his presidents. Not substance, but process, is what they learn from Argyris. He helps them learn how to change their behavior, how to become more effective problem solvers and decision makers. To make the same point, but in different words, Argyris helps his presidents appreciate the conditions that must obtain if they are to acquire valid information and what they can do to facilitate these conditions.

Learning for more effective action is not easy, Argyris emphasizes; his writings catalogue more failures than successes. He admits that he is unaware of any organization development success story in a total organization—that no existing organization has made the structural changes indicated for a fully developed Yb system. Argyris is enough of a realist to confess the failures and recognize the problems, but enough of an idealist to insist that the goal is worth all the striving, and that some organizations, and some presidents, eventually will achieve it.

Reprinted from Organizational Dynamics, *Summer 1974*

Dowling: A generalized question to start: Many experts argue that it's easier and more effective to bring about improvements in performance by changing structures and systems than by trying to change people's behavior directly. If I understand your position correctly, you would say it all depends—on the size and complexity of the change in structure and system necessary to effect the desired improvement and on the level of the individual in the organization and the degree of responsibility that he has. So yours is a conditional approach to organizational change. For example, you cite the classic case of Bill Whyte and the introduction of the spindle between the waitresses and the countermen that depersonalized the ordering process and defused their relationships. Previously, waitresses had competed for the counterman's attention in handing in orders. You might have accomplished the same thing if you had taken the trouble to have a very lengthy and elaborate confrontation session. But why bother?

Argyris: Right. What you just said makes sense, but let me add one other factor. If the person knows how to perform the new behavior you require—as in the spindle case, once they created the innovation there was no new behavior that they needed to learn—then it's quite easy to change behavior. But if the person doesn't know how to perform the behavior that you require, then that may be more difficult. For example, if we ask how management should behave to increase their subordinates' trust in them (and let's define trust as people's ability to take risks in front of each other), that kind of behavioral change—even though I haven't found many people against increasing trust—is very difficult to achieve. Most of my life is spent in trying to alter behavior and helping people to acquire skills they don't have that are essential to the new behavior they value and want to achieve.

Dowling: In other words, in teaching them new skills.

Argyris: Yes. And these new skills require new values. The second factor I want to add is to ask to what extent the new behavior is not performable without the cooperation of someone else. If I'm supposed to change something that only I have to learn, that's fine, but what if it's something that my colleague also has to learn before the change becomes meaningful? Let's assume that we're in a problem-solving meeting and, let's say, I see him completely misunderstanding my department's goals and doing this for political reasons—and he sees me as exhibiting the same behavior

76

for the same reason. Let's further assume that, as a consultant, you help me to see that I have been doing that to him and that you help me, somehow, to alter my behavior. That isn't enough; he's also got to alter his or I'm still going to be in trouble.

Dowling: I remember an instance that Chapple and Sayles give where several supervisors had responsibility for different steps in the credit operation; there was no end of backbiting and buckpassing among them. This problem was solved rather easily by simply putting them under the same boss—in other words, by restructuring the work flow logically and making the several steps the responsibility of a single superior.

Argyris: Because there the lack of cooperation had been caused by the way things were structured. However, let me add a point and pose a question. Did they need an Elliott Chapple to help them realize what was wrong? I think they did, but why did they need Elliott to do it? Didn't they have the intelligence to make that change on their own? So there's another issue that interests me: Not only how do you help organizations change, but how do you help them figure out why they needed someone else to bring about this change? This second criterion would not concern Elliott, while a management consulting firm might not want a company to develop that kind of intelligence, because that would lessen the need for consultants.

Dowling: I see your point. On the surface the restructuring seems obvious, but apparently they were locked in by their perceptions, and they did need a consultant to point out what seems, in retrospect, to be the logical solution.

Argyris: I have yet to be in an organization where my recommendations about structure or anyone else's are new to the people in that organization. Most of our recommendations are based on interviews and observations of people and I have found that, generally speaking, there is the intelligence within the system itself to solve any management problems. So, in addition to structural or interpersonal change, there is this other issue: How do you help organizations diagnose why it is that they need an outsider to solve problems they already have the intelligence and information to solve themselves? Of course, if they're unable to use the intelligence and the information effectively, obviously they need an outsider.

Dowling: You gave another instance of organizational change—Bob Ford's experiments at AT&T with job enrichment. There the structure of the job was changed without any consultation with the people whose jobs were being changed. The process was completely authoritarian. And yet it worked; the morale improved; the quality of work improved; attendance improved. Of course, you made the point that the changes worked in these cases because you were giving the employees more responsibility, even though they hadn't asked for it. Also, change was facilitated because each job was a self-contained unit.

Argyris: The change was top-down, all right. But the people in Ford's group had found out ahead of time that these college-educated customer representatives were fed up with their jobs; in effect, they had gotten some data as to what kind of changes these college reps would work best under. I know another case in the Bell system where employees were given more responsibility with positive results in terms of the worker, but the foremen were worried by the changes and went to the middle management and said they wanted more work. The middle management said, "Before we give you more work, which means we'll have to give up some of our work, we will have to approach the next level. . . ."

Dowling: ". . . and say what are you willing to give us so that we, in turn, can enrich the foremen's jobs by delegating some of these chores."

Argyris: Right. It worked all the way up to the vice-presidential level, and they stopped it because they didn't want to give up anything to the next level below. That's creating quite a credibility problem.

Dowling: I hadn't heard that before. I do remember that in that customer correspondence group there was one woman who was an exception. She said, "Look, if you give me more responsibility, I want more money; I quit." But this was only one out of over 120 employees. For the rest, having a more interesting job was sufficient reward.

Argyris: If, indeed, you increase productivity, it's terribly important to give an employee a fair share of the increase in productivity. Some companies are doing wonderful work in this area of job enrichment and some are using it in a god-awful way; it will backfire, and I'm glad it will.

Dowling: Have you followed the Emery Air Freight's application of Skinner's positive reinforcement?

Argyris: They applied it with salesmen.

Dowling: It began in sales, but where they've had the most concrete results is with customer representatives and people on the loading docks, where they've increased containerization utilization from 45 to 90 percent. It's the combination of continuous feedback on daily performance through records that workers keep themselves plus having the boss provide positive reinforcement according to a Skinner-type schedule. Skinner thinks that Emery's application of his ideas is immoral, because they boast of saving over $3 million, yet they have shared none of the savings with their employees. So far, they've gotten away with it. Maybe you're right, and it will eventually backfire or boomerang.

In terms of your assertion that with organizational change, structural change is only effective at levels where the level of responsibility is not great, how do you reconcile this with the structural changes Lord Wilfred Brown instituted at Glacier?

Argyris: That's a very good question. If I understand what went on at Glacier, I think they did what I believe in—in fact, I learned a lot from Glacier. What happened was that the psychiatrist Elliott Jaques began by working with Wilfred Brown and increased the degree of discussion, confrontation, problem solving, and trust at the upper levels. They then began to spread that new, interpersonal competence to the next level; in other words, they did not start with structure; they started by focusing on what I would call the interpersonal issues that influence problem solving. Once they did that, they began to make the structural changes.

My point of view is not that you should avoid structural change. However, I don't think you should start with structural changes; you should start by doing what Jaques did in the factory and then proceed to structural changes. If I understand the situation at Glacier, there was still some degree of top-down coercion, or imposition of structure. At the same time—and this has its parallel in other organizations—Jaques and Lord Brown developed a kind of structure that provided for increased choice, commitment, and responsibility for employees. So the resistance to this imposition of structure was less because employees saw that they were being given, in fact, greater opportunity for the control over their work lives.

Dowling: Through their elected worker representatives on the works council.

Argyris: Yes. I recall that Lord Brown told me that one of the first people he had as a representative was a communist trade union leader or shop steward, and people told him, "Don't let this guy on the works council; he's a troublemaker." Lord Brown replied, "No, we meant what we said. He's been elected and we've got to follow through." As I remember the story, it was the employees themselves who pressured him when he got out of line. They would say to him, "Look, this system is trying to be fair and you're not being fair in trying to buck it." Eventually, this man altered his attitudes and is now, I believe, a manager at Glacier. To summarize, I think the following has occurred: Lord Brown and Jaques started with unfreezing the organization, especially at the top. Second, with the unfreezing they learned a lot from the people below. Jaques spent a lot of time working at the lower levels of the organization, he fed back information, and together Lord Brown and Jaques designed a system that genuinely increased the control that the employees had. Part of that design was the opportunity to confront any kind of imposition, as well as the chance to take the initiative in creating new impositions, new structural changes.

Dowling: You mean the fact that any changes in basic management policies require the unanimous consent of both management and the employee representatives on the works council. Of course, there's also a formal appeals system open to any employee.

Argyris: That's what I mean—that the opportunity to confront the system is built into the system. The other factor that helps to make the system work is the innate British sense of fairness.

We've got to find ways of integrating what Lord Brown has done with what people like myself are talking about. I find his most recent book a fascinating one, but, as he says, there is nothing in it on motivation. His fundamental assumption appears to be that if you're a decent, civilized manager and you define a just system clearly and unambiguously, and if you define ways of changing that system or making it changeable, then people will really work hard. There's a lot of truth in his position; he's one of the few people who have come up with a relatively precise definition of what he means by a manager or what he means by a subordinate, and if people accept these definitions and function within them, you have a good working relationship. Where he and I might team up, figuratively speaking, would be for him to help develop these new definitions and for me to help develop a problem-solving interaction among the people so that they could confront these definitions and then internalize the ones they want.

Dowling: There's a little book since the one you're referring to called *The Earnings Conflict*, in which Lord Brown looks at the British society as a whole and expresses his fear that the British are losing that quality of fairness that formerly marked most of their relations. What's happened in England in the past months suggests that his forebodings are justified.

Argyris: I don't have any data for this, but I'd like to hypothesize that one reason this sense of justice, this sense of being willing to submit to what I'll call for a moment the "impeccable logic that is just," is deserting the youth in England is that it doesn't leave as much room for the expression of feelings as they need. They may, in fact, in another ten years go through what we went through in the Sixties with the hippie movement and the campus revolts.

Dowling: Assuming that you're right and that Lord Brown and Jaques began changes at Glacier in what you feel is the right way—first changing the values and the behavior at the very top—then it's clear how rare the Lord Browns are in the world. Your own piece in the *Harvard Business Review* on chief executive behavior as the key to organization development makes this point very strongly. The profile of the chief executive officer that emerges is of a man deeply committed to Theory X values and behavior. But not an inflexible autocrat, because he's perfectly capable of innovation, providing he does the innovating.

Argyris: But certainly he is an autocrat.

Dowling: I'm also reminded of the study that Mason Haire and several others did a number of years ago of over 3,000 managers in various countries. There would appear to be a managerial constant—that most managers felt their subordinates lacked qualities of leadership, were afraid of risks, and needed direction. In other words, when you initiate Theory Y organization development at the top of most organizations, the climate is singularly hostile.

Argyris: OK. You're getting at another crucial issue and my comments may be a bit long-winded.

I'm now working with a group of presidents, many of whom are represented in that article, trying to see what changes can be brought about. For example, I've worked with T-groups, and the idea was somehow to help people change their behavior. When we ask managers how they behave in dealing with people, they give us pretty straightforward answers. We study these answers and formulate them in the form of propositions: If you want to influence these kinds of workers, do the following things and you get the following results. The generalizations are pretty straightforward. We develop them from a lot of cases, and we call these the "espoused theories" that people have. Then we make tapes of the same managers' behavior under those conditions and we find that, for the most part, their behavior doesn't match their espoused theory, which is the kind of proposition the Haire study documented. People claim that they act democratically in dealing with other people when actually they behave autocratically.

We had started with the assumption that all human behavior is informed by some theory the guy has, a map that gives meaning to whatever he or she wants to do. If that's true, then it doesn't make sense for people to hold theories that they don't use or practice. So we went back to the tapes and we listened to their behavior and told them, "We are going to recreate the theories that must have been there in your minds." We called the resulting propositions their "theory-in-use" or their "theory-in-practice." We developed a model of the theory-in-use and we were able to show that one of the propositions of this model was that if you see someone else behave incongruently between his espoused theory and his theory-in-use, you didn't say anything, especially if the manager exhibiting the incongruency has power. In this way we could begin to see one reason why executives weren't learning about their discrepancies—they weren't getting any kind of feedback.

Now we're developing a new kind of what I'd like to call education for effectiveness—when I say we I'm referring to Don Schon, who wrote a book on organizational stable states and innovations. . . .

Dowling: Yes, I've read it. An exciting work.

Argyris: We've just finished a book together; we call it *Theory in Practice*, with implications for the redesign of professional education—how do you design education that will lead to more effective action? In this book we make the following kinds of generalizations: The best way to change behavior is not to focus on behavior; what you need to do is help people discover and make explicit their theory-in-use. If you help a person discover what his theory-in-use is, he can then decide whether he wants to alter it. If he learns how to alter it in an actual, on-going situation, you've helped him more than if you say to him, "You ought to be less autocratic."

For example, I have had people—presidents—who say, "Now I really see how autocratic I am; I'm going to change. I'm going to stop cutting people off when they talk to me." Later, we may tape his behavior and find that, indeed, he has stopped cutting people off, but either he increases his control over people in another direction or he keeps himself pent up as long as he can and finally reverts to his previous pattern. And people say, "You see, this is just a gimmick; this guy isn't really changing."

However, when we help him develop a theory-in-use, he sees that one of his ways of behaving is to control people in a certain way and with certain consequences, and if he's going to change, these values have to be changed. We begin to get a person who, first of all, has a much more realistic level of aspiration regarding how much his behavior is going to change—he realizes that he won't be a new person overnight, and second, realizes that he needs the help of the people with whom he's working. He no longer keeps thinking, "Well, I went to my T-group and I learned that I have to be less authoritarian. I'll try being less authoritarian by, in effect, becoming the opposite of what I was"—which is to withdraw. Instead, he might involve his peer group and say, "Look, I'm beginning to see some of my behavior; here's the theory I've been operating under among you people, and it doesn't make any sense to me now. However, I'm not going to change these values overnight and therefore, I don't expect real changes overnight in the way I work with you. I need your understanding and your help."

We've found that these presidents now have a map of why they behave the way they do, the values they hold, the strategies they tend to use, and the consequences that these strategies have on other people.

In a T-group, the strategy has been to create a vacuum and then have people project their behavior onto the group. In this new method of education for effectiveness we begin by recording a president's behavior, then abstracting five pages of it and listening to it.

Dowling: Do you mean recording an actual business meeting?

Argyris: Yes, an actual meeting. The president sends the recording to us and says, for example, "Here's my executive committee meeting for Wednesday," and we abstract from it, let's say, five pages. Next, ten presidents from different corporations meet here and read these cases in actual scenario form—no analysis, just what did the guy say and how did people react to it.

Dowling: They're reading each other's scenarios.

Argyris: Right, and their own. After reading the scenario they ask themselves what kind of a theory-in-use can they deduce from the transcription: To what extent is the president what we call Model 1, which includes Theory X but goes beyond it? Each president prepares his own diagnosis of his behavior while someone else in the group is doing the same on his case—so every president analyzes his own case and someone else's. Then they meet and exchange diagnoses. A president, for example, has the chance to show the group that he's developing some insight into his behavior; he may see that he was much more controlling than he had thought. He's challenged to do his best because he knows that when he's through someone else is going to analyze his case. We find that instead of worrying about who am I, what is my role (typical questions in T-groups), people are worrying more about how effective they can become. They're less interested in caring for one another and more interested in learning from one another and becoming more effective.

Because we have these maps of the theory-in-use, you don't need a vacuum to get sincere behavior going. Typically, the participant seems to rationalize as follows: "I've got a week; I'm not sure whether I'll really get to know everyone here or even get to trust everyone here, but what can I do to maximize my learning? How can I use the participants' resources to improve my understanding of my behavior?" In other words, using tapes makes people less dependent on each other; they have to worry less about caring for each other and interpersonal closeness and they worry more about effectiveness and competence and how to alter their behavior.

Dowling: I remember when you were explaining the relative failure of a top management group in organization development. All of them had had prior favorable experiences with T-groups, and yet the only time they actually showed any learning was when you were around. Once you left they reverted right back to their old behavior. I remember that one of the reasons you gave was that T-groups taught the wrong things, that there was very little emphasis on becoming more effective in group relations. . . .

Argyris: Or more effective in problem solving.

Dowling: Yes. The emphasis was on being evaluative and so forth. So in other words, what you're doing with this new approach is remedying what you diagnosed as the critical weakness in T-groups.

Argyris: Exactly; that's our attempt. By Thursday of a week's program each president has developed a pretty accurate map, we think, of his theory-in-use. Thursday night each one goes to his room and asks himself, "OK, this is my theory-in-use; what can I do to modify it? Tomorrow I'm going to present to the other nine people the action steps I'm planning on taking." We tell him, "When you come and tell us what you're going to do, don't give us your espoused theory. We want to know what you are planning to do, what you're planning to say." It's not enough for them to tell us they're going back to their group and try to be less controlling and listen more. In an effectiveness group, by contrast, the participants say, "All right, give us a scenario. What will you say, how will you do this, how will you reduce your control?" Maybe the president's response is, "I won't say anything." Well, that becomes the opposite of control.

Dowling: It's withdrawal.

Argyris: Right. It's not very helpful and it's not likely to be sustaining. And if that were the president's plan, we would point out the fatal flaws in his strategy. In any event, three months later each president sends us a second tape of his behavior and again we type up an excerpt.

Dowling: This is another tape of an actual meeting?

Argyris: Yes. The group meets here three months later to discuss the changes that they've been making. And I'm beginning to see change to a degree that I hadn't seen in T-groups. But the most important thing that I'm beginning to see—which I like—is that they're learning how to learn from a situation. There's no amount of training we can give them here that duplicates the variances and the complexity of the on-the-job situation. We can't even try to anticipate all the situations they're going to encounter, but we can help them to learn how to learn so that they can go back and alter their behavior through their own understanding of what is happening. One thing they realize is that they can't do it by themselves; the best way is to learn from their own work team.

Another difference in this kind of learning is that instead of saying, "OK, be less autocratic," we say, "OK, learn what your theory-in-use is and learn here how to alter your theory-in-use under conditions in which other people tell you they can't figure out what underlies your behavior." Then they try out their modified theory-in-use back home. Sometimes they come back and tell us, "Here was the trouble I had. I thought I was going to do this but it didn't work out." And the rest of the participants study the scenario and try to determine what went wrong and why.

That's my long-winded answer; I've forgotten the question.

Dowling: I don't remember the wording myself. But I recall that study of yours in which there was a substantial quantity of observable change in a consultant group. What impressed me most about that was that here were people who, in addition to changing their attitudes and behavior, also experienced a payoff as a consequence of their changed behavior. They had been reluctant to fire people, but now they found they were finally able to get rid of some imcompetent executives. They set up some new control procedures that reduced the frequency of missed deadlines. What I'm getting at is that in order to have any really effective change, you have to be able to internalize success—success that you can relate to the acquisition and application of your new values.

Argyris: Yes, because that success becomes the reinforcer of the new values and the new behavior. I thought you were going to say that the consultants changed because they were more intelligent than the other executive groups I'd studied. My own feeling is that they're not that much brighter than any other top-management group, but there's more pressure on them to be competent because there is immediate feedback from their clients. By contrast, I've been in an oil company where the president and vice-presidents knew what their market was and they felt relatively safe; in this case there was much less internal pressure—internal to themselves—to change. They argued that the inefficiency we pointed to as caused by their lack of openness was something they could afford.

Dowling: Since change is painful—why go through it?

Argyris: Yes, although some of the vice-presidents, especially the younger ones, responded that someday one of them might be president and, by that time, not able to afford it. But the feeling wasn't as compelling as in the consultant group.

Dowling: You referred in another example—a brief one that I hope you can expand on—to a division in a large electronics company that over a period of time systematically developed a group of executives who were willing to experiment, take risks, and so forth. I was wondering how they did it. What did top management do to make this development possible?

Argyris: In effect, we worked with the top level with tapes of their behavior until they had become much more effective, much more interpersonally competent. I want to be clear on one point: I'm interested in interpersonal competence, in such phenomena as openness and risk-taking and so on, because they have an enormous influence on rational problem-solving processes. I like to picture myself as a person who's saying, "Let's take a look at how emotions or suppressed emotions and so on gum up effective problem solving." I'm interested, in other words, in helping make rational activity more effective. I don't want to be viewed as a person who champions feeling over reason.

Dowling: You use the phrase "the rationality of feelings."

Argyris: Exactly. We were able to score the effectiveness of their problem-solving process. When they got to the point—unlike Company P, where they regressed every time I wasn't around—that they were able to reward each other and reinforce each other for more openness; then we took the next 40 people, rather than leaving it with just the top 20. That took almost a year. Then we tackled the next group of, as I recall, 60 managers. The results were best at the top and next best with the second group of 40. By the time we finished, it hadn't percolated as well among the lower group of 60 managers as we had hoped, but things were a lot better than they had been before. We didn't start at the second level until we were sure that there was a group of top managers who were going to reinforce the new behavior and not say, "Well, what the hell have you guys learned?" Not only did we spend a week with each group, but we worked with them in their actual problem-solving meetings and we taped their meetings after they came back and scored their performance and fed the data back to them.

As a consequence, top management began making structural changes. For instance, they realized that the design of their budgetary system was based on the assumption that you can't trust people, so they began to redesign budgetary systems. They also began to redesign their organizational structure.

Dowling: The last comment is a fascinating one. I remember being both intrigued and a little frustrated in a couple of your books because you made the point that if you changed interpersonal relations in the direction of Theory Y or your variation of it, Theory Yb, you also needed to make changes in administrative control mechanisms, structural design, and reward and compensation systems. But there were no maps as to what these structural changes should be if they were to be congruent with your Yb system. Maybe you're able to be a little more explicit about the structural changes that are desirable if you want to make the structure congruent with your system.

Argyris: I'm going to disappoint you, because I don't think that research has been done. On pay, for example, I think that in this country Ed Lawler and in England Tom Lupton and his group have focused most on these issues. In my book on integrating the individual and the organization, there was a section in which I tried to brainstorm the kinds of structures that will be needed. After brainstorming these ideas on leadership control systems and new kinds of structures I went back to a group of presidents and they said, "These are great ideas." I told them, "Fine, but we need to test them; there's no empirical data." This was in '64.

Dowling: Ten years ago.

Argyris: They said, "We'll be glad to support you, but not with this." I asked why, and listening to their responses was how I got interested in the interpersonal competence issue. They said they didn't trust each other enough to work together on anything so sensitive. That put me off on T-groups—all these presidents were alumni of T-groups. And hence this shift to education for effectiveness. At the same time I've been studying management information systems, I've also been studying budgetary systems, but I can't honestly say that I have the kinds of maps that satisfy me.

Dowling: What set me off was the comment about the electronics company where top management decided that since they had these new values, they wanted to revamp their budgetary system.

Argyris: I'm working now with a company that's doing some very innovative things. The president came to me and said, "What new kinds of pay systems are there for a Yb world?" When I told him I honestly don't know he said, "Well, we'd better find out; let's experiment." What he soon realized was that even if he knew what the right pay system was it would not work because it would be imposed. Even if he said, "I don't want to impose this on you, but here's something that's worked well in another organization. Would you like to use it?" the degree of imposition would be great enough that the internal commitment wouldn't be very strong. Can you afford to have low internal commitment when you're monkeying with the pay of your top people?

This man started at the top, so that meant that his top team did some real work on their own values, as a result of which they developed a new incentive compensation system for the corporate management group. Interestingly enough, they then asked, "If we're developing our own pay scheme, why shouldn't the people immediately below us also have a pay scheme?" Then they spent I don't know how many sessions trying to design a pay scheme for the divisional management groups. When they finally brought it to me I said, "Before you introduce it, let me ask you something. You had a theory that you couldn't impose it on yourselves; how can you impose it on the people below?" They hadn't invited them to any of their sessions.

Dowling: There was no participation.

Argyris: None. This realization surprised them; they saw that they were violating their own values. So they stopped where they were and brought in their subordinates—the people reporting directly to the president or vice-presidents—and told them exactly what had happened and involved them in the redesign. That's where they are at the moment. They're experimenting with what they say are insignificant amounts of money compared with the total salary package. But they intend to make the amounts significant.

I sometimes ask myself—and maybe this is a defense on my part—what would happen if we knew what the right structures were or what the right management information systems were and so on. Could they be imposed? I think they could be imposed on new organizations, but in an old organization I don't think it would work.

Dowling: In a new organization there's no value conflict.

Argyris: That's right. But in old organizations you may need to go through the unfreezing process. If you do go through the unfreezing process, then you should let the people pretty well design the structures themselves.

Dowling: When you stress the importance of beginning anything like this at the top I certainly see the power reasons, but I also remember Bagehot's marvelous phrase about the middle class being an imitative class. Maybe another factor here is psychological—that middle management is also an imitative class. In other words, they look up to and imitate the top brass.

Argyris: I don't know how to answer that. Let me speak first of middle management. In order for me to find out if they are an imitating class I'd have to factor out the impact of the authority of the people above them, which I wouldn't know how to do. So if they are imitating, it may be that the power factor is the whole story. There's one way of getting an answer, and that is to ask yourself where most of the innovations in a given organization come from. I know as many people in middle management as in the upper levels of management who are prepared to make significant innovations. I know a manager in a large company who was in the advanced management program at Harvard and who is now trying to do some really very simple things with job enrichment, but he's keeping it secret from his top people. So I can't go along with the class thesis, although it just might be true.

Dowling: The man you're talking about is taking a substantial risk.

Argyris: Yes, a tremendous risk, and he knows it. But that's the power issue.

Dowling: Why is he keeping it secret?

Argyris: Because he fears he'd lose his job, or the experiments would be killed. The other theory he has is that they would let him go on, but they'd call him some kind of a nut. Now, I'm told that the same thing is still happening at Procter & Gamble. There's a whole fascinating issue: Should people like myself go into organizations and collude with that kind of secrecy? Some people have said yes; I say no.

Dowling: Why do you say no? I mean, assuming that what the people are trying to do is congruent with the values you think should be introduced into the organization . . .

Argyris: I say no because I think in a world of unilateral power—as it is in the pyramidal structure—it may be ethically unjust and professionally ineffective to collude with the higher-level people in their ignorance.

On top of that, any academic has a position of credibility vis-à-vis inquiry to maintain. Should a professor in a university hide knowledge? I don't think he should.

Dowling: To get back for a minute to your friend in middle management who's instituting job enrichment and keeping it hidden from the boss; I suppose that he's hoping to get it out in the open after his innovation has proved its worth.

Argyris: That's right, and he'll show his work.

Dowling: In other words, what he's counting on is that his success will justify his actions.

Argyris: Yes, and I've been in situations where that's exactly what happened. It did work, and the management said, "We're sorry; we really goofed. Thank God you did it," and in other places where they said, "Don't ever do that again." The man didn't get fired, but he didn't advance, either.

Dowling: If top management were sufficiently authoritarian, success in itself might not be enough. I could conceive of him getting fired even if it worked.

Argyris: I'm told that there are some people in General Foods who are worried because their Topeka plant is so famous. "What are the new problems we're going to have; why did we even start this?" they ask. And there's apparently another group, thank God, that's saying, "Well, we made progress; we can't go backward, so we've got to go forward."

Dowling: You made an interesting observation that Theory X was hard on getting the job done but it was soft on the effectiveness of the system. Some of the most productive organizations had some of the most dry rot. Dry rot is John Gardner's phrase; you used "organizational entropy" instead. Could you expand on that?

Argyris: I've been in organizations in which you could point to losses of money, lessened commitment of effort, and so on. The comment people at the top made was, "Oh well, that's human nature." I remember one president who said, "Chris, 5 percent of the workers work, 10 percent think they work, and 85 percent would rather die than work. Now you can't change human nature." And I said, "How do you know you can't change human nature?" Then he responded with something like, "Middle management is full of clucks; we pay them more money than they're worth. You can't change that." So he's making assumptions about what cannot be changed that he has not tested. If he made the same assumptions about a product, someone would say, "Well, have you run a product test? How do you know you can't sell it or redesign it?" What I find is that most top managements permit the apathy, the indifference, the goldbricking to go on. And they rationalize it all as human nature.

Dowling: Isn't there another element there? It's the sort of thing that Likert is always talking about: You can have all sorts of human resources wasted and underutilized at the same time that the organization remains profitable.

Argyris: If what I am saying is true of all organizations—or darn near all—then all this dry rot gets incorporated into the price structure, because there's no one you're competing with that doesn't have that same problem. So it looks inevitable, like death and taxes. Only when we get some organizations that can really alter these conditions and subsequently alter their price structure—and it is happening with some organizations that are practicing job enrichment—then we will see that all these notions about a rigid human nature are not necessarily valid.

Dowling: Have you seen any reason to believe that the new development of human resource accounting is going to make any difference?

Argyris: First of all, I haven't found it taking off as fast as I would like, but that's true of all innovations. Some people who know more about accounting than I do tell me that there are problems endemic in the technical aspects of the system. But let me give you a theoretical answer. I know of no better way of getting some changes than by changing the basic language of management, and the accounting system is part of the basic language. So I would assume that if they can genuinely describe the human costs and if those get into the P&L statement, outside pressures will force a reluctant management to take some action.

Dowling: Organizational entropy is your answer to Lawrence's argument that "you show me the environment and I'll tell you what the organization should be." I suppose he's referring to the mechanistic-versus-the-organismic models; your argument would be that there is no mechanistic organization.

Argyris: To put it another way, even if there were, it would be temporary, because the entropy inside will get so high that even a place like the Bell System, which supposedly has a benign environment and is mechanistic, will have trouble.

Dowling: In the "Beyond Theory Y" article by Lorsch and Morse in the *Harvard Business Review*, an Akron plant is cited as the model of a mechanistic organization with very set schedules, policies, and rules.

Argyris: And everyone was happy and feeling competent. Even if we assume that all they said was true and the company is making plenty of money, it won't last. Look what happened at IBM. The engineering and marketing divisions had a monopoly of bright engineers; no good engineer would go into manufacturing, because there was no innovation going on. Then Tom Watson and others realized this and decided he wasn't going to have Akron-type plants. If the company was to remain prosperous, they had to encourage innovation at the manufacturing level.

Dowling: Was this Watson, Sr. or Watson, Jr.?

Argyris: Watson, Jr. I think the same is true of what happened at General Foods. There were some non-Akron-type people in the Akron-type plant. Some of these frustrated people eventually got to the top and said, "Let's make some experiments."

Dowling: The entropy you're talking about is a slow process. It's a little like Louis XV. After one generation of being happy, prosperous, and complacent with an Akron-type plant, then the deluge. You have retained a measure of distrust in situations where the people responsible for developing a program describe the marvelous things that have happened. There has to be an element of self-serving.

Argyris: They could do very easily what I try to do in my own work—provide tapes and say, "OK, mister, this is how I decide whether people have learned or not, whether they have changed or not. Listen to the tapes and make up your own mind." I do think that there are two reasons for optimism about the capacity of organizations to improve themselves: First, there are an increasing number of long-range success stories in subsystems, not in one total system; second, there is going to be a greater predisposition on the part of younger managers to build on these success stories. I don't think ten years ago you could have predicted that General Foods would have done what it did do, but it was some of the young top people who saw the necessity for doing it. I should add a few words of caution. It's going to take a large team, not a small one, to develop a truly successful total organization.

Second, I don't think we have the necessary competence among most OD people. Not only are too many of them tied to the old T-group values of closeness and not concerned enough with effectiveness and competence, but many of them don't know enough about teaming up with people who know something about microeconomics or financial analysis, budgeting processes, management information systems—and all these things have to go together. Therefore, it will be quite a while before we develop a successful organization.

Dowling: Have these successes within subsystems—you mentioned parts of Polaroid, IBM, TRW, and Corning Glass—have they followed a common approach to organization development?

Argyris: I don't know their approaches but I can tell you that things like T-groups, team building, intergroup rivalries being explored, the redesign of work—all of these have been included in the development process. But how they have used them I don't know in detail.

Dowling: I remember reading accounts of job enrichment and job redesign at Texas Instruments at the foreman level. It was more or less successful, depending upon the amount of support that the foreman received from his immediate superior. In other words, it was a spotty business, depending on how much reinforcement, reassurance, and approval the foreman got, despite the fact that top management was formally committed to the concept. I suppose you would approve of the fact that the lower and middle managers had an option as to whether or not to follow this commitment. It wasn't forced on them.

Argyris: Yes, but I would also add something else. Some of those middle managers may, in fact, disbelieve the top people. They watched the top's behavior. The top can say they really mean it, but some of these middle men can be very cagey. What Texas Instruments didn't show were the real reasons why some of its supervisors didn't support the job enrichment program. They could write us a narrative by bringing some supervisors who weren't supportive into a room with some who were and asking, "Well, what prevents you from giving support?" What if someone says, "Well, I think you've got to be kidding; it's a new trick, a new fad"? What can we do to unfreeze that? The person might say, "Well, I'll tell you what you can do. Give me a boss who behaves differently than mine behaves." All right; let's bring in the boss. You see the direction I'm going in. If one middle manager fears job enrichment because of his boss, the two people are regarded identically. They're both looked at as people who aren't supporting their foremen. But there's quite a difference. The only way to get at this difference is if the bosses are also confronted with their behavior.

Dowling: There could be another element in the job enrichment program at Texas Instruments. The lack of support or commitment might be a form of resentment on the part of some middle managers whose jobs were not being similarly enriched.

Argyris: That's a good point. That's one more reason I start at the top of the organization. I don't know the situation at Texas Instruments, but certainly at the telephone company there are plenty of young middle managers who would like a lot more enriched work.

Dowling: It might be useful to compare you with Ren Likert to put your approach to organizational change in a context. Your ideal or model of a manager is very close to Likert's System 4 manager. I think the primary difference is how to get there—how you move toward achieving a System 4 or System Yb.

Argyris: OK. I like System 4 management, but I think there are conditions under which System 1 management is the most effective, especially for unimportant decisions.

I think you're right in that Ren and I are very close in terms of our goals. If I focused only on his writing, I'd have to agree that there might be a difference in how to get there, but if I focus on him as a human being as I know him, it's hard to think of things on which he and I would differ. He would think of unfreezing the top; he would consider T-groups as an alternative; he would consider using research results to unfreeze the organization—he was one of the first to do it and I do the same thing.

Dowling: I would think of him as being somewhat more directive and authoritarian in terms of establishing a model. To me that's an important distinction.

Argyris: That may be true. Ren is much more of a believer in persuading people to make certain kinds of changes. I believe in the autonomy of organizations to design and choose for themselves. I'm now trying to write up this material on the change in presidential behavior, and one of my fundamental assumptions is that the most important resource an organization has is valid information—or information that is validatable. Not people, not machines, but valid information is the most important resource in any kind of organization.

Dowling: What are the preconditions for obtaining valid information?

Argyris: Let me begin with the individual. The higher the self-acceptance and self-awareness, the lower the probability that a person will be defensive. The lower the probability that he will be defensive, the more open he will be to feedback. But he's got to get feedback that isn't itself defensiveness-producing. So if you're a pretty open individual and I say you're closed and I keep pushing it, there's a point at which you understandably may stop listening. The feedback you're getting is not particularly useful and helpful feedback. But then you can also say the higher the self-awareness, the higher the self-acceptance, the lower the probability that someone will give distorted and defensiveness-producing feedback. So one of the preconditions in human beings for obtaining valid information is increased self-awareness, increased self-confidence and self-acceptance.

Another condition is a condition of choice—to what extent can people choose, make choices, and to what extent are they held responsible for the choice. The more the person can be held responsible for the choice, the higher the probability that he will seek valid information and will not be satisfied with information that is not very valid or that isn't validatable. Another is a sense of essentiality. If a person feels a sense of essentiality in the organization family or whatever, there's a higher predisposition for valid information.

Conversation with
B. F. SKINNER

B. F. Skinner is, in the opinion of his professional peers, the most influential psychologist in the country. He is already one of the best known among the general reading public. Certainly he is the most controversial psychologist. Whence the influence? Whence the celebrity? Whence the controversy?

Skinner is a behaviorist, which means that he seeks the explanations to human behavior not in the mind within but outside in those conditions in the environment that collectively determine behavior. His first fame came through the design of the "Skinner box," a controlled environment in which rats, pigeons, and eventually men underwent transformations in established patterns of behavior in response to changes in the environment.

Take one famous experiment with piegons. Food was the reinforcer that moved the pigeon to behave in a particular way. Giving the food to the pigeon when it made the desired response was the reinforcement. *Operant* is the term Skinner used to define the property upon which the reinforcement depended—in this case, the height to which the bird had to raise its head before it would be fed. The change in the frequency with which the head was lifted to this height Skinner called the process of operant conditioning.

All operants grow stronger through repetition—Rome wasn't built in a day—and some operants are inherently stronger than others because they produce consequences of greater importance in the life of the pigeon—or the life of the individual man. Pigeons and man alike

Reprinted from Organizational Dynamics, *Winter 1973*

behave not because of the consequences that are to follow their behavior but because of the consequences that have followed similar behavior in the past. In Skinner's terms, this is the law of effect or operant conditioning. Says Skinner, "Operant conditioning shapes behavior as a sculptor shapes a lump of clay. Although at some point the sculptor seems to have produced an entirely novel object, we can always follow the process back to the original undifferentiated lump."

Skinner's early reputation came from repeated demonstrations of the law of operant conditioning with pigeons and other animals. When he moved on to man—and his writings and researches have focused on human behavior for the past 25 years—he became both famous and controversial.

He held that man's behavior was every bit as controlled as the pigeons'—the difference lay in the number and complexity of the determinants. Freedom was an illusion; when J. S. Mill asserted that "Liberty consists in doing what one desires," he merely begged the question by failing to look behind the desires themselves and asking what accounted for them. The distinction that makes sense to Skinner is not between freedom and control, but between feeling free and feeling controlled, between acting to avoid something—negative reinforcement—and acting to gain something—positive reinforcement. In the former case, the individual feels coerced and controlled. In the latter, he feels free.

Skinner goes beyond description to prescription. He isn't satisfied with enumerating the various controls that together make up the technology of behavior, but he goes on to specify the ways in which the technology available can be used to create a better world.

In fact, Skinner would argue that enlightened men of good will have a responsibility to employ the controls toward benevolent ends. As Skinner points out, the technology of behavior is ethically neutral; it is available on equal terms to villain and saint. "The industrialist may design a wage system," he maintains, "that maximizes his profits, or works for the good of his employees, or most effectively produces the goods a culture needs, with a minimal consumption of resources and minimal pollution." We also suspect that Skinner still adheres to the view he expressed in *Walden Two* over twenty years ago: that the techniques are in the wrong hands, the end product of most manipulation being private profit or personal aggrandisement.

In other words, Skinner elevates the manipulation of behavior towards benevolent ends to the level of a civic responsibility, which raises the question whether or not it is fair and accurate to label Skinner a psycho-administrative fascist, to conclude with Stephen Spender that he advocates "fascism without tears."

The answer depends largely on how we define fascism. If we mean an ideology that exalts nation and race, then there is not a trace of it in Skinner. On the other hand, if we mean an ideology that asserts the positive value of economic and social regimentation, then there's a strong strain of fascism in Skinner's thinking.

The more interesting and significant question is, what goals does Skinner think the technology of behavior should be employed to reach? At two levels, the question is comparatively easy to answer. Skinner is for the maximum use of positive reinforcement and the minimal use of negative reinforcement that leaves the individual feeling controlled and coerced. And if we want Skinner's vision of the ideal society, we need only read *Walden Two*. If he's amended or altered his vision, we are unaware of it.

At the specific, pragmatic level it's much more difficult to answer the question. In general, Skinner's answer would be that benevolent ends are those that enhance the survival of the culture and of mankind. However, Skinner concedes that survival is a difficult value because it is hard to predict the conditions a culture must meet.

In reading a piece entitled "Freedom and Dignity Revisited" that Skinner wrote for *The New York Times*, the conditions that in his view enhance the survival of today's China are clear—he writes with obvious approval of the young Chinese who wear plain clothing, live in crowded quarters, eat simple diets, observe a rather puritanical sexual code, and work long hard hours for the greater glory of China—but it's impossible, at least based on what we have read of Skinner, to draw up an equivalent list of specific conditions for our own culture.

Given a sufficient threat to the culture we suspect that Skinner would justify the use of negative reinforcement and aversion therapy. Skinner might even approve of the drastic aversion therapy administered to Alex in the film "A Clockwork Orange" to make him good. Given the menace that the bad Alex presented, society realistically had only two choices: permanent incarceration or a drastic form of aversion therapy. This is only conjecture. We know that in the same *Times* article Skinner took issue with the reported statement of Anthony Burgess, author of the novel on which the film is based, that "What my parable tries to state is that it is preferable to have a world of violence undertaken in full awareness—than a world conditioned to be good or harmless." Dr. Skinner dissents—as would a good many other people, ourselves included.

100

To what extent does Skinner beg the question of the specific conditions that enhance our culture—the conditions that the technology of behavior should be employed to advance? The question is a difficult one to answer. As the conversation that follows makes plain, Skinner advocates some quite specific conditions in industry. The bigger social picture is not as clear nor are the mechanisms by which the destined changes will be arrived at.

Skinner consistently denies that the controlling he advocates will be done by a benevolent dictator or an equally benevolent behavioral engineer. When a bearded youth at a symposium at Yale on Skinner's ideas asked him "Who is going to program this whole thing?" Skinner replied that it was not a matter of someone pushing control buttons but of "the gradual improvement of the practices controlling the survival of the culture." At times the improvement in practices almost appears to be self-generated. Skinner asserts that "in certain respects operant reinforcement resembles the natural selection of evolutionary theory. Just as genetic characteristics which arise as mutations are selected or discarded by their consequences, so novel forms of behavior are selected and discarded through reinforcement."

These remarks on Skinner present a very partial and personal view of his ideas undertaken because our relatively brief conversation with Skinner gave us only enough time to probe the application of his ideas to business. For his general views we recommend his books, especially *Walden Two*, *Science and Human Behavior*, and *Beyond Freedom and Dignity*, in which he has restated them with unexampled grace, clarity, and passion. Not the least reason for Skinner's celebrity is his command of the written word; like Freud, he is a distinguished stylist as well as a profound and original thinker.

Dowling: You draw the analogy between operant conditioning and its role in cultural evolution and natural selection and its role in genetic evolution.

Skinner: Yes, and I think it's important, too, because selection is a very different kind of causality. Darwin's views came very late in the history of intellectual thought, and the way in which human behavior is shaped and maintained by its consequences has taken an even longer time to surface. That's what we've been studying in the laboratory for the past 40 years now, and we've discovered that when you arrange certain kinds of consequences, certain types of behavior are selected.

Dowling: You have come under a good deal of criticism on the grounds that operant conditioning destroys autonomous man and minimizes freedom. If I understand you correctly, your answer would be that the freedom that is being defended has been an illusion all along.

Skinner: The real distinction is between whether we are really free or whether we feel free. I want people to feel freer than they feel now. When you act to avoid punishment, or to avoid any kind of unpleasantness, you *have* to act and you don't feel free. But if you act in order to produce positive results—what we call positive reinforcements—then you feel free, and I'm all for that. I want to get away from punitive control, the kind of control that is used by governments with police and military forces, or that is exercised over students by teachers who threaten them with punishment if they don't study.

Dowling: Do you feel that punitive control is widely used in industry?

Skinner: There is more of it than you might think. Many people consider a weekly wage a positive reinforcement. You work and you get paid. But you don't work on Monday morning for something that is going to happen on Friday afternoon, when you get your paycheck. You work on Monday morning because there is a supervisor who can fire you if you don't work. You're actually working to avoid the loss of the standard of living maintained by that paycheck.

On the other hand, if you're on piece-work pay, you are positively reinforced for what you do, and you build up a very high tendency to respond—so much so that labor unions and other people who have the welfare of the worker at heart usually oppose that kind of incentive system. Salesmen are usually on both a salary and a percentage basis, because you can't send a supervisor out with every salesman to make sure that he works. He works for the additional commission, but it doesn't wear him out as a straight piece-work schedule does, because he has the salary to support him. Straight commissions work well but cause trouble. The commission system in brokerage firms, for example, often leads salesmen to exaggerate opportunities and pull other tricks that cause trouble for the firm.

Dowling: Witness that student in Philadelphia who opened accounts without any money and without even showing up in person. Let's talk a little more about punishment. I wonder if you could illustrate the various controls available to the manager as forms of punishment and what you feel are the alternatives to punishment.

Skinner: When a supervisor points out that a person has done something wrong, he is mildly punishing him. His comment is a threat in the direction of his being discharged or possibly laid off without pay. And when a supervisor thinks his job is to move around a plant and discover things being done wrong and to say "Watch that" or "You got into trouble with that the last time," he establishes an atmosphere that really doesn't benefit anyone. True, the worker may be less likely to do things wrong, but you can get the same effect if the supervisor simply discovers things being done right and says something like "Good, I see you're doing it the way that works the best." Supervision by positive reinforcement changes the whole atmosphere of the workspace and produces better results. A constantly critical posture on the part of the supervisor encourages bad morale, absenteeism, and job-changing. You get the work out, but at an exorbitant price. With positive reinforcement, you get at least the same amount of work, and the worker is more likely to show up every day and less likely to change jobs. In the long run, both the company and the worker are better off.

It does not cost the company anything to use praise rather than blame, but if the company then makes a great deal more money that way, the worker may seem to be getting gypped. However, the welfare of the worker depends on the welfare of the company, and if the company is smart enough to distribute some of the fruits of positive reinforcement in the form of higher wages and better fringe benefits, everybody gains from the supervisor's use of positive reinforcement.

Dowling: What about those occasions in which punishment is inevitable? Let's take a hypothetical case: The supervisor catches three of his workers shooting craps behind the machine when they should be working the machine. Under such circumstances, in which the imposition of punishment is really inevitable, is there one best way, one best method of applying it?

Skinner: I can't solve a problem like that sitting here in my office. I'd have to go into a given organization and see what's going on. I daresay there are times when you need some kind of punishment—docking pay, giving a verbal reprimand, threatening discharge, that kind of thing—but what you've just said is a clue to the kind of thing that would be better.

Why *are* the workers shooting craps? Look at the so-called "contingencies of reinforcement." All gambling systems pay off on what is called a variable-ratio schedule of reinforcement. That's true of lotteries, roulette, poker, craps, one-armed bandits. They all pay off unpredictably, but in the long run on a certain schedule. Everyone would benefit if work could be organized so that it also pays off on that schedule. People would then work, and they would enjoy the excitement that goes with possessing a lottery ticket that may pay off at the end of the week. Management could solve some of its problems by adding a bit of a lottery to its incentive conditions. Suppose that every time a worker finished a job, he got a lottery ticket, and at the end of the week, there was a drawing. More jobs would be done, with greater pleasure.

Look at a room full of people playing bingo. They sit for hours, listening with extraordinary care to numbers being called out and placing counters on numbers with great precision. What would you give, as an industrialist, if your labor force worked that hard and that carefully! The bingo player works hard and carefully because of the schedule of payoff. It's a very poor one, because in the long run all players lose, but it commands an awesome amount of labor from people, with great precision and concentration.

Some industrial systems could be redesigned to have that same effect. And people would enjoy what they were doing as much as they enjoy playing bingo. Everyone would gain.

Dowling: Has it ever been tried in industry?

Skinner: I don't know, but I suspect it has. It has been tried in education very successfully, although it has not yet been widely adopted. But let's take an example of how you could use a lottery to solve the problem of absenteeism. With today's high wages, missing a day's wages doesn't much matter. But suppose you have something like a door prize every day. When you come to work, you get a ticket, and at the end of the day there's a drawing. Then a man will think twice before staying away. If absenteeism is a real problem, a reasonable prize per day might solve it.

Dowling: What's the relationship between the ratio or frequency of the reinforcement and the size of the reinforcement? And what effect do they have on productivity?

Skinner: The size of the reinforcement is, of course, important, but the schedule of reinforcement is more so. With a lower organism like a pigeon, we can get a fantastic amount of activity with very small amounts of reinforcement if we put it on an effective schedule. I've seen a pigeon peck a little disk on the wall ten thousand times in return for three seconds' access to pigeon feed, then go back and peck another ten thousand times. It is a long process but it's possible to build behavior up to the point at which more energy is expended than is received in the reinforcement.

Dowling: What analogy, if any, is there between the pigeon pecking ten thousand times and the worker in industry?

Skinner: I should hope there would be none. But there are many examples of so-called stretched schedules in everyday life. For example, people may be fond of fishing in a particular stream, but slowly they fish it out. The first time they catch the limit, the next time not quite so much, and finally they go back where they catch very little. They may seem foolish to those who have not had the same history.

Dowling: In talking about the effectiveness or the lack of effectiveness in the incentive systems, one of the reasons that a great many people have found that incentive systems have not paid off is that the incentive system came up against the informal group organization and against the competing and conflicting reinforcement provided by the group. You have said yourself that the group is an enormously powerful reinforcer, far more effective than any individual. Would you comment on the impact of informal organization and the informal group on the operation and relative ineffectiveness of many incentive systems?

Skinner: One question to ask is whether the group is right about it. If people are working on a piece-rate basis and the group has set a quota, presumably the schedule is having an unwarranted or even a dangerous effect. That's one thing. And if a new person comes in and starts producing beyond the quota, he will be punished by the others. They are protecting their own interests by refusing to let the schedule work them too hard, and they could be right.

But if they are holding production down to a level at which the plant is being used inefficiently, you have to improve the contingencies. The workers will come round if you make it genuinely worth their while and provide a reasonable balance between what they're being paid and what it costs them in effort and fatigue. Piece-rate schedules as such may not do the job, if the group sets a quota and punishes anyone who exceeds it.

Dowling: When you say that what needs to be done in the case of a low-producing group whose output is below what an objective observer would describe as reasonable is to improve the contingencies, what specifically do you have in mind?

Skinner: It is important to remember that an incentive system isn't the only factor to take into account. How pleasant work conditions are, how easy or awkward a job is, how good or bad tools are—many things of that sort make an enormous difference in what a worker will do for what he receives.

One problem of the production-line worker is that he seldom sees any of the ultimate consequences of his work. He puts on left front wheels day in and day out, and he may never see the finished car. There are also industries in which what is being made isn't worth making, and there is no good reinforcement if the worker is not producing something people need.

I can't take a specific problem of that sort and solve it without knowing all kinds of details. Suppose I were an engineer in the bridge-building business and you came to me and said, "I want to put a bridge across a certain river—tell me what to do." I couldn't tell you. I'd have to go and see the river, see what traffic the bridge is going to handle, what the nature of the terrain is, and so on. Just because I knew all about bridge building wouldn't mean that I could tell you what to do until I'd looked into things. Even if I knew all about incentive systems—which I don't—I couldn't solve a particular problem without looking at the situation.

Dowling: Are you familiar with William Whyte's piece in *Psychology Today?* I think he calls it "Persons, Pigeons, and Piece Rates."

Skinner: I believe I read it. I think he makes a point that some schedules don't work as anticipated, but that isn't quite true. They work as *I* anticipate, they're just not well applied. We have clearly demonstrated that schedules that work with pigeons work perfectly well with human beings. Other things are involved, however. If I were a pigeon, I could upset an experiment, so that things wouldn't seem to be working very well, but I should do so only if the circumstances induced me to do so. It's a question of knowing all the relevant facts and not simply of trying to solve a problem with one principle as if it existed in a vacuum.

Dowling: Whyte talks about the conflicting stimuli that operate frequently in an industrial situation. You've got, for example, a worker on incentives who is also encouraged by the suggestion system to submit ideas for improving work methods. In a sense, the suggestion system is a positive reinforcer—he will get an award if management accepts his improved work method. On the other hand, he knows that there's a chance that the incentive system will be changed because of his suggestion and that he will lose out. In addition, his buddies and peers will get no award, and they will also suffer from the incentive changes. Another example of conflicting stimuli would be the case of a man who knows that the rate is relatively loose and if he puts out he is going to make a very handsome week's pay this week, next week, and maybe the week after. On the other hand, he knows that when other workers have behaved similarly the industrial engineering department has come in, restudied the job, and tightened the rates. I think we're talking about conflicting stimuli.

Skinner: I'm not sure that "conflicting stimuli" will explain it; these people are behaving exactly as you would expect under these conditions. You don't expect an elevator operator to recommend an automatic elevator, and I'm not surprised when a man does not submit a suggestion that might cut him out of a job. You can't expect a man to make suggestions that will damage him in the long run, even though you give him a prize. What are described as "conflict situations" do not mean that there is anything wrong with operant conditioning. People are behaving exactly as they ought to in the cases Whyte described.

Dowling: In other words, it's an illustration of just how complex the variables frequently are. Speaking of variables, one phenomenon that has always fascinated me is rate busting. In a work group, under incentives, you might have maybe one or two out of thirty people who seem interested only in money; social approval or companionship means absolutely nothing. How could you describe the rate buster in terms of operant conditioning?

Skinner: You put it very well: The rate buster is not controlled by his peers. Their censure or punishment is not important enough to keep him within the quota. The group doesn't control him, and therefore he's controlled by the schedule. The result doesn't violate any principle; it just shows the complexity of things.

Dowling: It would seem that there are considerable differences from individual to individual in the power of money to reinforce.

Skinner: Not necessarily. The opposing condition may be more powerful. If you offer me a given amount of money to do something dangerous, and I accept, it may mean that danger is not very aversive to me, or that money is very reinforcing. You cannot tell which.

Dowling: To get more to the general question of designing a compensation system, some people claim that if you want to improve performance and modify behavior, you should take whatever money is available and distribute almost all of it to the top performers—in other words, give them a really sizable reinforcer and more or less forget the rest.

Skinner: These are practical problems that I can't solve from here. But in general it is important that a person's pay should represent some reasonable fraction of what he contributes to the company. I remember a case in which salesmen were making calls in business offices. They could do two things: they could make appointments by phone, in which case they would see people pretty well up in the company but make few calls per day, or they could make door-to-door calls, in which case they would make many more calls but see people much further down. (Actually, they weren't making sales on the spot, just describing the service involved; the sales came through later.) From the point of view of the company, it was important that they saw the top people, because they were the people who actually bought the service, but the salesmen were paid in terms of the number of calls they made. An effective compensation system should reinforce the behavior that is worth the most to the company.

Dowling: Job enrichment is one of the great cries now. There is a feeling that youthful workers are less interested in money than their parents were, and more interested in a job where they can control many of the conditions under which they work. How would you relate job enrichment to your own psychology?

Skinner: I would not want to try to define "job enrichment." In interpreting what is happening with young people today, we have to take into account some very great changes that have occurred in the last generation. My father worked hard all his life because he was afraid of going to the poorhouse when he grew old. He wouldn't need to worry about that now; he would be on Social Security. People used to be afraid of losing their jobs; but now there is unemployment insurance. In other words, we have greatly reduced the significance of the money earned in a job. Diminish the significance of money, and other reinforcers obviously become important. What reinforcers do I mean? The work pace, schedules, how far you go in getting to work—these things become enormously more important. Forget about piped-in music. Look at the annoyances associated with the job and get rid of as many of them as you can. If, by moving the company into the suburbs, you can have your employees living close in, that's an important consideration.

Another question is whether what you're doing is worthwhile. People are much more alert to the ultimate value of things—for the culture and for the world—whether you're polluting the environment or using resources wastefully. Could you get any satisfaction from working in an industry that was making something that you regarded as worthless, or dangerous, or unnecessarily polluting?

Dowling: In the list of substitutes for money as reinforcers that you have just mentioned, you haven't given much recognition to controlling the conditions under which you work—if you want to put tags on it, to democratic or participative management. I gather you don't give them much of a role.

Skinner: The democratic principle lies in letting the worker tell you what he likes and doesn't like. He may not be the person to decide how to get rid of what he doesn't like or how to produce what he does like. Industry is a beautiful example of the failure of a control and counter-control to produce effective contingencies. A hundred years ago, someone said this in the *Scientific American:* "Management wants as much work for as little pay as possible and the worker wants as much pay for as little work as possible." So what happens? They get together and do something called bargaining. Incentive conditions emerge as a result of a bargain. And it's often a bad bargain all around. The conditions are not really very efficient as far as management goes, and not very pleasant as far as labor goes. If most people are bored with their jobs, it's because the system is the product of a battle between opposing forces. Someone should design incentive systems with the dual objectives of getting things done and making work enjoyable.

Dowling: We recently did a survey for the first issue of *Organizational Dynamics,* in which we asked several hundred top managers what use they made of psychologists. The results were paradoxical: Top managers felt that there were many problems the psychologist could help them with, but there was very little inclination to use them. Only about 3 percent of the people surveyed had used psychologists and, even so, they used them sporadically on minute tasks. Which raises the question, what do you think psychology has contributed to industry, and what do you think it could contribute?

Skinner: I'm not a specialist in industrial psychology. I have only a casual acquaintance with the kinds of things done by Douglas McGregor and Abe Maslow. They do not strike me as being particularly effective. You can classify motives and still neglect contingencies of reinforcement, and the contingencies are the important things. Behavior modification is beginning to get into industry, and that may mean a change. Up to now it's been most effective in psychotherapy, in handling disturbed and retarded children, in the design of classroom management, and in programmed instruction. It is possible that we're going to see an entirely different kind of psychology in industry. Unfortunately, there are not yet many people who understand the principle. It is not something that can be taken over by the nonprofessional to use as a rule of thumb. It requires specific analysis and redesign of a situation. In the not-too-distant future, however, a new breed of industrial manager may be able to apply the principles of operant conditioning effectively.

Conversation with
GEORGE C. HOMANS

George Caspar Homans is a scion of what is probably America's most distinguished family, the Adamses. Interesting, but of little moment. Perhaps. But consider the following passage:

> Given the chance, I have always deserted anything that might have contemporary practical importance or that might lead to reforms. I have deserted the twentieth century for the thirteenth, social pathology for primitive kinship, industrial sociology for the study of small groups. It may have been mere escapism. . . . My nerves may have been too weak for the modern world. What never failed to interest me was not sociology as an agent of change or as a means of understanding my immediate environment but sociology as a generalizing science. What were the best possibilities for establishing generalizations? What were the main intellectual issues? By what handle shall we lay hold on it?

The whole passage gives off an aroma of atavism. We think of four generations of Adamses searching for certitude and universal principles, of John Adams and John Quincy Adams and their preoccupation with natural laws, of Brooks Adams and *The Law of Civilization and Decay*, of Henry Adams's attempt to apply the Second Law of Thermodynamics to the movement of human history. The tone, moreover, is pure Adams—the self-deprecating irony, the hyperbole, and even the comment about his nerves. The letters of his distinguished granduncles Henry, Brooks, and Charles Francis Adams are full of complaints that their nerves were too weak for the modern world.

Reprinted from Organizational Dynamics, *Autumn 1975*

The search for universal principles may be a familial preoccupation, but the directions in which George Homans has pursued his search are contemporary and owe little or nothing to his ancestors. Intellectually, Homans is a hybrid. A would-be poet who majored in English literature at Harvard, he has ranged widely in his attempt to educe universal principles about the behavior of men as men from frequently recalcitrant data. He studied social pathology with Elton Mayo, and as a young man, he wrote an excellent brief introduction to Pareto (with Charles Pelham Curtis), whose principles he embraced briefly as an antidote to Marxism. His historical research culminated in his study *English Villagers of the Thirteenth Century*. Best known as a sociologist and as the author of a classic in the field, *The Human Group*, published twenty-five years ago, he lacks a degree in sociology. His membership in The Society of Fellows, a frankly elitist organization (a kind of platonic academy on the banks of the Charles River), exempted him from degree requirements. Among its other alumni are B. F. Skinner, William F. Whyte, McGeorge Bundy, and Arthur M. Schlesinger, Jr. In forty-five years, he has gone the course from aspiring poet to being what he calls "an ultimate psychological reductionist," a self-confessed believer in that branch of behavioral psychology whose chief seer is Skinner.

What general principles has Homans ended up with? In wrestling with the data on medieval villages, kinship patterns in primitive societies, and interpersonal relationships within small groups in industry, what has he found that they have in common? The conversation itself is largely about the attempt to answer that question. But let us mention one example that somehow eluded us during the interview. Homans's general conclusion is that "the ultimate explanatory principles in anthropology and sociology, and for that matter in history, were neither structural nor functional but psychological." As one of the unhappily rare instances that demonstrates this thesis, he cites the fact that tribesmen in a variety of primitive societies tended to be "distant" from anyone set in authority over them. The reason is clear: Persons in authority had frequent recourse to punishment or the threat of punishment in controlling their subordinates, but men as men tend to avoid both punishment and its source—a basic proposition of Skinnerian psychology and a proposition that lies at the core of the problems between superior and subordinate in any organization.

Last, Homans makes clear wherein he differs from Skinner—that is, the respects in which Skinner the great behavioral psychologist is not a great social psychologist. In essence, Skinner has not been much concerned with problems involved in applying his theories in the workaday world. His attitude seems to be that somehow, because his theories are true, they must ultimately prevail—the delusion of prophets from Mohammed to Marx. Homans, despite his professions of escapism, has been more concerned "since my Puritan background taught me that nothing valuable could be obtained without hard work. The facile solutions came under moral suspicion." This includes, as the conversation makes clear, the facile solutions to social problems advanced by Skinner.

Dowling: You once wrote that if sociology doesn't teach students something that they can use effectively in handling men, it is nothing. In your two best-known books, *Social Behavior* and *The Human Group*, what are the most important lessons for operating managers?

Homans: That is very difficult to say. I am older and less optimistic now than when I wrote that. In the book *Social Behavior*, I was enunciating one form of a very general theory of social behavior—what I call behavioral psychology. In a crude sense, those principles have been known to mankind for a long time. In that book, I tried to show how these principles accounted for the development of face-to-face behavior in small groups. *The Human Group* is a rather different kind of endeavor in which I describe the more empirical relationships that seem to hold good in various small groups that I studied in a variety of cultural settings.

   As far as what good my work does people, I'm sorry to say that it does much more by way of alerting people to what may go wrong than it does in telling them what they can do about it. But don't think that sensitizing people to what may go wrong in dealing with small groups of people is without its virtues. What I teach my students is much less a guide to action than it is a process of sensitizing them to what may happen so that they won't be surprised or angry when it happens to them. It's an advantage to know that something is apt to swing around and hit you in the back of the neck even if all you can do is duck.

Dowling: In your article "The Sociologist's Contribution to Management in the Future," you referred to a kind of checklist of important factors in industrial behavior that sociologists had begun to develop—a checklist of items that managers could neglect only at their peril. What things did you have in mind?

Homans: I didn't have a checklist in mind as much as a set of principles. Nowadays, I think of items such as the principles that if an operation or activity is rewarded, it's likely to be repeated and that the higher the value of the reward, the more likely it is to be repeated—what I call the success proposition or the law of effect.

Closely related to it is the rationality theory or proposition that every man, in choosing between alternative actions, is likely to choose the one that has the greatest value along with the strongest likelihood of being realized. To put it in simple mathematical terms, the larger the excess of probability times value (P x V) for one action over the other, the more likely it is that a person will take the former action. Of course, the person may be wrong, his perceptions may be mistaken, and the results of his action may turn out to be bad for him. But that doesn't invalidate the general principle.

There is also a crucial principle that others and myself call the frustration-aggression principle.

Dowling: That one I don't remember.

Homans: It's crucial both in human affairs and also in pigeon affairs. If people or pigeons expect a particular result from their action on the basis of their past experience and they don't get it, there's likely to be an emotional reaction. The emotional reaction may express itself, if it's not too costly, in some kind of aggression. It's a principle that explains much of the behavior we observe every day.

Dowling: Would the principle of distributive justice be another term on your checklist?

Homans: Yes, and it is at the root of a lot of conflict in industrial society. People only perceive justice in their relations with other men when each man's profit or reward is directly proportional to his investments and his costs. Among the factors that come under the heading of a man's investments—at least what he thinks are his investments—are, for example, age, sex, seniority, and acquired skills.

Dowling: I recall your discussion of the cash posters and the ledger clerks in the accounting department of a utility company. The ledger clerks were the senior people with the more responsible and demanding jobs and with less autonomy, yet they were paid no more than the cash posters. And they thought it was unjust.

Homans: They were paid no more. And in discussing the case, I drew one administrative implication: You are asking for trouble if your relative pay scales don't correspond to the employees' concept of what is just. The trouble is that you have everything lined up at one moment and have achieved what I call status congruence; the next moment there's a slight change in operations, and a group starts making new claims for itself. Now, I don't think you can ever completely straighten them out. Some people start perceiving the situation as unfair again. Distributive justice demands not only that higher investments receive higher rewards in one respect but that it do so in all respects. In the case of the cash posters, I think management was mistaken—not foolish, but mistaken. Management paid the cash posters a relatively high wage partly because they didn't think they could attract people for lower pay. They thought it would be a hell of a lot harder than it in fact was.

Dowling: Maybe there was an element of paying for monotony. The job was so dull, management thought it had to reward the cash posters with money since they weren't rewarding them in any other way.

Homans: I think they also had that in mind. There was another factor. Not very long before, the job had been done only by men. In fact, there still was one man doing cash posting, although I didn't mention him in the study. And at the same time, there were higher wage rates for men than for women in comparable jobs. So there was a historical element in the relationship between the ledger clerks and the cash posters.

Dowling: When I read this story, I thought of a study that Ed Lawler conducted at a small plant in Columbus, Ohio in which the rank-and-file workforce redesigned the pay system according to their sense of distributive justice.

This is a case of distributive justice in action. They discovered that the total pay packet didn't increase very much when they did it—by 6 to 9 percent. But the relative distribution of pay among groups of employees changed radically.

Later, when they measured employee reactions, they found that salary satisfaction was phenomenally high and that overall job satisfaction had increased greatly. I wonder why we don't see more applications of the theory of distributive justice in the compensation area? The costs to the organization would appear to be small in relation to the benefits.

Homans: Whether or not you can do things piecemeal depends very much on circumstances. How many employees did the company have?

Dowling: It was small—a little more than 100 employees.

Homans: You might do that with a group that small, but at Boston Edison Company, for example, to have raised a general discussion of salary rates and wages might have resulted in irresolvable arguments among different work groups.

If everyone knows what everyone does and it's a reasonably homogeneous group, you can do something along the lines of the Columbus plant. There are other fascinating concepts in this area of distributive justice that entertain me. My friend Elliot Jaques studied the Glacier Metal Company and decided that the way to measure the differences between jobs was on the basis of the time span of decision—the amount of time that lapsed before an individual's actions were reviewed. I always have thought that, in theory, this was as good a principle as any. He worked out on paper a system that seemed to me a very fair way of distributing rewards, but no one in the company would buy it when the time came.

Dowling: As I recall, it was the union that would not buy it. Wilfred Brown [the managing director] would have bought it.

Homans: Yes, I'm sure he would have bought it.

Dowling: There was a study at one of Honeywell's plants in which they determined whether in fact the workers' concept of equity in pay corresponded to their perceptions of the time span of discretion. The study didn't alter the way anyone was paid, but at least we have one piece of research that confirmed Jaques's theory.

Homans: We always struggle toward distributive justice, but any change in the operation of a particular group may throw the balance out of kilter. You have to go through it, but it's an endless task that defies completion. I suspect that as various groups take on different tasks with slight differentials in difficulty and responsibility, companies develop a very large range of pay grades with small steps between grades. Eventually you reach the point where someone says, "This is intellectually and organizationally a mess. Let's simplify it." So you put in six or seven very simple pay grades across the board and the process begins all over again. Perceived inequities foster the creation of fresh differentials.

As an example of correcting an inequity, four of the senior ledger clerks were given slightly higher levels of pay because they had been there a long time and were said to be group leaders. In fact, they didn't do any group leading, but this helped to justify the pay distinction.

Dowling: Another administrative lesson that you drew from the case of the cash posters and ledger clerks was that you invite dissatisfaction and discontent if you move higher-status people, even temporarily, into what they regard as a lower-status job. As I recall, the higher-status, more responsible ledger clerks were bumped into the lower-status cash poster jobs whenever it was necessary.

Homans: Yes, and they didn't like it one little bit. There are different principles of justice that conflict with one another. What would have happened at the Boston Edison Company if you had done it the other way and had some of the better cash posters start doing some ledger-clerk work? The union probably would have insisted that they be paid more money. Everyone talks as if somehow it is possible to devise an industrial system in which everyone will be absolutely happy. But you can't do it.

Another pay subject that interests me is the size of wage differentials. Jerry Scott (who is now deceased) and I went to Detroit after World War II to investigate wildcat strikes. During the war, the wages of the less-skilled workers had been raised, but controls had been put on the wages of the higher-skilled workers. While a differential still existed, the size of the differential diminished, and this was one reason, I think, for the wildcat strikes. I believe the general tendency in American industry over the past 20 years has been in the direction of increasing the size of differentials. The pressure of the unions has been more or less in that direction.

Dowling: In *Social Behavior,* you described bomber crews in which there were very good human relations and very high congruence, and yet these very happy groups were also remarkably ineffective.

Homans: Well, there were no social tensions in the sense that there were people with high skill but low status, or vice versa. That's what we mean by status congruence.

Dowling: What interests me is whether, as a general principle, there is a reverse relationship between high congruence and effectiveness.

Homans: I'll bet you cannot prove that. But it was fascinating in this particular case. Actually, the relationship was curvilinear: Very high congruence was associated with low effectiveness, middle-level congruence was associated with high effectiveness, and very low congruence was associated with ineffectiveness.

Dowling: That still leaves the question of why very high congruence was associated with ineffectiveness.

Homans: We don't know the answer. We could have known only by carrying on direct observations, interviews, and so on. Maybe everyone related so well to one another that they relaxed as far as their efforts to bomb were concerned.

Dowling: Do you know of any other studies that support the same general thesis?

Homans: No, I don't. I was very entertained by it. That's why I cited it. Obviously, there are plenty of situations in which the adjustment of workers to one another may be so good that it gets in the way of work. Yet S. D. Clark's study of checkout counters at supermarkets suggested that congruence was positively related to effectiveness there.

Dowling: Somewhere in *Social Behavior* you made the statement, and I found it somewhat related, that very often the employee who is the most satisfied is the least productive.

Homans: The difficulty is that there are so many confounding variables that I wouldn't like to state that as a general rule. What I tell my students is that there is no general relationship between productivity and satisfaction.

Dowling: I think your exact words were: "Often, but by no means always, the more satisfied a man is, the less productive he is." I would agree with you that there is no general correlation between satisfaction and productivity. A couple of recent reports by two large groups, one at N.Y.U. and the other at Case Western Reserve, surveyed the research. Looking at everything that has been written on the subject of the relationship between satisfaction and productivity, they came to the same conclusion: There is no general correlation between satisfaction and productivity.

The Case Western Reserve study found that satisfaction among rank-and-file workers tends to be associated with the amount of discretion they have on the job, while productivity depends on rewards, recognition, feedback on performance, and levels of pay. Productivity, in other words, is a function of reward.

Homans: Productivity isn't a direct function of reward. From all we know about piecework systems—and this follows from the elementary principles of behavior—if you have a linear payment system, such as piece wages in which you are paid the same amount for each unit produced, eventually the time comes when you have enough money and other rewards become relatively more important to you. This is one of the reasons for putting ceilings on production.

Dowling: You mean within a group.

Homans: Yes, within a group. This allows for the social kinds of rewards that may get in the way of production. Productivity does not go up in a more or less straight line, even if you make really big money at the end. Of course, there are always exceptions. Human behavior is very complicated.

Dowling: The only major exception I can think of is the famous Lincoln Electric Company, where workers turn out twice as much work and earn twice as much money as workers doing similar jobs in other companies.

Homans: Yes, that's the one I was thinking of. Now, the problem is that I think no company can continue doing this indefinitely. I don't know what the situation at Lincoln Electric is now.

Dowling: I read an article recently that claimed that the workers at Lincoln were still outproducing everyone in the electrical industry. Maybe the answer is that with all the publicity Lincoln has received over the years, it has become a magnet for rate busters.

Homans: My view is that we all can be rate busters if the circumstances are right. I recall a study of moonlighting jobs that showed that when people really desired extra money, they worked like mad and didn't worry about group control over production at all.

Dowling: That's interesting. In other words, they took those jobs only for the money, and their regular jobs provided their social rewards.

Homans: Apparently. We don't know the answer.

Dowling: I attended the symposium last fall marking the fiftieth anniversary of the Hawthorne experiment. You were a close associate of Elton Mayo and you have written extensively about Hawthorne. What do you see as the chief lesson of Hawthorne?

Homans: If you want to understand organizational behavior, you begin with the slow, laborious task of observing how workers actually behave in the shop. That's the lesson of Hawthorne. If was the first time that in a systematic way people looked really carefully at some of these things. People sneer at Hawthorne, but there has been no study since that has examined better the kind of things that actually occur.

Roethlisberger and Mayo's great contribution was not so much new factual information as it was a method of observing and, above all, listening to people when they talked to discover what really was bothering them—or not bothering them and affecting their behavior.

Dowling: In other words, the new idea was the value of painstaking, close observation of an actual situation.

Homans: Yes, close observation of an actual situation. The kinds of things that were found in the bank wiring room have been found in different degrees and different ways in hundreds of places since then. People knew some of these things, but the care with which the study was done provided the real lesson.

Dowling: Do you think the orthodox interpretation of the relay assembly room is the correct one in terms of exchange principles, the exchange of increased productivity in return for increased attention?

Homans: Increased attention, increased freedom, less pressure of supervision—a whole string of changes. The relay assembly test room showed the power of some of these factors when they are applied to a small group. The difficulty with the application of psychology and sociology to business is in the ability to generalize. You always can do it with a team of 10 or 15, but can you do it across the board in a plant? The difference between your small group and the rest of the plant may account for many of your results.

Dowling: In other words, what is commonly identified as the Hawthorne effect, the positive consequences of being treated like someone very special and receiving much attention, can't operate when everyone is treated the same way.

Homans: That's the difficulty. When people talk, which I think they do far too glibly, about making industrial work more interesting, more satisfying, and less alienating—to use that nasty word—I don't think it refers to anything very definite. The problem is that you always can do it with a small group, but it's awfully difficult to do it with any large-scale operation. No one has done it very effectively.

Dowling: I know that Chris Argyris claims he has never seen a successful example of organization development outside of subsystems—nothing large scale. Texas Instruments has applied job enrichment to thousands of workers but always on a department-by-department basis, and many more thousands of Texas Instruments employees still have unenriched jobs.

Homans: I think that job enrichment can be implemented. Not that everyone wants job enrichment, but that's a different question. Industrialists should realize that you should do it because it is good in itself and not because it will increase profits.

Dowling: Volvo in Sweden, for example, is pretty clear about why it has instituted job enrichment. Not because they thought productivity would increase but because they had terrific problems with turnover and absenteeism.

Homans: It might make a difference there.

Dowling: You have a system in Sweden—incidentally, the head of Volvo was terribly unhappy about it—in which the rank-and-file worker is paid whether or not he shows up for work. So there is an extra incentive to make the job more interesting.

Homans: That's a very different ball game.

Dowling: I thought of job enrichment when I read your discussion of the study done by Nancy Morse that showed that workers responded positively to general rather than close supervision. However, at the same time their perceptions of inequity increased and job satisfaction tended to diminish, first, because with more responsible jobs, their levels of aspiration rose and, second, because despite more responsibility, they weren't paid more or promoted more frequently. What do you think of this phenomenon in terms of job enrichment? You have enriched the job by giving the employee more responsibility, but at the same time, he has made a new investment and he believes that he should be more rewarded with a raise in pay or a better job. As you have pointed out, any satisfied desire tends to create an unsatisfied one.

Homans: In almost all cases job enrichment would be a good in itself, but I don't know what effect it would have on productivity. It might have a more positive effect on absenteeism. The more I work in this field, the more complexities I see. For some people, the end result of job enrichment might not be increased job satisfaction if it means that you have to pay close personal attention to a particular kind of activity and that interferes with your social interaction.

Dowling: In other words, on balance the decrease in social interaction might outweigh the increase in job interest.

Homans: Yes. You were talking about Volvo. Do you know why the American auto workers who went to Saab-Scania to look at job enrichment didn't like what they saw?

Dowling: Their reaction, I gather, was complex. Part of the answer is that they were there only for four weeks. Also, they were strangers to each other. More importantly, they were strangers in a foreign land. If the six workers—four men and two women—had spent six months in Sweden instead of six weeks, their reaction might have been different. Also, the group apparently preferred the assembly line because it required less concentration.

I often have wondered about the two women in the relay assembly test room who were replaced. Are they an example of the kind of people who won't respond to job enrichment?

Homans: I don't know. There is a point about the Western Electric research that does credit to the honesty and ethics of the researchers. They had long interviews with the women in the relay assembly test room and also with all the people in the bank wiring observation room. And they suppressed those interviews. This was a deliberate decision when Roethlisberger and Dickson were writing their book. They suppressed the interview record to preserve the privacy of individuals. I think the interviews are probably still at the Harvard Business School.

Dowling: At the Hawthorne symposium, Robert Kahn from the University of Michigan delivered an interesting paper in which he claimed that the relay assembly test room has been misread all these years.

Homans: What is his theory?

Dowling: His theory, in a nutshell, is that real participation has real effects. And he claims that it was the participative element in the relay assembly room that accounted for the increase in productivity.

Homans: Fritz Roethlisberger certainly recognized this. The girls were consulted on every change. That may well have been an element, but I don't think it was the only one.

Dowling: There was an overall increase in productivity—from 20 to 60 percent.

Homans: One of the things that hasn't been explored in the Volvo kind of situation, or in a situation like the relay assembly room, which really is very different, is whether productivity, by definition, can increase indefinitely. What happens in one of these situations when everything becomes routine?

Dowling: What do you mean by routine?

Homans: Well, no further change occurs. Part of the excitement is that change is occurring; you're being consulted about everything. Now, what's the steady state situation? I'm not sure whether you could have sustained increased productivity in the relay assembly room. Of course, it did increase for five years. But presumably there would have come a time when there would be no further increase.

Dowling: The relay assembly was not abandoned because it was running out of steam.

Homans: No. It was abandoned because of the Depression. When you can stimulate people through personal attention, through participation, and through treating them differently from other employees, what ultimately happens when being consulted, participating, and so on become a matter of course? Then what do you do? Does this treatment lose some of its value when it becomes routine?

    I don't know the answer. Of course, I'm in favor of all the experiments that have been tried. What always interests me is the ambiguity of some of the results. Very few methods seem to hold good across the board. The results vary with circumstances. One of the questions that very much interests me is what happens when some of these things become routine. Maybe the positive results continue; on the other hand, people may become satiated. I don't know the answer.

Dowling: What do you suspect?

Homans: I suspect that participation is probably a continuing reward for people. I think giving people close attention is probably a continuing reward. But I'm not sure about this. I'm even more bothered about the generalization problem. Suppose you had participation, not the kind of participation the relay assembly workers had, not in one small group, but in the whole plant. In such cases, people might decide that they are participating, that they have a say about what happens, and that they should not produce more. I will confess that I am a bit of an old cynic.

Dowling: In other words, the participation, recognition, and so on were rewarded by a productivity increase of 20 to 60 percent among the women in the relay assembly room. What you're saying is that there is far from a guarantee that the continuation of participation will lead to a willingness to produce say 50 percent more.

Homans: Especially if it's plantwide. In the case of the studies made by the Michigan people at Prudential Life Insurance, participation was encouraged to the extent that the group was allowed to decide that it wouldn't work for a couple of days.

Dowling: Not only was the study terminated, but the vice-president who was responsible for implementing it was fired.

Homans: That I didn't know. Why was it terminated?

Dowling: My understanding is that the study was terminated because the workers wanted to extend participation into spheres that management thought were none of their business. In other words, it's one of those instances where success killed the experiment.

Homans: Old-fashioned authority has some advantages, which have been forgotten, and to organize participation on a large scale leads us into the difficulties of any democratic system: How do you organize participation in such a way that reasonable results occur when many people don't have the time to participate? I have a maxim that entertains me. There are extraordinary limits on possibilities of participation because of the time people have available. If you participate all the time in decisions on what you're going to do, obviously nothing is done. That's driving it to the extreme. When you're talking about reforming an industrial system, you have to talk about something that can be operated across the board. With much attention, very skilled people, and small groups, reform always can be successful in some sense. But then people jump from this to something that's going to operate across the board and reform the whole industrial system. They forget the Homans principle that no society, no governmental system, or no industrial system can work successfully if it depends on extraordinary abilities on the part of the people who run it. It has to be operable by ordinary damn fools like me. And that's what bothers me about Chris Argyris, for instance, toward whom I'm very sympathetic in some ways. I don't think the system he has in mind can be operated by ordinary damn fools.

Dowling: I think Chris would concede that the kind of system he advocates—System Yb, as he calls it—would be extraordinarily difficult to set up and operate. He never has seen it in operation yet except in small units, although one medium-size company currently is working very hard at becoming a System Yb organization. Chris is committed to System Yb as an ideal, but I don't think he's too optimistic about making it operative on a large scale.

Homans: When I refer to ordinary damn fools, I don't want to sound like a snob. I'm including ordinary high-level executives with good abilities but without extraordinary abilities or training.

Dowling: You associate yourself with the ideas of Skinner. On the other hand, I was struck by your observation that Skinner is a great psychologist but not a great social psychologist.

Homans: He certainly isn't. The interesting thing about Fred, whom I've known for years, is that his behaviorism is too pure for me. I claim that *Walden Two*, which he takes very seriously as a social design, by his own principles won't work.

Dowling: By which you mean . . .

Homans: For example, Fred has the kids in the *Walden Two* community very closely and carefully trained by expert psychologists. The amount of time and effort necessary to provide this close behavioral training would cost more in reality than any community could afford. That's one of the directions I have in mind.

Dowling: Also, on a broad scale you would come up against the scarcity of human resources. In other words, how many people are there around to do the job?

Homans: Yes. You have to employ some people in productive activities such as raising food. I once figured out that something like one-half the population would be concerned with closely training kids according to behavioral methods. Although behavior is generated according to the rules of behavioral psychology, it isn't deliberately created. It's created by contingencies that happen by chance. If you do a cost-benefit analysis of *Walden Two*, for the benefits derived it may be cheaper to let the kids be raised by the ordinary traditional methods. Another problem is that Fred does not face up to the horrid problem of status and power.

Dowling: What do you mean, "Doesn't face up to it"? It's been years since I read *Walden Two*.

Homans: Fred has people rotating among jobs; that's part of his design. And he thinks there won't be any question of one job being superior to the others in some social sense. But they will.

Dowling: Your basic contention is that status is a reflection of power, and power in turn is a reflection of the ability to provide services and rewards . . .

Homans: That are scarce.

Dowling: Therefore, you are going to have differentiation in status and power and the ability to distribute rewards in any situation.

Homans: I don't think Fred looks into this sufficiently. The freeloader problem also is something that he looks into too lightly. It is the reverse of the high-status problem.

Dowling: I know what a freeloader is in common parlance, but I'm not very clear about the freeloader problem in *Walden Two*.

Homans: In any collective effort, there always is the problem of the man to whom you cannot deny the advantages, the rewards of the collective effort, even though he hasn't contributed much to it himself. In communities such as *Walden Two*, this would be a serious problem.

At one time Fred was thinking of actually participating in a community, and I said—this may have been enough to stop him—if you do it, let me be there as an observer. The group that has come closest in many ways to realizing the Skinnerian kind of community is the kibbutz. They are first-rate communities, but even though in theory all people are equal and rotate among jobs, the status problem does arise. People who contribute the most in some sense do receive more rewards—not monetary rewards but things such as the opportunity to send their children to universities.

Dowling: One thing that always bothered me about *Walden Two* was the assumption that the length of time you have to spend on a job should be dependent on how unpleasant the job is. The most unpleasant jobs require the shortest service. This is predicated on the assumption of a universally accepted definition of what is pleasant and unpleasant.

Homans: That's right.

Dowling: And this strikes me as contrary to the diversity of human nature.

Homans: What I'm going to say also is implied by human nature. If the unpleasant jobs are paid significantly more than the more pleasant ones, some people are going to seek the relatively unpleasant jobs. Suppose it's a relatively pleasant job to be a boss. As a department chairman, I know that this isn't always true. But suppose being a boss is relatively reward-ing to many people. If you pay them very little and you give the people who drive tractors, mow hay, dispose of garbage, or cook relatively high pay, you might end up lacking what in fact you most require—that is, leadership ability in the proper positions.

Dowling: Yes, but wouldn't the person who is attracted to a leadership role be the kind of person to whom the satisfactions involved in being the boss would be more attractive than higher pay?

Homans: Perhaps, but I think you would have to be very careful about the tradeoffs involved.

Dowling: How about its application to the industrial situation? In Bill Whyte's article "Pigeons, People, and Piece Rates," he said that although he can buy Skinner's basic principles, he cannot buy his application of them. He thinks that Skinner vastly oversimplifies the problems involved in applying his principles.

Homans: He certainly does. That's what I mean when I say Skinner is a good psychologist but a very bad social psychologist. The fact is that Skinner still believes, although I told him he was wrong at least 20 years ago, that piece rates will steadily increase production. They won't. One of his notions was that on a random basis, every so often when you pull a lever, a pile of money will fall into a bag right by the machine. You need a quick payoff, a random payoff, which will mobilize the energies that are mobilized by the one-arm bandit, in order to make the piece-rate system pay off. I always thought that this was not a bad idea but wondered whether you could make the notion of increasing earnings by chance acceptable to any union.

Dowling: I would doubt it. One application of random reinforcement in industry cited by Walter Nord is a hardware company in St. Louis that used a variable-rate schedule as the antidote for excessive absenteeism. If an employee had a perfect attendance record for a month, he was eligible for a ticket for a prize worth $20 to $25, with one prize available for each 25 eligible employees. After six months of perfect attendance, employees were eligible for a drawing for a color television set. After 16 months of the program, sick-leave costs were down by 62 percent. This kind of random payoff is much more likely to work with absenteeism than it is with productivity.

Homans: After all, although we see the energy expended on the one-arm bandit, we don't see anyone spending all day for five or six days a week working it. You could practice random reinforcement only on jobs where the operation was very simple because if the job required any degree of discretion, the temptation to not go through all the motions you have to before the payoff occurs would be hard to resist. If you had a set-up man in a machine shop whose work required much discretion and care, and at the completion of his task you paid him nothing or a large amount of money on a random basis, there might be a tendency on his part to cut corners. But if the man were performing a completely repetitious, standardized job where discretion wasn't involved, it might be worth trying.

Dowling: Do you know any instance where it has been tried?

Homans: No. Fred and I used to talk about it. But we never went beyond the talking stage.

Dowling: Let me give you a hypothetical situation where you might begin applying the principles of behavioral psychology. Let's assume that you are a new plant manager and you find a department in which the number one norm is low productivity. In this department, productivity is well below what anyone thinks could reasonably be achieved without undue fatigue. Your problem is somehow to turn this norm around or at least make a dent in it. Where do you start?

Homans: I am becoming more skeptical all the time about my capacity to change people's behavior. First, I would try to discover what the hell is going on. Talking nondirectively to people in the department might help a little. I probably would not offer the low producers higher piece rates. If I did, my approach might be resented by other people in the plant. This would be another instance of distributive justice: People in effect would be rewarded for not behaving well if you offered them more pay.

Dowling: In other words, you would avoid the squeaky-wheel-gets-the-grease syndrome.

Homans: If you had a union in the plant, you probably could not cut the rate in order to make them toe the line. If there weren't a union, I might try that approach. At least, it would be compatible with distributive justice.

Dowling: It also might depend on the labor situation in the particular community and on whether jobs are scarce and people think twice before they risk the loss of their jobs.

Homans: It wouldn't be a bad idea to try talking to the people and say, "Look, productivity is much too low here and it's going to affect the solvency of this company, which should make a difference to you." It might not help, but on the other hand, if you approach people with your problem, it conceivably might make a difference. I've been a ship captain, and this kind of problem didn't arise. For the last five years, I've been a department chairman, and I've never discovered how to make my professors and staff answer letters on time. Of course, I have no means of changing the payoff structures for them. Sometimes I talk to them, but it doesn't seem to help.

Do you think it would be possible if productivity were really low to see what could be done by way of group discussion? One of the things that's interesting in studies about a severe restriction of production is that it's terribly boring trying to look busy all the time. Unless employees are very resentful of the company, I don't think it would be impossible to achieve some real gains through group discussion.

Dowling: One of the points you made is that if people think the company is unfair and the company wants production, withholding it is the sweetest revenge employees can have.

Homans: But it's still very boring.

Dowling: One conclusion might be that through group discussion, you as plant manager would try to find out whether the company was perceived as being unfair and in what way and what could be done to change the group's perceptions. You cited an example in which output was low because conditions in the department you studied, and in the company as a whole, were such that workers could expect little advancement in pay or rank in return for higher output.

Homans: Sure. That's what we call the prediction study. That's Roethlisberger, Zaleznik, and Christensen, assisted by Homans.

Dowling: As I recall, the dominant group in the operation was Irish in origin.

Homans: About half the department was Irish. In effect, social rewards were the chief rewards obtainable. Since the Irish received more than their share of social rewards—they were very clannish and friendly among themselves—they were more satisfied than other workers.

Dowling: They were the leaders in restricting production.

Homans: That isn't a fair statement. They really didn't severely restrict production; rather, they didn't produce as much as they could. They were something like the workers in the bank wiring room. They didn't produce as much as they conceivably could, but at the same time, their production was reasonably satisfactory to management. On the other hand, they consciously restricted production. One of them, the girl whom we used to call the queen bee or the den mother, who was the dominant figure in the group, once said, "We don't restrict production; we produce restriction." But they weren't viciously cutting production as an act of revenge against management.

Dowling: But social rewards were more important. Didn't some of the other groups outproduce them?

Homans: That's right. There was a group of middle-class workers, most of them Yankees rather than Irish, who acted like rate busters, perhaps not so much because of any Protestant work ethic but because this was very aggravating to the dominant group.

Dowling: In other words, they derived satisfaction from showing them up.

Homans: Yes. Or doing what the others didn't condone. There's nothing more rewarding, when you're treated as an outsider, than to show complete contempt for the rules of the dominant group. "He only does it to annoy because he knows it teases," as the line goes. The people who were really low producers were not members of the dominant group, which was largely Irish. They were the old-timers, some of whom were German—old-time craftsman types who worked carefully but very slowly. These were the people who really produced on a low level.

Dowling: How do you explain their low productivity?

Homans: Their thinking was dominated by a tradition of quality. It wasn't as if general quality were low in the operation, but they just were particularly careful.

Dowling: In other words, they received their rewards from doing high-quality work. Did quality count in the kind of job they did?

Homans: One reason we chose that place was that there was a wide range of different kinds of jobs, including highly skilled jobs. Some fascinating things happened. There was a lot of horseplay. One time, a man hugged one of the women and broke one of her ribs. As usual, there was a certain number of things that you didn't mention.

Dowling: What happened?

Homans: The queen mother, who also was the secretary of the union, got the woman out of the plant and to a doctor without management knowing about the incident, which was a firing offense.

Dowling: Let's move out of the plant and look at the bigger picture. You associate yourself with Skinner in believing that freedom is an illusion—that man thinks he is free when the behavior that society makes appropriate for its citizens is the behavior they think is good.

Homans: I like to think of liberty as a beloved discipline.

Dowling: Right. A beloved discipline. You also believe that the illusion of free will is going to be saved by cost considerations. What do you mean by that?

Homans: In a way, the issue of determinism is a bogus one. All of our behavior is absolutely determined; however, because you don't know how it's determined, except in certain crude cases, it doesn't make any difference. You still retain the feeling of freedom. Suppose we knew much more about the general laws of behavior than we now do. Because we don't know the circumstances of a man's past history, we still would not know how the laws would apply in his particular case. Suppose we not only knew the general laws, which in many ways we do, but also the circumstances of a particular person's past history that might affect his current behavior. Further, suppose that we could design a computer and feed into it all of the general propositions and the given conditions. Suppose we could do all this. Would the result be worth the cost of doing it?

Dowling: How do we know?

Homans: My bet is that it wouldn't be. We only would be proving what, in a funny sense, we already know.

Dowling: We have a start on the general propositions, the principles you previously have cited. You described yourself as "an ultimate psychological reductionist"—a description you called horrible. I would agree.

Homans: I'm not sure we have them all, but we have some general propositions that I believe apply to all the human sciences. That's all I mean by "ultimate psychological reductionist." But you may have the general propositions and not be able to use them. You may remember the example I cited concerning my war experience when I was skipper of a mine sweeper. It makes a big difference what the magnetic field of a ship is. This had to be neutralized or we'd set off mines under the ship. I knew that scientists believed they had mastered the principles of electromagnetism. But they couldn't predict the magnetic field of a ship. What does this mean? General propositions are crucial, but you also must know the circumstances to which they are applied.

Dowling: In this case, as I recall, they were fearfully complex.

Homans: They were fearfully complex because they involved past history. But that's true of man as well as iron. It cost more than it was worth to try and calculate and therefore predict the magnetic field under the ship because it depended on factors such as the heading on which the ship was built, the latitude and longitude of the place where it was built, on the

133

way it traveled over the oceans of the world, and how much it had been battered by the sea. Scientists knew the principles of electromagnetism, but they didn't know the past history in sufficient detail to apply them. This is usually true of man.

Dowling: In other words, it wasn't the absence of the computer that was the crucial problem but the absence of the appropriate and necessary data to feed into it.

Homans: That's right, although I think it might have required a special kind of computer beyond the capacity of any we had then.

In human terms, it is hopeless. All of us believe in determinism at times—that is, experimentally believe in it. At other times, we believe we're free. Our behavior is completely determined, but it doesn't make a damn bit of difference to me because I can't predict it. I can't show how the behavior of different men, behavior exemplifying the same general propositions, combines over time to produce particular results. The trouble is that the past behavior that affects—determines if you will—present behavior is linked together in complex chains, creating the illusion of freedom. I like to quote Justice Holmes, who also was a determinist. He used to say, "The way the inevitable is brought about is through effort."

Dowling: Holmes also made the comment that while Marxists believe that the laws of human history are moving inexorably in a given direction, they are committed to moving them along in that direction.

Homans: That's the same idea.

Dowling: Sometimes when you read Skinner, you sense that we're just around the corner from the point where we will have the technology and the technicians to create the perfect community.

Homans: The question is not whether behavioral principles work but whether you can use them to get certain results, which is a very different proposition. You and I now are behaving according to behavioral principles, but I'm not trying to change your behavior in a particular direction. Skinner talks as if I could manipulate you if I wanted to. That is a great mistake. The reason it's a great mistake is this: If you have a group of retarded children, you can, as my friend Bob Hamblin has done, apply behavioral principles to change their behavior for the better. Everyone calls this immoral now, although I don't see why. What's wrong with helping a retarded child read better? Even though behavior is all determined by behavioral principles, to deliberately obtain the results, you have to have control over the circumstances. What Fred never has realized is that the cost of gaining that control would be more than most people would be willing to pay. You can do it when you have people in an institution.

Dowling: And you can do it with a child in a Skinner box.

Homans: Of course, there's a lot of guff talked about the Skinner box, but the Skinner box was just a convenient method of keeping a child warm and comfortable with a lot of freedom—with no diapers or any constraining stuff around.

Dowling: I don't know that I've ever seen an adequate description of the Skinner box.

Homans: Everyone thinks of it as a machine—like the machines used to reinforce pigeons. But it wasn't. It simply was a large box in which a child could lie on a comfortable set of pads. He crawled around in the box, and the excrement was removed by a roller. When you wanted to play with the kid, he was taken out. He was much less imprisoned than he would have been with diapers on and covered with a blanket in a crib. It was a convenient way of taking care of kids in their early months. Why this bothered the liberal community so much I never have been able to grasp.

Dowling: Your point is that you can control the circumstances when you have people in institutions and when you have very young children, but you cannot control circumstances in a society like our own.

Homans: Yes. Fred says, "We will design a culture." But even if you know what the design of a good culture is, how are you going to get in a position politically to put your design into effect?

Dowling: I remember an article by Skinner in *The New York Times*. I gather he had been to China. My impression was that Maoist China was closer to his version of an ideal society than our own. He talked about young Chinese wearing plain clothing, eating simple diets, observing a rather puritanical sexual code, and working long hours—all for the greater glory of China.

Homans: I don't know about that. I have been to China, but not since Mao. What I don't understand from most of the accounts of people who have been there since is how the controls actually operate. All you see are the results of the controls. What I should like to know, for example, is how the government makes sure that a collective farm delivers its quota of grain.

Dowling: Given our democratic society, you would have to change it completely to impose the kind and degree of controls that go along with redesigning a society.

Homans: That's right. But Skinner somehow still believes that because his principles are true, of necessity they can be deliberately used and will be in the immediate future to obtain certain results. They will not be unless we find ourselves in a situation where we are able to mobilize more control over people than we normally do. The fact that the principles are true doesn't imply anything about what you can accomplish with them.

Conversation with
WILLIAM F. WHYTE

William F. Whyte, who is a professor at the New York State School of Industrial Relations at Cornell University, is probably the best-known and most distinguished successor of the line of anthropological observation of employee behavior that began with the bank-wiring room in the Hawthorne experiment (in which researchers sat back and watched and became part of the furniture). As a member of Harvard's elite Society of Fellows (a group of scholars-in-residence whose most celebrated alumni are McGeorge Bundy and Arthur Schlesinger, Jr.), he knew the pioneers in this work—Elton Mayo and Fritz Rbethlisberger.

His first book, *Street Corner Society*, a vivid study of life and mores among the street gangs in Boston's North End, was followed by a series of fine-grained studies of organizational behavior in such different locations as Chicago restaurants, Oklahoma oil refineries, a Midwest steel container plant, and a fine-glass-blowing plant in New York State.

What distinguishes Whyte and his students, among whom are Chris Argyris, Leonard Sayles, and George Strauss, is their insistence that for theory to be sound, it must be built on a foundation of field work and observation. Ivory tower musings or questionnaires are not enough.

Whyte, in particular, emphasizes the impact of technology upon managerial behavior. Obviously, the technology of an oil refinery is vastly different from that of a restaurant. It is the job of the behavioral scientist to ferret out just how the differences in technology and work flow affect the appropriate leadership styles, staff-line relationships, reward systems, and so on. Whyte also maintains that technological change, an

Reprinted from Organizational Dynamics, *Spring 1975*

ever-present factor in many organizations, almost inevitably brings about changes in human behavior.

Altogether, in his many books and articles, Whyte probably has shed more light on the many-faceted change process than any other behavioral scientist.

Dowling: In the studies that you have done in recent years comparing the culture of agricultural systems in Latin America and in other places, you obviously have drawn on some of the concepts that you developed earlier and found useful in industrial organizations; I'm thinking of concepts such as the importance of diagonal and lateral relations and the necessity of providing integrators and coordinators to link organizations. In these studies of different countries, cultures, and types of organizations, have you developed any new insights that you think would prove useful in understanding organizational behaviors, or has it been more a matter of confirming previous concepts?

Whyte: I've learned more about the relationship of culture to organizational behavior, but I can't point to particular lessons that I've learned, say, in Peru, that are applicable here. As I was examining Peruvian organizations, I began to recognize that vertical or hierarchical relations seem to be stressed much more in Peru than in the United States. The U.S. orientation reflects our democratic ideology and a different sort of class structure, in which you're supposed to avoid domineering behavior. These features of our culture make it easier for us to develop satisfactory horizontal and diagonal relations so that you don't have to keep appealing to the top to solve problems that arise between different parts of the organization.

I began, then, to see that this sort of flexibility that we take for granted in the United States has not been recognized in management literature, which still seems to be oriented around the management hierarchy—the relationships of the person to his boss, and so on. So I came to recognize through working in another culture that our flexibility in handling authority is a source of great strength in our organizations. I even have a hunch that this has a lot to do with the success of U.S. management in the Common Market countries. It's not money—there's plenty of money in Europe—or even technology that has given us a margin of superiority. Instead, it's a style of management, which hasn't been explicitly recognized.

Dowling: In terms of the Peruvian versus the American culture, do you find differences in achievement motivation, which McClelland's theories hold to be a key to relative industrial growth and development? In other words, are the Peruvians less achievement-motivated than we are?

Whyte: Yes, and I think it goes very deep into the culture. For one thing, you find there is no satisfactory single-word equivalent in Spanish to our word "achievement." You have to talk around it to get at the idea. The same is true of our word "thoroughness." The great heroes of Peruvian history have been men who were spectacular failures; they gave their lives in causes that failed. They displayed courage, self-sacrifice, and many noble qualities but not achievement as we are accustomed to think-ing of it.

   Of course, I think this is changing. The current government is bent on its own version of development, and has pushed aside the so-called old oligarchy. New sorts of people are coming up. But I don't know to what extent they recognize this kind of cultural and psychological problem.

Dowling: McClelland claims that the achievement curve in the United States is on the downgrade, even among middle-class students who traditionally had the highest achievement scores. Do you have any comparable figures for Peruvians?

Whyte: We found, in our surveys in Peruvian high schools, major social class differences in a number of items that we think are related to achievement motivation. The public high school boys show a much higher achievement drive than the boys in the elite private schools. However, this survey was made in 1962; it would be interesting to resurvey to see what changes have taken place and whether these social differences have persisted.

Dowling: What would your guess be?

Whyte: Probably there would be less of a distinction between the two types of students now that the government is pushing new approaches to education and giving new dignity to manual work. The government is also trying to promote an ideal of cooperative work to replace the emphasis on individualism that formerly characterized the society.

Dowling: Another possible explanation for the superior record of U.S. organizations might be their flexibility in introducing major changes. In the past, you have written much about successful interventions and change. Your feeling, in general, is that it is more effective to begin change with structural change, which almost inevitably forces behavioral change in its wake. But I think you would also agree with Chris Argyris that ideally the two types of change should run in tandem.

Whyte: I would put the emphasis on the structural side. But then you also have to ask if the involvement of the top people is necessary, as it's likely to be in any structural change. If the top people don't see the need for the structural change, your first step in intervention would have to be to work with them in assessing these problems, putting them in some kind of frame of mind where they could appreciate the value of structural changes.

Over the years, the dichotomy of structure versus process has been overplayed. In the group dynamics movement, the thrust has been that process is everything—that you change people and everything else falls in place. Now, Chris Argyris doesn't hold this extreme view. In a number of places, he has recognized the importance of structure even though he has worked primarily on process. The biggest payoffs are to be obtained by giving more attention to structure; but one has to move back and forth between structure and process.

If I were going into an organization to do consulting or to do research and people told me that X, Y, and Z were not performing well, that there was conflict between this department and that department, my first step would be to examine the structure carefully. Not just the formal structure as it appears on paper, but the work flow, the patterns of interpersonal contacts, the rewards and penalties, and so on—data that could be viewed pretty objectively. Then I would get people in the organization involved in examining the structure and seeing to what extent the structure itself might create or intensify conflicts. At the beginning, almost everyone will say that conflict arises because of personality differences, and that since it's well-nigh impossible to change a mature personality, you had better put new people in those positions. You may fire them or not, but anyway you move them out of their current jobs and put more compatible people in.

However, you may find, in the first place, that this approach is impractical because the people in those positions—the people in conflict with each other—may have certain abilities and knowledge that are needed. People with personalities that might be more compatible might lack the abilities required for the job. Beyond that, structure is often at the root of the conflict. Put new people in and they're going to get involved in the same kinds of controversy. Concentration on the social process, at the expense of structure, may lead to a kind of catharsis every now and then as people talk out their problems and relieve their tensions and sometimes develop new insights in the process. But unless those insights lead to structural changes, you will be stuck with the same problem you had before.

Dowling: Your classic case of the spindle, where you defused the conflict between the waitresses and the countermen by depersonalizing the relationship and having the waitresses put their orders on the spindle, is an example of eliminating the conflict without any change in the personalities involved.

Whyte: It's interesting how many people have commented on the spindle—that very simple piece of technology—and what it accomplished. Of course, we also observed that the countermen who got along relatively well with the waitresses, compared to the ones who didn't get along well, had quite different ways of organizing their work. They lined up their orders in the most efficient way to fill them. The work moved faster, and so the girls, in general, were more satisfied and stopped shouting at the countermen. This had nothing to do with the countermen's personalities; the difference was in how they organized their work. Management, interestingly enough, was not aware of this difference. Management would tell you that X gets along well with the waitresses and Y doesn't—implying that the reasons were a matter of personality. The trouble is that if you say "personality," you have a big black box that you can't do anything with, whereas if you ask yourself, "How do X and Y organize their work and their relations with the waitresses?" then you may see some objective differences that are independent of personality. And that gives you clues as to how to improve the situation.

Dowling: You say you can't change personalities. But when I read the Tremont Hotel case, one point that really struck me was the change in the personality of Kraus, the resident manager. He started out as a prototype of the Prussian martinet. Now initially, as you pointed out, the change was superficial. He pretended to change because he was afraid that if he didn't, the boss would fire him. But later, he did internalize this change; after his boss left, he continued an effective working relationship with Wiley, the personnel man, even though the things that Wiley was doing went against Kraus's basic nature.

Whyte: I should rephrase what I just said about personality. When working, as one ordinarily does in psychotherapy, on a mature individual (just a one-to-one relationship), changes are very difficult to bring about. And it's really not practical to attempt it in an organization. But if you change the situation in which the individual is working so that he experiences different rewards and different penalties from before, his behavior will change to some degree. And this change will be described by people as a personality change. He's not the same man he was before. How deep-seated that goes I really don't know. I don't think, for example, that Kraus ever developed much insight into what our approach was, but he did come to recognize that some of his previous actions had created trouble for himself as well as for others and that letting Wiley help him to smooth these relationships seemed to work. To what extent he was changed deep down inside (whatever that means), I don't know. I'm glad you brought it up because I ought to modify my flat statement that you can't change personality.

Dowling: At the level of operating behavior, it is possible to induce modifications. Is that a fair statement?

Whyte: With Kraus, a man in his late fifties whose success was based upon giving orders and threatening people with dismissal if they didn't obey, it's rather much to expect him to make a major personality change or develop a whole new view of the world. With a younger person who finds himself in a different sort of situation and one in which different behavior is rewarded, he might gradually change and become genuinely comfortable with, say, a more participative style of leadership.

Dowling: One of the changes that you made in the Tremont Hotel was in reward symbols. Previously, all the tangible symbols were organized around cost controls. You introduced a different set of symbols. Henceforth, managers, including Kraus, were to be evaluated, rewarded, and/or punished in relation to turnover among their employees. Here was an example of where the change in the reward system, or the symbols, induced a change in the surface behavior.

Whyte: Yes, that's important. One of the persistent problems in trying to help people to do a better job in a human sense—in business—is that the systems for keeping track of costs have been very highly developed. It's only recently that behavioral scientists have begun to work on the possibilities of measuring gains and losses in the value of human resources. We have known for a long time that a certain type of manager could go into a new situation, cut costs, and make a very good record, by the traditional measures, within a short time. And yet, he could leave the organization in a very deteriorated state. That was possible because there have been no regular means of measuring the state of the human organization. Now we have some of the technology. I think surveys can be useful along this line, particularly if they are done periodically so that one can chart trends.

Dowling: You mean the kind of survey done by the Institute of Social Research at The University of Michigan. They make a specialty out of measuring the human organization on a regular basis.

Whyte: Yes, that makes sense. One could also look at items such as absenteeism and turnover where we have some cost estimates. However, we need to develop other measures that will eventually reflect or be reflected in the economic output of the organization—measures that expose the ruthless manager who looks good by liquidating many of the valuable human resources of the organization.

Dowling: We have talked about changing the symbols of rewards in order to bring about a change in behavior. It would seem equally important to change the rewards themselves. In another article in this issue, we talk about a division of Corning Glass where new business teams were never judged effective until the people who made up these teams began to be rewarded on the basis of their contribution to the teams as well as their performance in their functional responsibilities. When they were evaluated, rewarded, and promoted half on the basis of their contribution to the business teams, their performance on the business teams improved tremendously. Do you think this is a common problem in project teams or business teams—that management sets up these teams but fails to change the reward structure?

Whyte: I think it is. One of the deficiencies in organizational behavioral research for many years was downplaying the role of money and financial rewards. We need to ask ourselves: "How do you relate money to this particular social system?" If you want people to devote their time to this effort, it can't be done by fiat. We need to ask how are we going to reinforce this new behavior. How are we going to reward it economically and otherwise? People always define their primary role as that on which they get evaluated.

The general lesson is that when you institute any structural change, you have to think of the other changes that need to go with it and support it. Changes in the structure of evaluation and monetary rewards are perhaps the most necessary as well as the most frequently overlooked.

Dowling: Talking about reward structures—do you see any hope or any advantage in using employee participation to set salary or wage scales?

Whyte: Efforts are being made with promising results so far. I don't want to mention names of companies because I don't know if they are ready to report on it. Personally, I'm interested in something even more far-reaching—looking at the labor-managed enterprise as a system in which people who work in the organization elect representatives who choose their managers, and so on—the kind of structure that is developing in Yugoslavia. We're looking at something like that in Peru, where the government is trying to push private industry toward this kind of scheme. I'm going to be spending some time in and around the city of Mondragón in Spain, where over the last 30-odd years there has developed first a sort of vocational technical school and then a series of enterprises. The last I heard, they had 11,000 people working under this system—from making furniture to such sophisticated items as machine tools.

I don't think the Holy Grail is in Mondragón, Yugoslavia, or Peru, but I'm interested in looking at different systems of organizing work and studying how they operate. I'm not looking for any one best way because I think that relates to culture, the economic environment, and so on. Apparently there are a number of different ways in which an economic enterprise can be organized and function successfully according to various measures. It's clear, however, that if you go in for employee participation, the leadership requirements for the foreman, superintendent, manager, and so on become quite different. You still need the direction, instruction, and supervision, but within the confines of different social system changes. One question that puzzles me is this: If you move

144

toward the autonomous work groups at the lowest job level, what becomes of the foreman?

Dowling: At the well-known dog food plant in Topeka, they don't have foremen any more. The foremen initially were used to train the workers to take over some of their previous functions. In a sense, they worked themselves out of a job. And in Scandinavia you have a number of cases in which autonomous work groups function quite efficiently without foremen.

Whyte: Still, these autonomous work groups have to be coordinated in some way to the total plant, and the total plant to the political and economic environment. There must be management people involved in that coordinating and facilitating process. I haven't seen anyone describe these new roles, and I'd like to see it done. We don't yet know the social requirements for effective leadership in the worker-managed system or in a system where work groups possess a good deal of autonomy.

Dowling: One clue, and I'm drawing again on the dog food plant, is that autonomous work groups may be composed of very special people, a kind of elite. The 70 employees at Topeka were selected out of 700 applicants on the basis of fairly exhaustive interviews, tests, and so on. Part of your answer may be that your problems of coordination are minimal if you get the right type of employee in the first place.

Whyte: Yes. Also, you have to distinguish between setting up a new plant and converting an old plant. It's much tougher to establish a new system in an old plant. And unless we learn how to do that, we may face a situation in which we can develop satisfactory human systems only if we scrap all the old plants.

Dowling: In a developed country like ours, that would be impossible. But to get back to autonomous work groups: Do you buy the assumption that given the opportunity, most rank-and-file workers would respond positively to becoming a member of such a group?

Whyte: There would be transitional problems. People would be anxious about plunging into the unknown even though they don't like what they are doing now. A number of years ago, Arthur Turner did a study on the automotive assembly line. He had the notion that if you introduced job rotation on these lines, it would improve the workers' sense of well-being. But when he talked this over with a number of them, he found them very resistant to the idea. His diagnosis, which was probably correct, was that they didn't know if they could cope with that sort of change.

If I were advising a company to go in this direction, I would also advise them to expect some resistance at the start or at least some anxiety on the part of the workers. Maybe they could leave open the option of going back to their old way of working if they didn't like the new setup. But I think people can get used to broader responsibilities and more varied work and eventually find such work more satisfying than their old jobs.

Dowling: In one experiment, at Motorola, employees had the option of assembly-line operation or a system under which a small group is responsible for assembling a total product, or at least a total component. The division was 75 percent to 25 percent—75 percent opted for the enlarged, enriched job; 25 percent said, "Leave me alone. I choose the assembly line."

Whyte: Yes, alternatives are critical. Employees should be given their choice between job enlargement or not, whenever this can be done within the economic and technological limits of the firm.

Dowling: Have you seen the piece in *The New York Times* on the U.S. auto workers who observed Saab-Scania's engine plant and said they preferred the assembly line? How would you interpret that? It's contrary to the prevailing belief that workers appreciate job enlargement when they are given a chance.

Whyte: Of course, this was a very short exposure in a foreign environment, which was probably anxiety-provoking in general. I wouldn't expect workers just automatically to love an enriched job. Another aspect is that some jobs are so routine that a worker can do the job without giving it much attention. He can talk with other people, daydream, and so on. When you enrich the job, there is more responsibility, and he has to give it more continuous attention. At the same time, you may not have added enough to the job so that he can really take pride in craftsmanship. On balance, you may not have made the job more attractive.

Dowling: You mentioned Turner a few minutes ago. Wasn't there a study by Turner and Lawrence that showed a great difference in reactions to an enriched job between people who came from an urban and a rural culture? The people who came from the rural culture responded very positively to having a job enriched, assuming more responsibility, and having something that required greater concentration and constituted a challenge. In this study, the people from the urban culture didn't like it and resented it. They were interested in money and in having the fewest possible demands made on them. Have you seen any confirmation of this thesis?

Whyte: Not as it bears on job satisfaction. In my first study of the oil industry back in 1942–43, however, I found striking differences in workers' receptivity toward the union drive that was going on at the time. The workers who grew up on the farm, working under papa, and who had had very little of what sociologists call peer-group interaction, tended to relate to the foreman as though he were their father, whereas the boys off the street corner tended to have the sort of horizontal loyalties toward the work group that seemed to facilitate union organization. The people who worked for their old man over the years—in isolation and interaction with only one authority figure—were conditioned to accept management and resist the union.

Dowling: We were talking about participation by workers in designing salary and wage structures. I've heard of one instance (you may be familiar with it) of a plant in Columbus, Ohio, where the workers participated in the redesign of the salary structure. You might think, "My God, you can't do this; they'll steal the plant." In fact, while the total salary bill increased by only 7 to 9 percent, the distribution of the total among jobs was changed very drastically, to reflect the workers' perceptions of the relative worth of these particular jobs. Subsequent surveys showed a level of salary satisfaction vastly higher than what had existed before. Would you think this experience could be duplicated, or is it a real freak?

Whyte: I like to look for freaks. Put it this way: I think we have much more to learn if, instead of looking at the standard organization, we look around for people who are doing something that is distinctively different—that is, if they seem to be getting away with it. Then I think we need to move in, and not only do surveys, because surveys only give you measures of attitudes; they don't tell you how anything comes about. We need to document how these changes were made and how this system operates—in which ways it is different from the way it operated before.

I remember that when I first heard about the Scanlon Plan, I was excited. Here was something novel, interesting, and promising. I still think there is a lot to be learned from the Scanlon Plan. Over the years, Scanlon himself and those who followed him were primarily concerned with proving to the public that this system was successful. So far as I know, a really intensive research study of the Scanlon Plan—one that would provide practical guidance—has never been written.

Dowling: Most of what I have read has an evangelical flavor.

Whyte: Yes. Larry Williams, with whom I work, has been studying a plant that recently abandoned the Scanlon Plan. It's too bad we couldn't compare it with a similar plant that made a success of the plan. The big problem in behavioral science today is that a lot of interesting things are being done where the surface indications are that some successes are being achieved, yet the people reporting these successes are more interested in the missionary side and in spreading the gospel. We know a plan or approach is successful, but we're given no in-depth understanding of what made it work. If I were a manager, I would be more impressed with a person who came to me and said, "Well, here is a plan with these potentialities, and these limitations, and it is likely to work in these circumstances, and not to work so well in these others [. . .]" than I would with the fellow who comes in and says, "I have the answer." In other words, I think the Scanlon Plan would have caught on better if we had some systematic studies not only of successful Scanlon Plan attempts, but of unsuccessful ones, along with an analysis of the adaptations that people have made of successful cases.

I doubt that there has ever been a situation in which the plan that people started with was the one they ended up with—even assuming it was successful. You achieve some progress, but then you always see some problems you hadn't anticipated, and you make some adjustments to meet those problems. So the system that you have a few months down the road is quite different from what you thought you instituted. If no one is going to be on-site describing this system and analyzing what happened, then the person who is trying to sell the Scanlon Plan or any other change model is in the position of not really knowing what he's selling. It's partly a problem of research technology: Social scientists have mainly depended on the survey, which gets at the attitudes, perceptions, and beliefs but doesn't get at the social process.

Dowling: Then, to your knowledge, there is no instance where a research team going in and studying a Scanlon Plan wasn't connected with one of the groups actively engaged in selling the plan.

Whyte: I don't know of any. I do not doubt that Joe Scanlon and his followers have had something to offer. It's just that it hasn't been sufficiently documented so that we understand what it's all about.

Dowling: One change model that you have studied is Skinner's theory of operant conditioning. From the article that you wrote, "Pigeons, Persons, and Piece Rates," I gather that you think Skinner's reinforcement theory has both merits and weaknesses. How would you summarize its utility and its defects?

Whyte: I'm not in any basic disagreement with Skinner about the value of operant conditioning (the law of effect or operant conditioning being that man's behavior is determined by the consequences that have followed similar behavior in the past), except regarding his view that it's very simple to apply. In *Walden Two,* he tells you nothing about how the rates were established. When the reader comes on the scene, the jobs have been established, along with how long you have to work on each one. There's no explanation of how they came into being.

Dowling: Aren't the rates established primarily on the basis of assumptions as to how unpleasant each job is, with the most unpleasant job earning the most credits? Of course, the board that sets the rates assumes that everyone will define unpleasant jobs in precisely the same way.

Whyte: Certainly that's a false assumption. One of the major problems in applying operant conditioning to the working world is not that people don't respond the way that Skinner says they do, but that the real world of the factory and offices is a lot more complex than Skinner allows for. You have to relate the rewards to the reinforcement schedule and to a wide variety of different activities that may be valued quite differently by different people. Skinner doesn't deal at all with the social ramifications of installing such a system.

What prodded me to write "Pigeons, Persons, and Piece Rates" was hearing him interviewed by Bill Buckley. At one point, someone else brought up the case of the Chicago school system, where it was alleged, probably correctly, that most of the pupils weren't learning much. And Skinner said that in a year's time, he could take over the Chicago school system and get all the teachers teaching according to his principles and all the pupils having a dandy time learning. A scientist should not be held accountable for what he says on a TV program, where he is trying to be provocative. I think if you had pinned Skinner down, he'd back off from his statement. But the example was so far out that it suggested complete lack of consideration of the social milieu, the economic situation, and so on. If Skinner had said, "Let me work on one school, or maybe even one classroom, and get something started that we will then be able to spread," I would have said, "Fine, let's go ahead." By making grandiose claims, he's not serving to develop what I think is an important set of ideas regarding motivation.

Dowling: You have specifically used the example of conflicting stimuli for the incentive worker who has a money-saving idea. His plant has a suggestion system. If he submits the suggestion through the normal channels and the suggestion is accepted, he's going to get an award. But as you pointed out, the award is a one-shot deal; it's possible that the introduction of the award-winning idea will lead to a modification of the rate. He might actually be penalized in the end. He also faces the fact that his buddies in his peer group aren't going to get any money, and to put it crudely, they may end up getting screwed along with him.

Whyte: Skinner's answer would be, "That's not the way that you set up an operant conditioning system. Either you have a single stimulus or you have various stimuli that all point in the same direction." But in the work situation, you have to deal with a complexity of social and economic factors that are just out of bounds for Skinner. I'm agreeing with Skinner that behavior tends to be shaped by its consequences. Okay. But then, I'm saying, "How do we structure the consequences so as to secure the behavior that we want to produce?" That's the problem.

Dowling: You're saying that Skinner is postulating an industrial setting so simple that it is unreal?

Whyte: Yes. If I were trying to design a work situation, then one of the bases with which I might begin is operant conditioning; but then I would add there are going to be all sorts of stimuli impinging upon these workers, and some of them are going to move them in one direction, and some are going to move them in the opposite direction. Which way do we want the worker to move? And can we modify the stimuli that are unproductive? Skinner, as far as I can see, doesn't face the problem. I suppose he considers it trivial. But any management concerned with operant conditioning has to face the problem.

Dowling: If you're talking about the incentive system and workers exceeding standards and being properly rewarded, then the Skinnerian model only fits the rate buster, who, as people have been demonstrating for 30 years, is a rare bird—maybe one worker out of every 20 or 30.

Whyte: There may be a few more than that, but they constitute a small minority. The standard incentive system is designed so that it works as it is supposed to, with only a small minority of the workforce—certainly fewer than one in 10 who respond almost exclusively to monetary incentive.

The problem with providing positive reinforcers for the piece-rate worker, as I explained in my article, is that we're talking about observation and measurement procedures rooted in a network of relationships among the person, the time-study man, the supervisor, and other workers. To give one example, the rate itself is the result of an elaborate contest between the workers and the time-study man. The latter knows he is being fooled, but he has no precise way of knowing how much. To the measurements he makes, he plugs in an estimate of how much he is being fooled. If the consequence is a rate that most workers feel is not right, money will be ineffective as a reinforcer because the workers won't exert what they regard as excess effort to obtain incentive pay.

Dowling: So in nine-tenths of the situations operant conditioning inevitably fails?

Whyte: Skinner would say it fails because it's not properly applied. To which I would reply, "Okay, but to apply your psychological theory, we have to take some major steps in social analysis and in managerial leadership."

Dowling: For instance?

Whyte: Well, on this question of the conflicting stimuli in the plant suggestion system, I would be inclined to get around that by trying to work toward some kind of incentive that is broadly shared among a group of workers or a department or even a whole plant so that any suggestions that individuals might develop would be discussed with their co-workers in the first place. The worker advancing a good idea would get recognition from his fellow workers rather than being considered disloyal to them. In other words, I would restructure the incentive system to avoid the major cross-purposes we typically find. That means making a change not only in the incentive system per se, but in the way that people work together in the plant. A lot more decisions would have to be made on the basis of group discussions.

Dowling: Do you go along with Skinner's belief as to the importance of the randomness of reinforcement? Random and unpredic   le are two characteristics he thinks are extremely important.

Whyte: I understand that according to his theory, it's not necessary that each time a pigeon pecks correctly, it gets a reward. But we are talking about people now, not pigeons, and if the rewards are only very sporadic, I wouldn't expect results. I would expect, from some of the things we've been studying, that many people respond better to reinforcement and rewards that occur often—like 75–90 percent of the instances rather than 25 or 50 percent. If you've been existing in a pretty deprived situation, where the world around you is hostile, then maybe you're not going to respond an incentive that will maybe pay off now and then. On the other hand, with more experience in getting rewards, you may not need them as often to stimulate additional effort.

Dowling: The Emery Air Freight Company is the only company that has applied Skinner's ideas on a large scale. They found that the key to the effective use of positive reinforcement was the frequency of feedback. They had various groups of employees keep daily performance measure on themselves, and productivity went up as feedback was given every day of the month. But when the same workers got this performance feedback on a daily basis only one week out of every four or five, performance reverted back almost to its previous low levels. This leads to the question: In terms of any kind of effective intervention, how important is feedback—giving employees, on frequent and regular intervals, the answer to the question: "How am I doing?"

Whyte: What psychologists call "knowledge of results" I think is crucial.

Dowling: Or you could call it also "evidence of competence." Providing regular feedback is one way of developing feelings of competence among employees.

Whyte: I've often heard subordinates say, "I must be doing all right because the boss hasn't given me hell for three months now." The absence of negative feedback is interpreted as positive, but it's a pretty weak positive. It doesn't have the reinforcing character of some positive encouragement, but then, as you say, the Emery people recognize that a positive reinforcement doesn't have to be personal. In fact, on a daily basis personal feedback is hardly practical. It would be pretty silly to tell a boss to go around and pat his people on the back all the time. But if you have a system producing records related to performance that workers think are fair and accurate, then it's bound to be useful, and give them a great sense of satisfaction.

Dowling: One fascinating point is that although Emery has saved $3 million over a three-year period by using positive reinforcement, the company hasn't shared a dollar of those savings with the employees. Skinner, by the way, regards Emery's use of his theories as "immoral."

Whyte: I would be surprised if the Emery employees don't catch on eventually and say, "Look, how about sharing some of those savings?" Management people frequently kid themselves that there are many ways of getting more work out of people without rewarding them more. I don't think there is any ideal formula for sharing benefits. But it seems to me that although any management that moves toward some kind of participatory approach would get a very positive reaction on the part of workers, it would also not be long before they asked for more money. For example, if work is restructured so that you no longer need a foreman, just occasional attention from someone in higher management, it's bound to occur to the rank-and-file worker pretty soon that the salary of that foreman is being saved by what the workers are doing. They may not say, "Let's take 100 percent of that foreman's salary and divide it up among us," but they're bound to say, "Well, the foreman got $1,000 per month; maybe we should have $600 of that. Let's talk about it." At which point higher management's representative is likely to say, "That's not what we meant by participation."

Dowling: I raised this question in relation to the dog food plant, in which all the first-line supervisors disappeared after the employees took over their function. And the answer was: The question has never come up. One answer seems to be that workers are paid not on the basis of the jobs they actually do, but on the number of jobs they have learned to perform. They are very well paid in relation to what they made before and in comparison with workers in the area with similar skills. Surveys have revealed a remarkably high level of wage satisfaction among employees. Another part of the answer could be—I'm just speculating—that up to a point, the intrinsic satisfaction would be seen (maybe subconsciously) as being more important than extra money. Workers would be so satisfied with their jobs that it wouldn't occur to them to ask for more money.

Whyte: You might be right up to a point. But then I think (and here I'm just guessing) that workers would become concerned with the apparent inequity. "All right, we are happy on our jobs; we appreciate this opportunity to do more interesting work and be more creative and so on. But we also recognize that this is saving you a whole lot of money. And why should all of the savings that result from our efforts go to the company?" I can't imagine that this idea would not come up sooner or later. Maybe because existing wages are above the market level, or the union has not been very effective, it will be later rather than sooner.

Dowling: The dog food plant is nonunion, which is probably an inhibiting factor in this case. In comparing the Tremont Hotel and the Weldon Company, you mentioned that you had a large number of interventions in both cases and that it was awfully hard to pinpoint any one intervention as being decisive in bringing about the changes. Also, in both cases you had a very substantial time lag between the principal interventions and any measurable results. In the case of Weldon, you achieved a big decrease in turnover but not until after the program had been in effect for two years. In the case of the Tremont Hotel, it was several months after the research program had terminated before you had a substantial decrease in turnover. In other words, the sequence seems to be this: A very considerable improvement in employee attitudes toward management, cooperation with management, improvement in morale and so on, followed a long time afterwards by improvements in various measurements of performance. How do you explain the time lag?

Whyte: I have come to expect it. Maybe one has to think in terms of some phenomena as being at a surface level, while others, like turnover, are at a deeper level. Quitting a job is a pretty fundamental thing. By contrast, attitudes toward the job may fluctuate up and down without precipitating the decision to quit. I don't mean *unconnected*. While we didn't have survey measures, we had all sorts of indications at the Tremont Hotel that employees felt better about their jobs and appreciated the group meetings and having the chance to talk with Edith Lentz, the field worker, about their problems. But all of that was going on at a time when the turnover rates were still quite high. They began to drop slightly within the year we were working there, and after we left, they dropped sharply. I may be just rationalizing when we take credit for their dropping later as a kind of delayed effect of our efforts.

Dowling: Didn't business, in general, and business at the Tremont Hotel turn sour in the year after the project terminated? To what extent did the change in the external environment account for the decrease in turnover?

Whyte: That's what we don't know. The only way we could have answered that question would have been if we had turnover figures from the other hotels in the city, and they were not available. We just had the impression that the Tremont turnover had gone down more rapidly than that of other hotels, but we couldn't prove it.

Dowling: This ties in with the story I wrote recently on the application of Rensis Likert's ideas in a GM plant in Atlanta ["At GM, System 4 Builds Performance and Profits," *Organizational Dynamics*, Winter 1975, pp. 23–38]. Survey feedback showed considerable improvements in workers' feelings about the plant, their jobs, and so on. But the performance indices fell at the same time worker-satisfaction figures were on the increase. It was two to three years before there were any substantial improvements in grievance reduction, quality, downtime, or labor costs.

Whyte: That is important to recognize. I suspect that a lot of improvements in organizations are due to changes in leadership styles that don't seem to produce quick results.

Dowling: Even so, the change in leadership style may have to begin at the top of the organization; otherwise, the effort is likely to be restricted to whatever subsystem initiated it. In *Money and Motivation*, you had the case of the paint room in which the girls set their own work pace, productivity went way up, morale went through the ceiling, and so forth. But the plant manager stepped in and canceled the change. The girls in the paint room were making more money than other employees in much more skilled jobs—and all hell broke loose. What do you think? Do you think there is a strong argument for top-level involvement and commitment if any change effort is to be successful?

Whyte: Yes, but if we think in terms of a multiplant company, I would prefer to work primarily at the plant level. I would try to get the top people to take a quasi-experimental approach. One of the problems in any bureaucracy is the notion that if you have a good idea, you should do it everywhere. It is much sounder to take an experimental approach and say here is an idea that looks promising, but it might not work. Since there is some risk involved, we don't want to do it everywhere. In addition, we don't have enough people who understand the idea to begin applying it on a large scale. Let's begin at one plant where we have a manager who is particularly imaginative and willing to try new things. Let's work with him in developing the program. Then I would structure the situation so that the top people are constantly informed of the progress made by the program. In other words, give the plant manager considerable autonomy in developing the program, but at the same time, keep top management in continuous touch with the program. That way, if it's successful, top management will identify with the change effort and demonstrate a real interest in extending it to other parts of the operation.

Conversation with
DAVID McCLELLAND

David C. McClelland, professor of psychology at Harvard, is best known for his studies on achievement motivation over the past 30 years. In fact, his assumptions about what motivates people are more complicated. He divides people into three basic categories. First are those whose basic dominant motive is achievement; second, those whose dominant motive is power; third, those whose dominant motivation is affiliation.

The achievers are the artists and creative people. In the business world, achievement is the appropriate operating motive for entrepreneurs in charge of small business on the make, scientists in research and development laboratories, and salespeople. They are concerned—frequently to the point of obsession—with personal accomplishment, but are relatively unconcerned with controlling other people.

Everyone favors achievement; power, in contrast, has a bad reputation. Yet, as McClelland demonstrates, power is the appropriate operating motive for most managers in organizations. The problem is the confusion that has unfortunately arisen between the desire for personal power—dominance and manipulation—and the desire for socialized power—that is, the desire to exercise influence on behalf of other people. Successful managers, who by definition must work with other people to get things done, typically rank high in their need for socialized power.

People who are dominated by the need for affiliation usually make ineffective managers—or, to borrow the title of an article by McClelland, "Nice guys make bad bosses." Why? Affiliative managers are not running a department; they are conducting a popularity contest. They

Reprinted from Organizational Dynamics, *Summer 1972*

find it difficult to say no. They play favorites, compulsively persuading themselves that any employee with whom they have developed a personal rapport is also an effective employee.

What distinguishes McClelland from most psychologists is his belief in the malleability of human nature, his insistence that we can learn to develop within people the pattern of motivation that is appropriate to their calling in life—within limits, of course. The person who starts off hopelessly deficient in the achievement motive cannot be trained to become a high achiever, but significant motivational changes can and do occur, in large part because they become *self-reinforcing*. Whenever a manager experiences intrinsic feelings of accomplishment—for example, as a result of reaching achievement goals that he has set for himself—he tends to seek out further opportunities to repeat these feelings of accomplishment. A beneficent cycle has been set in motion. McClelland, as the conversation will show, has much more to say about the dynamics of achievement motivation and achievement training.

Dowling: Dr. McClelland, how would you characterize people who are high in what you have called the "N ach" factor—that is, people with a strong need for achievement?

McClelland: They're people who spend a lot of time thinking about how to do things better, shorter, and more efficiently. They're very concerned about cost efficiency, input-output ratios, getting to the office in a shorter space of time, and so on; and they spend a lot of time thinking about those things.

When we test people for achievement, we measure how they think, not their attitude toward achievement. Everybody approves of achievement. But our measure is how often they think about achievement. We get a measure of it by getting people to tell stories suggested to them by pictures—the so-called thematic apperception test.

It's not really a test; it's a way of getting a person to talk out loud in a relatively free situation so that we can see how often his thoughts revert to doing a better job.

Take the example I used in *The Achieving Society*. The picture shows a boy sitting at a desk with a book open in front of him. To most this would suggest daydreaming or simply reading. But to a boy high in achievement motivation, it might suggest that the boy is taking an hour-long written examination. He is two-thirds finished and trying to think it through. He is dissatisfied with himself; he has studied hard, but he can't recall all the answers; and so on. Such a boy would obviously be someone who cares a lot about achievement.

Dowling: You made the point, I recall, that tests and questionnaires were an insufficient way of determining achievement, the impression being that too many people will try to please the trainer by giving him the answer they feel he wants.

McClelland: That's right. Men give answers they think are socially desirable. People will always say they're interested in achievement if you ask them. But if you check up on them, they may never think about it. They may think often about buying things or who they're going to have a date with, but seldom about doing things better. Many studies have shown that what people think about spontaneously, rather than how they respond to interviews and questionnaires, is most likely to show up in their subsequent actions. Oddly enough, even people who from our point of view score high in the need for achievement will often rate themselves low. The reason is that when you ask them if they're interested in achievement, they interpret that to mean, do you want to be a big man, a success? A manager? President of the company? And very often they don't. They are interested in doing a better job—not necessarily in controlling other people.

Dowling: In other words, they've got power confused with achievement?

McClelland: That's right. They've got power confused with achievement. It's the most common confusion we run into. Now, I'm not saying that power isn't important for managerial jobs. It is. Managers have to be concerned about power. But achievement is really more appropriate for what we call the individual contributor, the individual salesman; the sales manager is another thing altogether. In fact, a person with high need for achievement—the crackerjack salesman who gets promoted to sales manager—is often quite unhappy.

Dowling: Like the scientist or engineer who gets promoted to be a manager of scientists and engineers. He does it because there's more money and status in the managerial job, but when he gets it, he finds out that money and status don't mean that much to him.

McClelland: Yes. The salesman as sales manager knows that he doesn't have personal responsibility for the sale any more. He's managing other people who do the selling. He personally can't get feedback on how well he's doing any more in a managerial job because he's got all these crazy guys working for him. He knows what their records are—but he didn't do it; they did it. He doesn't know whether his managing is responsible for it or not. So a lot of the characteristics he likes in a job are missing in a manager's job.

You see, in addition to the thought characteristics, there are certain action characteristics of people with a high concern for achievement. They are very interested in the kind of task that is neither too hard nor too easy. A moderately challenging task is the one they prefer. The reason for that is obvious. If the task is too difficult, they'll fail. If it's too easy, they can't feel any sense of achievement because anyone could have done it. So the first characteristic they have is a desire to find moderately risky tasks, although subjectively, when they're doing the task, they don't feel that it's risky. A manager who makes a decision, even though objectively he's taking what other people would consider a risk, never feels he's taking a risk, if I can make that distinction.

Dowling: Part of this stems from self-confidence?

McClelland: Yes. He feels it would be a risk if someone else did it, but it's not a risk if he's doing it.

Dowling: In fact, as I remember, you've written that these people have an insight into their potential. In other words, not only do they feel it isn't too great a risk, in fact it isn't.

McClelland: That's right. They're usually better at it. They've calculated their costs and found improved ways of doing it. And their chances are probably better than average. It's a moderate risk only from the viewpoint of the average person doing the job. Maybe from the viewpoint of their doing the job, it's much better than a moderate risk.

Another characteristic we find among achievers is that they're very much interested in tasks in which they can get concrete feedback on how well they're doing. And on many jobs it's very hard to get concrete feedback on how well you're doing. Your boss can tell you that you're doing a good job or a bad job. But that's not what these people want. They're not interested in the opinions of other people, which they feel may really depend on whether they wear the right kind of tie or have the right kind of wife or something like that. They're interested in the task itself giving them feedback—like selling. A salesman, in a sense, doesn't care what his sales manager thinks. He sees how much he sold and how much he earned.

They keep a track record—a useful analogy. If you're a runner, you can literally keep track of what you're accomplishing. In a sense, it's almost irrelevant whether the coach says "good boy" or not. You know whether or not you shaved a tenth of a second off.

Another thing the high achievers like are tasks in which they have a sense of personal responsibility for the outcome. If they don't have it, obviously they can't feel any satisfaction from doing it.

Now there are several kinds of work situations in which you don't have much personal responsibility. One is when the decision is made by a committee; in a sense, all you're doing is carrying out somebody else's orders. Another is when you're simply not in a decision-making spot. You may be a subordinate, and you're told what to do. High achievers don't like that because they need to feel that the decision was theirs.

Dowling: Wouldn't it have something to do with the size of the decision and their own estimate of their capabilities? People can make small decisions, but if there's a gap between their estimate of their capabilities and their decision-making range, as it were, they're still going to be unhappy.

McClelland: Yes. There has to be a feeling at some point that they have some range of choice.

The third thing high achievers don't like is a gambling situation. A gambler may take what he considers a moderate risk, but one of these people couldn't derive any satisfaction from winning a bet because he would feel it was just a matter of luck. Instead he wants to feel that any success of his was the result of personal effort.

Dowling: In other words, achievers don't like to feel they're the pawns of fate.

McClelland: Yes. They're really very uncomfortable with that—or with any factors that are completely beyond their control. Of course, that's basically why achievement-oriented people are pretty negative about political interference, or any other kind of interference, for that matter.

They get upset if they did a good job as far as planning and organizing are concerned, but then the ultimate decision as to whether it's go or no-go is in somebody else's hands.

For example, there was a community action agency in Kentucky where we were doing some training in achievement motivation. Well, I talked to an employee of the agency who had been working very hard at improving some of the run-down shacks in the hills of eastern Kentucky. There's a regular program for home improvement, provided that the man is willing to work on his own house. Well, he'd gone around and talked to each of the men, diagnosed what was needed by way of money and materials, got the man to agree to how many hours he was going to contribute, and filled out the necessary forms. Then he sent his proposals to the regional office for this program in Atlanta, and they didn't even answer his letter. That's pretty frustrating if you're high in achievement motivation—as this man was. It was totally beyond his control as to whether he would get any money to complete that job.

Dowling: You've written at length about the factors that, at any one point in time and in a culture, produce a comparatively large number of people who are high in achievement. I say comparatively large numbers because I'm sure that you obviously do find some high achievers at any time in any civilization. But they seem to exist in striking numbers in some periods rather than in others. Why?

McClelland: I don't know as much about this as I once thought I did. But we tried to find out what were the critical factors causing a nation to increase its concern for achievement as represented in the mass media or popular literature, songs, plays, children's books, and so on. When I wrote *The Achieving Society*, I was working largely on child rearing, and we had data to show that if parents stressed achievement and set goals for the child that were high, but still goals he could reach, and let him decide on how to reach them, that child would develop strong achievement motivation. But then the question is, how did the parents get concerned with achievement? You have to push it back, and now we really don't know. We have a kind of pluralistic view of the possible causes of rises of achievement motivation throughout history. For example, religious reform movements may increase the desire to improve over the old way of doing things.

I wrote about a Mexican village that had been converted to a kind of Fundamentalist-Protestant Christianity from a very sketchy form of

Catholicism. The Protestant converts were very idealistic and felt that they were better than the people in other villages. And we felt that this sense of superiority entered into their motivations and made them more concerned about doing better at everything. So ideology, I think, is pretty important. But then you still have the question of where does the ideology come from. In this case it came from a Protestant missionary group that visited the village. But that hardly explains a lot of other cases that I've run across.

Dowling: I remember that one very interesting case was the Ibos, in Nigeria, and their honorary societies. The young men wanted to get into the honorary society whose membership was open only to people who had achieved wealth and status. Therefore, the family and the young man himself tended to become achievement-oriented because it had a high operational value, given the goals of that society.

McClelland: Yes. They have a kind of honorary society system, and you have to accumulate a certain amount of wealth before you can get elected to one. Recognition is in the form of achieved status—you can achieve renown by achieving in the economic sense, whereas in a lot of systems you can't. In them, it may depend on your lineage, who you're related to, whether or not you wield power in the community.

But if you push these historical questions back, you still have the question of why the Ibo had that kind of society in the first place. They might have had high need for achievement first, which led them to create these particular honorary societies that stressed economic achievement.

Dowling: The data just aren't available on that.

McClelland: No.

Dowling: What about the situation in Pakistan where all the investment came from a few small groups?

McClelland: They were tiny minorities in a few trading communities. This raises the whole issue of whether opportunity creates motivation; the opportunities were there, but only a comparative handful of Pakistani took advantage of them. Traditionally, Americans have tended to argue—oddly enough—for what you could call a rather Marxist interpretation of history, the prime mover being what happens in the environment, especially in the economic sphere, rather than something inside the minds of men. Western economists take the same view as Marxist economists. If you've got an economic opportunity, that supposedly stimulates people to take advantage of it. However, history shows that the process is by no means automatic. There have been lots of opportunities lying around for generations that people haven't taken advantage of.

At the time of the rise of ancient Greece, there were other civilizations living in that same area. Nobody did anything about those great opportunities. At the time of the exploitation of overseas trade under the British, they didn't have any great advantages over all the other European countries that might have done the same thing if they'd wanted to badly enough.

It's hard for me to explain all of history just in terms of external events. Some of these motive forces certainly determine the response to the environment. It was very common, particularly in the twenties, to argue that this response was genetic. That's nonsense, because if you take a given racial stock, say on the peninsula of Greece or in Great Britain, you find them responding very vigorously to opportunities at some times in their history but not at other times. Yet the genetic stock is the same.

Dowling: The only thing you can say, then, is that the achievement motive, in order to have any practical consequences, has to be linked with opportunities.

McClelland: No question about that. And we have data to prove it. If you get a lot of achievement motivation and you don't have the opportunities, you're likely to get a lot of public disorder and violence. Countries are increasing their achievement motivation all over the world, and if they don't, at the same time, increase opportunities, then they're in for trouble. There's a new study of countries with high achievement orientation but low educational opportunities. The man who did the study used two measures: The proportion of kids of high school age who are actually in high school was low, as was the opportunity to get ahead, but achievement motivation was high. Then he simply counted the number of assassinations, riots, and other types of "domestic violence," and he found that the particular combination of high achievement motivation and limited opportunity was bad news for the country. Countries with low achievement motivation and low opportunities showed less domestic violence.

To some extent you could use the United States as an example of the same thing. When we tested the black population fifteen years ago, it was only the tiny Negro middle-income group that had high achievement motivation. The lower-class black had very low achievement motivation in the sense of not being interested in getting ahead. He fulfilled the stereotype of the lazy Negro, but of course, he was not interested in achievement for a very good reason: He didn't think it would do him any good if he tried anyway. And it probably wouldn't have, because of the lack of opportunity.

However, the general concern for achievement has been rising in the black population—probably faster than the opportunity structure has improved. This results in impatience and violence among blacks and many idealistic young people who are not black. Oddly, I think a lot of the violence comes out of idealism rather than despair—or at least out of despair that is a consequence of the idealism. They want to bring about change fast; they don't want to be told by older people that it can't be done, so we have to move now on many fronts if we wish to avoid more turmoil.

Dowling: The success of achievement motivation training among lower-middle-class, poorly educated Negroes seems to offer some hope of dealing with the achievement side of the achievement-opportunity axis.

McClelland: This work began almost accidentally, in the sense that we ran across a group of black fathers—it was kind of a father's club in Roxbury—and they were looking around for something to do; they heard about this achievement motivation training, and somebody volunteered to put them through a course. Most of them had criminal records, and I think that only one of the whole group had graduated from high school.

Dowling: I'll take back my comment about lower middle class.

McClelland: Actually, they don't like to use the term "class." That's sort of an income thing and they consider themselves all underclass, which they are to some extent. This group really has done quite well. Some went into business for themselves after training; almost all have better jobs and higher incomes. A number formed a group called Massachusetts Achievement Trainers, which has been quite successful in offering motivation training to blacks and other disadvantaged people.

They trained a group of lower-middle-class black businessmen in Washington, D.C. They did own small shops, but very small—dry cleaning establishments and things of that type. And these men also did quite well. We followed them up six months after training and found that eight had already started new businesses. Of course, there are a great many programs that seem to be developing black capitalism. What we've urged ever since we discovered the importance of opportunity combined with motivation is that motivation training really should be given in connection with a loan program of some type. That way you link motivation to opportunity. In one case in Atlanta, a bank-sponsored motivation training activity is under way. The actual training is being done by the staff of the Behavioral Science Center, a company which I helped found and with which I'm associated as a consultant. BSC also received a contract from A.I.D. to do some training in Ecuador for small businessmen in connection with a Small Business Loan Program of five million dollars.

Dowling: In some cases achievement training has resulted in concrete economic achievements among the participants; in other cases it hasn't worked so well, or it's failed. How do you account for the differences?

McClelland: Certainly there are circumstances in which it doesn't work. I think the main thing is to realize that achievement training by itself is really appropriate only for a rather narrow band of occupational opportunities. It isn't particularly appropriate for managers. BSC now gives managers an organizational development package, which combines some achievement motivation training with some power training and some instruction in managing motivation.

A clearer case where achievement training wouldn't work is when you take eighth graders out of the eighth grade, run them through courses in achievement motivation, then put them back in the same school without touching the school. We've regularly found that achievement motivation training helps some, in the sense that their grades go up a little bit after the training. But this improvement disappears after a year or two. You see, this is a case where you're plugging people back into an opportunity structure that doesn't mesh with what we've trained them to try to do.

Dowling: The structure doesn't support them at all.

McClelland: No. Because, for example, we train them to take moderate risks, like deciding how many problems they can do in the time allotted. Well, the teacher gives them no choice at all. She says do this many problems by next Friday. And we say set your own goals and achieve them in your own way. But because the teacher sets the goal and the path to it as well, the student can get slapped down for deviating from either.

In another study we compared two organizations in Mexico; one was very authoritarian and not developing very rapidly, while the other was growing very rapidly. We tested the top executives on the need for achievement and then tested them again three years later. And we found that the level of achievement motivation in that slowly growing company—it was barely maintaining its own—was quite a bit lower among the top people than among the top management in the fast-growing company. Furthermore, three years later it was worse, because the executives with high achievement motivation on the first test had either left the slow growth company or scored lower. Again you have a case where lack of opportunity prevents the development of achievement motivation and would certainly limit the gains from any achievement training.

Dowling: That reminds me of a study done years ago by Fleishmann at an International Harvester Plant. He found out that people going to a human relations course learned new ways of behaving and looking at their subordinates, then they came back on the job and found out that their boss wasn't behaving any differently and their peers weren't behaving any differently, and it produced frustration.

McClelland: We had a beautiful case of that in one company. The Behavioral Science Center was training some salesmen, and the company's idea was that here were some men who were not quite bad enough to fire, but they weren't turning out enough sales to justify the company's keeping them, either. We thought that maybe achievement motivation had the answer. And so we foolishly accepted the contract and we ran them through the achievement motivation course—and wow! Their performance started to improve right away; one guy sold more insurance the month after training than he had sold all year before. But we were never invited back into that company. We thought the program was a big success. It was very naive of us to accept the company's identification of the problem, because the managers began to get very upset and to feel threatened by these high-producing salesmen; they felt that their own jobs might be in danger. They didn't know what the salesmen had learned. And they began to be very uptight about what was happening.

Dowling: They saw a power threat.

McClelland: Sure. Well, it was present. From then on, BSC—and any consulting organization should feel this way—doesn't take for granted that the company has correctly identified the problem. Also, you need to give a full explanation of what your training is designed to accomplish—otherwise you'll get into all kinds of trouble.

Dowling: It reminds me of some cases of small groups of executives who underwent sensitivity training, got religion, then came back and again found an environment that was hostile to everything they learned. In other words, I think it would be fairly safe to say that motivation achievement training only takes and is only desirable in certain organizational climates.

McClelland: Right. We concentrate on finding out what kind of climate a company has as a first step. We do a little diagnosis, because often a company doesn't know what its organizational climate is. A company that encourages achievement motivation and rewards people for good performance instead of criticizing them for poor performance has a quite different climate from one that doesn't do these things—and incidentally is likely to be doing better.

Dowling: What kind of management training should a company with a highly structured authoritarian environment have?

McClelland: It always depends on how well they're doing. If they're making a lot of money and everything's going along fine, they don't need it. You've got to be in trouble before you want to do something or make any changes.

Dowling: I remember in the Indian study one thing that surprised me was the absence of correlation between the achievement motivation scores and the change scores. Those people who scored the highest on need for achievement to begin with were not necessarily those who changed the most. On the surface, at least, it looks like a contradiction.

McClelland: It came as a surprise to us, too, although there's one study showing that those who were initially higher did a little bit better. But it isn't a close relationship. In a way, that suggests that the training is more valuable, because you don't have to select people in terms of this initial characteristic. They can acquire it during training so that they can perform better afterwards.

Dowling: In the Indian study, didn't some of the people translate their new awareness of themselves and their goals into power attainment rather than achievement?

McClelland: I'm not sure they did it on purpose. I think they were trying to be achievement-oriented but only succeeded in being power-oriented—the "big man syndrome," as I call it. They had raised their level of aspiration, but to them, that really meant being more important.

The one predictor of beneficial training that we found was desire to change—in psychological terms. There was a substantial gap between their real selves and their ideal selves.

Dowling: Of course, the other important correlation was between opportunity and change. Those people who were the heads of business, or at any rate were in the position to powerfully affect the decisions in the enterprises, made the most change.

McClelland: That's right.

Dowling: Could you summarize the four principal techniques used in the achievement training study?

McClelland: We borrow a lot of techniques that are becoming popular among many different types of management training seminars. One of the four major inputs, as we call them, is formal instruction in the research findings about the achievement motive: what it is, how you measure it, how you determine how much you have, what the action characteristics are that go with thinking like an achiever, and how you recognize them in other people. This is what we call the achievement syndrome.

Essentially, we make the following proposition to people who are in business: We've found through all this research that the achievement motive is an important element in success—not the only element, but an important one—for entrepreneurial positions in life. If you're in that kind of position, and you want to be more successful, we have every reason to believe that if you think like this and act like this, you'll be more successful. So this part of the training is just straight information-giving.

The second major element is what we call self-study, which is part of many other courses in which people learn about the way they think and the way they act from games, tests, and so on. In this way they can see where they stand relative to the achievement ideal. For example, in the second course in Kakinada, India, people wrote down six stories suggested to them by six pictures—to find out how strong their achievement motive was. Another somewhat more bizarre but quite effective form of self-examination was to ask each man to think of the words he would like to have inscribed on his tombstone and turn them in the next morning.

Dowling: In short, they answer the question: Who am I?

McClelland: Actually two questions: Who am I? And am I an achiever? They presumably they make some kind of decision about whether they want to change into an achiever or not. There has to be some kind of commitment to change or there won't be any. That gets you into the third element, which is goal setting and planning. If I want to be this kind of person, how can I specifically act in the next six months in my business to bring about change? There is a very elaborate goal-setting exercise that participants go through, which is then evaluated by others in the course.

Dowling: Yes, I remember. Groups of four or five reviewed each plan, the idea being that otherwise the individual might satisfy himself with generalities. The group is much more critical.

McClelland: Yes. Exactly. The plans drawn up are usually much too general. Actually, we've found in following up these people that it isn't the specific plan so much as learning how to make a plan that's important. Because often when they get back in their jobs, they'll find that the plan was impractical and they'll abandon it. However, they're much more likely to think of another one, having once been through the process.

The fourth characteristic is what we call interpersonal supports or group supports. The fact that you usually do this in groups and that the group often belongs to the same company or comes from the same community helps people to continue to focus on their goals. They go back and meet occasionally and give each other reinforcement.

Dowling: In the cases where the course lasts up to ten days and meets in a kind of retreat setting, they get lots of support from the staff and from each other.

McClelland: Right. Our final analysis of which inputs were most important wasn't as revealing as we'd hoped it would be. We thought we might find that some particular ingredient in the training was essential: If it were present you'd get the desired end result, and if it weren't present you wouldn't get it. What we found was that the larger the number of different inputs, the greater the output, in the sense that the more things you did and the better you did them, the better your results in terms of improved entrepreneurial performance.

Dowling: Isn't training in the achievement motive a common element of all programs?

McClelland: Yes. The achievement syndrome at the very least provides a framework to explain what you're doing and why you're doing it.

Dowling: What about the prestige factor that's also present to a greater or lesser degree in all courses?

McClelland: Yes, it's one element that helps get people's attention. More and more I'm convinced that for motivational change or attitude change or any behavior change to take place, you have to grab people's attention.

We go through life, through certain routines that capture our thinking processes and our action patterns day after day after day. Basically the problem a change agent has is to disrupt that in some dramatic way and make people pay attention for the moment to something else. Now, the prestige inputs, as we call them, are simply devices for grabbing people's attention. That is, they may pay more attention to someone from Harvard, or someone with scientific backing, or a successful entrepreneur than they would to the guy down the hall.

Dowling: I was impressed by that brief instance you gave of the "hello-goodbye syndrome"—where the person who has a brief contact with a prestigious psychiatrist sometimes shows as good results as someone who has undergone extensive psychotherapy.

McClelland: Right. Man in the white coat, impressive building, someone caring for me, someone caring who's really an expert. There's also the Harvard Test of Inflected Acquisition—the Rosenthal effect, we call it, after the professor who demonstrated it. He showed that when teachers expect school children to do better in terms of test results, they in fact score them better, even though the test results are faked.

Dowling: I gather there are two elements involved in the prestige factor: First, you're telling people that they can expect to change; and second, it counts that the people who tell them they can expect to change have prestige in their eyes.

McClelland: Yes. Because the people doing the testing have prestige, they'll believe them.

Actually, we use many sources of prestige suggestion. With the Bombay courses, for example, we stimulated people to think they were going to change by our choice of words in the initial brochure—we stated quite boldly that the purpose of the course was to "increase," "create," and "stimulate" the entrepreneurial spirit and managerial effectiveness. We also buttressed our arguments with all kinds of prestigious props— years of scientific research, Harvard University, and association with the Bombay Management Association, an organization with a big local reputation.

Dowling: To change the subject drastically—does the achievement motive throw any light on the discontent among students today? I'm thinking of the fact that most students come from middle-class families in which you would have a bias toward business and in which you'd expect to find the achievement motive fairly high. Maybe I'm mistaken.

McClelland: I think that there are several things involved. Part of the discontent comes from the desire to do a lot of things in the world that their parents didn't do, which is—after all—fairly normal. As I said earlier, achievement-motivated people choose moderate risks—they want to do at least a little bit better than was done before.

If you come from a home where your daddy has made it—bought his house in the suburbs, a car or maybe two cars, and so on—and you have some achievement motivation, where do you go from there? Can you look forward to doing more of the same? Living in the suburbs just like your father? No. Achievement theory says that you have to do a little better than he did. Does that mean a bigger house? Well, that somehow doesn't appeal to most students. Instead, they've moved out on another tack and said, "Maybe we can improve the social machinery for delivering goods and services to the poor or to the blacks." Actually, it's right in the American tradition of trying to do a little bit better than your parents did.

Dowling: In other words, the achievement motive still exists, but it's seeking other worlds to conquer.

McClelland: Yes. The norm has changed. And what's good enough for daddy, who may have moved up from real poverty, is certainly not good enough for the son, because he's already up there. He has to move the next rung up the ladder.

And apparently what's not appealing to the kids—I must say I admire them for it—is just more acquisition of material goods. If you've got one car or two cars, what good is three cars? Diminishing returns set in. If you've got a nice ranch-style house, what's good about one twice as big? It really doesn't provide much achievement satisfaction. There's more achievement satisfaction in trying to make the system work so that all people are involved in it, let's say. But, of course, what students are finding is that it's going to be really tough. That may not be a moderate risk; it may be a really big risk to try to do that.

Dowling: Hence, the frustration.

McClelland: Hence, the frustration. Yes. it's certainly not easy to get things moving as fast as they would like.

Dowling: This talk about father and son reminds me of the accounts I've read over the years of the way in which Joseph Kennedy brought up his children. He obviously worked on their achievement motives. On the other hand, he very consciously directed them against going into business.

McClelland: He also worked very hard on their power orientation. They are the best-educated people I know in the power area. I've written a lot on power motivation, because it has a bad reputation—you're not supposed to be power-oriented. And that's because of a misunderstanding between what we call the desire for personal power—dominance, manipulation—and the desire for socialized power—that is, to exercise influence on behalf of other people. And it's this more socialized power that goes through political channels. What I've read about the bringing up of the Kennedy boys is that they were fiercely competitive and had a lot of both achievement and power training. You see, competition, in a sense, is both achievement and power: You want to beat the other guy, but you also want to do well. And I think because of the traditional Irish interest in politics, this was a new world to conquer and Joseph Kennedy also equipped his sons superbly to deal with the power game. They understood the influence game; they understood the political process and how to make it work.

Dowling: The other element about the Kennedy boys' bringing up is that business was never praised as a career—apparently business was never discussed at all. And a sensible thing, too—there's a case in spades of daddy having three cars.

McClelland: We find generally among the so-called upper-class students at Harvard that they really can't aspire economically. We have had achievement motivation training in my undergraduate course in motivation, not because we want to increase their achievement motivation, but because this turns out to be a good way to teach the subject of the course. And you have boys who say quite frankly, "I can't possibly surpass my family or my father." If you're a Rockefeller or someone like that, it's ridiculous even to think about it.

Dowling: So like young Laurance Rockefeller, you go to Harlem or you go into politics—like his uncles Nelson and Winthrop, or his cousin John D. IV.

McClelland: Sure. You have to move into a different field. Generally upper-class people have lower achievement motivation, and they shift to power or influence instead. The British have a better name for it when they talk about the difference between statesmanship and manipulation—that's the difference between what we called socialized power and personal power.

Dowling: If our achievement motivation is declining—at least among middle-class and upper-class youth—it must have increased tremendously in Japan since World War II.

McClelland: Our data on Japan were conflicting. At the time I wrote *The Achieving Society*, the children's textbook data did not show that Japan was very high in need for achievement. However, those textbooks were written during the MacArthur occupation, when American advisers were a major influence in what stories were getting into Japanese textbooks. So I thought there was good reason not to believe it too much. The contrary evidence was that Osaka High School students ranked very high on achievement motivation. We were more willing to believe that than we were the textbooks. And of course, since then the evidence is that the Japanese are fantastically high in achievement motivation. The other interesting thing about those Osaka data was that, with one exception, it was the only group that we ever tested anywhere in which the working class—the so-called lower-class—was high in achievement motivation. In every other country it's the middle class that's been high in achievement motivation. The exception was a Jewish group in this country in which achievement motivation was high—and equally high for lower-, middle-, and upper-class Jews. And that's like the Japanese. Everywhere else the middle class ranks higher than either the upper or lower class.

Dowling: The upper class is presumably higher than the lower?

McClelland: Yes. That's the way it is among the WASPs. We found the same distribution in Germany and Brazil—everywhere but Japan. That's very significant because that means that the upwardly mobile people in Japan—the little people—are also high in achievement motivation. And that predicts a tremendous economic success for the country as a whole. It's like the Jewish success in the United States. Study after study has shown that, of the ethnic minorities, the Jews have done the best on the average. It's a very interesting parallel.

Dowling: What's the overall trend of achievement motivation in the United States?

McClelland: As far as we know, we've definitely gone down—it's arguable how far down; we don't have solid enough data. We're certainly down from what we were before World War I, and the high point, as far as we know, was in the period from the 1890s to 1910. On a comparative basis, we're still slightly above the world average.

On the other hand, the need for power is going way up in this country. It's been going up steadily, and I think it's extremely dangerous. All you have to do is read the newspaper every day to discover how everyone is getting power-oriented. It's dangerous because the need for affiliation is also going down, and if you have an increase in need for power and a decrease in need for affiliation, then you get people murdered right and left and general violence. We reported that finding in *The Achieving Society* for other countries, and we are seeing the same pattern of domestic violence in the United States. I predicted this trend ten years ago, and unfortunately the prediction has proved true.

Dowling: Could you also make the generalization that this decline in the achievement factor in the United States is on a sufficiently large scale to indicate a declining rate of economic growth over the next 10 to 15 years?

McClelland: I'll have to be honest and say I think my data are not good enough to predict with real confidence. But the future doesn't look good. In balance, the need for achievement seems to be declining; that indicates we would show a declining rate of economic growth over the next ten years.

Dowling: What are the countries that are ahead of us in terms of this factor? Is Japan at the top of the heap?

McClelland: Of course, it's the most visible one. Other countries showed high when I did my research back in the 1950s—and there were some surprises. France was high then, and France at that time was talked about as the sick country of Europe; no one expected much of it economically. Germany was high then, and Germany has done very well in the last decade.

Dowling: That shouldn't have come as any surprise.

McClelland: No, that wouldn't have been a surprise. I know other countries that I think are going to surprise people—India and Pakistan. People were a little overwhelmed at the problems of India, including the Indians. My data suggest, however, that India is not going to do too badly. Her economic growth isn't going to be phenomenal, but the Indians should do fairly well economically—if they don't fall apart politically. The problem is just to hold the fabric together long enough.

Dowling: What about the birth rate?

McClelland: I tend not to be so alarmed by that as some people. Not that I'm against population planning, but I think it puts the emphasis in the wrong place. Basically, the philosophy of people who want to control the birth rate is essentially a philosophy of scarcity. We have limited resources and we must cut back. Now, that undermines achievement orientation as an ideology. The achievement philosophy says, look, we'll create more resources. So my answer to the population people is that philosophically I object to their prophesies of doom from overpopulation; practically, of course, I don't object to family planning, particularly where people are motivated to achieve anyway. But I think there's a chance of creating new resources to keep up with the increasing population, and that philosophically that encourages an achievement motivation.

Conversation with
KENNETH E. BOULDING

Kenneth E. Boulding, professor of economics at the University of Colorado and director of the Program of Research on General and Social and Economic Dynamics, Institute of Behavior Science, is a protean man. The latter of his two titles barely suggests the range of his interests—economist, ecologist, systems man, humanist, philosopher, poet, and active member of the Society of Friends. He has served at various times as president of the following organizations: The American Economic Association, The Peace Research Society, and The Society for General Systems Research. The marks of achievement and recognition are evident: 27 books, including two volumes of sonnets—what other economist can talk about his published sonnets?—and innumerable articles and 23 honorary degrees from universities here and abroad.

So much for kudos. What about his thinking? The conversation, of course, will reveal much more about that question than this brief introduction can possibly cover. But we can mention a few highlights that impressed us.

He possesses a special insight into the operations of our society, which probably arises out of a combination of his intellectual breadth and depth and the fact of his being an outsider. Boulding, an Englishman from Liverpool, came to the United States when he was already 27. Traces of the accent remain.

Two illustrations of his insight: Another Englishman transplanted to the United States, the philosopher Alfred North Whitehead, once wrote that a "society could best be classified in terms of the some-

Reprinted from Organizational Dynamics, *Autumn 1977*

bodies whom, in fact, it satisfies." Boulding, using this classification, categorizes the United States as a society in which the poor and the rich are exploited for the benefit of the middle class—a seminal insight. In the conversation, he cites the state universities in which rich middle-class students are subsidized as prime proof of his thesis.

Another insight is what he calls the aristocratization of that same middle class. Progressive affluence sustained over a sufficient period of time has been accompanied by a weakening of the work ethic and the kind of conspicuous consumption traditionally associated with the upper class. As we have indicated, Boulding is much more than a conventional economist.

He is difficult to classify or categorize because he is an original. Take his dismissal of the labor theory of value as "simply wrong." Why?

"Labor produces nothing, just as raw materials in the ground produce nothing. It's the process of organization by which labor is hired, employed, and directed, by which raw materials are brought together, by which machinery and buildings are assembled, by which processes of production are organized, which in fact create the product. Labor by itself is an inert mass incapable of producing little more than scratching a meager living from the woods. The organizer who really creates the product, however, almost has to be either an owner or controller of property."

In short, Boulding has turned Marx upside down and substituted a capital theory of value for the labor theory of value. Strong and original stuff and, as the conversation reveals, vintage Boulding—and a rare vintage indeed.

Dowling: Let's begin by talking about what you call the grants economy and how it mitigates or redresses the inequities and inefficiencies of the exchange economy. I suppose the best place to start is by defining the term.

Boulding: A grants economy is an old idea. Economists have long recognized one-way transfers. I define a grant as a one-way transfer of economic goods in contrast to an exchange, in which you have a two-way transfer: I give you something; you give me something. This isn't to say, however, that noneconomic goods in the form of gratitude, well-being, and so on are not passed in reciprocity for both economic goods and noneconomic goods.

Dowling: Chester Barnard had a phrase: "What you get in return are ideal benefactions."

Boulding: What we tried to do in studying the grants economy is really to systemize it and view it as a major sector of economic life that has a certain unity to it and that contains certain governing principles.

Another way to look at it is that, whereas exchange involves rearrangement of assets among the exchangers, the sign of a grant is redistribution of net worth. If I give you $100 and you give me a nice smile in return, your account doesn't recognize the nice smile.

Dowling: In other words, you give me $100, I give you a nice smile; you have $100 less, and I have $100 that I didn't have before.

Boulding: Exactly. That's the accountant's way of viewing the transaction. So the redistribution of net worth forms the most important parts of the grants economy.

Then we distinguish between explicit grants, which are simple transfers of economic goods of some kind that an accountant recognizes, and implicit grants, which represent those redistributions that occur as a result of changes in the price structure, in taxes, or subsidies and in quotas, restrictions, and regulatory operations of all kinds. This, of course, is a particularly interesting aspect of a grants economy because it's very often hard to say what the distributional impact on particular operations is. And studying this phenomenon is an important part of economics.

We see this in the study of the incidence of taxation. On the whole, I regard taxes as part of the grants economy. On the criterion of transfer of net worth, they certainly are. When I pay my taxes to the federal government, my net worth goes down. And the federal government's net worth goes up, even though I may get unaccountable benefits in return.

Dowling: They're indirect and very difficult to measure.

Boulding: Very difficult to measure. You might argue that just as we have environmental impact statements, we should have distributional impact statements, and it is beginning. The Bureau of Reclamation is supposed to do this now. I think this should be a very general part of the information system. When you do anything by way of laws, of regulations, of policy making—anything of that sort—there is always redistribution, so a distributional impact statement would usually be appropriate in such instances, and these statements would often turn out to be very surprising.

Dowling: Why would they be surprising?

Boulding: Because the economic system has immensely complex interactions. Things pop out where you don't expect them to. The redistribution aspects of almost all policies are usually very different from what the authors of these policies or even the supporters of these policies expect.

I have developed what I call a law of political irony, which says that everything you do to help people hurts them. While there are notable exceptions, many cases illustrate the law. The incidence of taxes is an example. Incidence will run through the system, taxes will be passed on, rearranged, and passed on again. People will adjust, and the principle is that the adjustable will adjust, the unadjustable will be stuck with the tax. In time, the incidence of taxes tends to fall on the people who cannot adjust.

Dowling: Or who can't pass the tax on.

Boulding: Right, who can't pass it on. This means, on the whole, people with inelastic supplies and demands. The more inelastic the supply of anything you provide, the more likely you are to end up with changes you cannot adjust to, by definition. A good example is, if New York gets into trouble, what are you likely to end up with? Well, you're likely to end up with the landowners suffering a decline in land values. The other people will adjust; many will move out of the city. This will mainly affect land values. The one thing that cannot be removed is Manhattan Island. There is no way of towing it away. That is why land values tend to reflect, as it were, the distributional impact of last resort.

The prize example of this is the impact of the tobacco quota. Back in 1934 we put a quota on the tobacco of all the farms that happened to be producing tobacco. You go down to Kentucky, to tobacco country, today and you'll find two physically identical farms but with one worth six times the value of the other. One has a tobacco quota and the other doesn't. This is all capitalized in the value of the farm. This was a free gift of the American people to the owners of land that happened to be producing tobacco in 1934, and it's very hard to justify.

Dowling: It has never been extended to farmers who took up tobacco farming after 1934?

Boulding: No. If they want to grow tobacco, they have to buy a quota from the descendants of the people who were growing tobacco in 1934. It's fantastic. Another example was Lyndon Johnson's fortune. It was made in television as a direct result of franchises granted by the federal government. As such, it's a free gift from the American people.

I have innumerable examples of this. Any kind of quota, any kind of licensing, any kind of restriction of this kind will create these grants, and they're usually very hard to justify.

In this little book that I've just been editing, there are some interesting articles that demonstrate the federal subsidies to housing— Fannie Mae and Ginnie Mae. All those Maes end up generating the middle class, and they all result in taxes on the poor and the rich for the benefit of the middle class.

Dowling: As a member of the middle class, I should probably applaud.

Boulding: It's a real problem. In fact, one could define social democracy as the process by which you subsidize the middle class in the name of subsidizing the poor. You see so many examples—public education is a good case in point. State universities are a shocking subsidy, in this case to the rich middle class. We found that at the University of Michigan the family income of our students averaged in the top 10 percent of the family-income distribution. I'm pretty sure the same is true here in Boulder. They are quite heavily subsidized, and they are subsidized by rather regressive state and local taxes, sales taxes that fall heavily on the poor. The system is extraordinarily hard to justify. I hope that after careful study of the grants economy, particularly the whole incidence of distributional impact, we can get a little more sophistication about these matters.

Take, for example, the much-touted "new international economic order." It's much like the Holy Roman Empire, which, in Voltaire's words, was neither holy, nor Roman, nor an empire. This is not new, maybe it's international, but it's certainly not economic, nor is it an order. If it works out at all, it will be a subsidy to the rich people in the poor countries. This is *what* cartels always do; this is what OPEC does.

OPEC subsidizes the rich in its member countries. It doesn't benefit the poor very much.

Dowling: Isn't its marked increase in size one reason why your grants economy is becoming more important? I'm thinking that when you're talking about GNP—my figures are fairly recent—60 percent of GNP in Great Britain ends up in government accounts. I think we're up to 35 percent in the United States. This, it seems to me, is a rough indication of the growth of the grants economy.

Boulding: One thing, of course, is to look at the grants economy as a totality. When you do that, you find that the most important institution, by far, is the family—and that's still true. James Miller of Michigan did a study of this in 1968, I believe, in which he came to the conclusion that about 30 percent of GNP is redistributed in the family—that is, it consists of grants from parents to children, children to parents, wives to husbands, husbands to wives, and so on. Direct redistribution through government was about 7 percent of GNP—it is a rather larger amount now—with about 2 percent of GNP additional from private charity, foundations, grants, and so on. So, at that time, the grants economy might have been 40-plus percent of the GNP—30 percent of which was still in the family. We don't really know how far the rise in public grants economy has simply displaced the grants economy of the family because we don't have any early data.

Dowling: You can certainly guess with Social Security tied to increased costs of living, and so forth, that you obviously have a diminution in one aspect of the grants economy and that is in children who support parents.

Boulding: Of course you do. I supported my mother in her old age, but my children have no intention of supporting me. We have the teachers' pension fund system. It isn't only just the government grants economy. It's also the pension fund system, which transferred part of this out of the family into the financial market.

Of course there's a tricky problem with all of this. Many items that look like grants may be deferred exchanges. It certainly used to be true that you supported your children in the hope that they would support you in your old age. It was a kind of investment. In most parts of the world this is still true. This is why the population is so incredibly intractable in the poor countries. In a country like India, the only hope of a secure old age is to have four sons, and any population restriction is highly unpopular, as Mrs. Gandhi discovered. So things that look like grants in the short run turn out to be an investment. All investment, in a sense, is deferred exchange.

Dowling: You quoted Miller on the family being the largest source of grants. Obviously these proportions have changed since his figures.

Boulding: I don't have any current figures on this. But I'm sure the government's grants are over 10 percent of GNP now. A fair test of this is the difference between the total government budget—which is about 35 percent—and government purchases of goods and services. Purchases of goods and services at federal, state, and local government levels are still, I think, only about 23 percent of GNP. So the difference should be about 12 percent. This is a figure off the top of my head.

Then you have to add to that, as I say, the incidence of redistribution. There are direct redistributions in terms of agricultural subsidies, loan subsidies, and all these things. Then you would have to add to that the whole indirect redistribution. It's hard to assess items like prohibition of branch banking or the regulation of public utilities. The point is that the grants economy has two effects: It affects the distribution of economic wealth, and it also affects the allocation of resources. I suspect, for instance, that our subsidies to the banking system result in a banking system that is really too big. I suspect it's the same with the airlines.

There are some interesting problems on how you adjust supply and demand in this case. In education, I would like to see much more use of the price system. The grants economy in education would go to the student rather than to the institution, as with the old GI Bill of Rights. On the whole, I would finance higher education through setting up educational banks. Colleges should charge students the full cost of their education. Then your federal educational banks would lend the student however much he or she needed with the loan to be repaid by a lifetime surcharge on his or her income tax. It would only be one or 2 percent surcharge on income tax. If the student earned a good income, he or she would pay it back. If the student became a hippie, he or she wouldn't have to.

Dowling: In your writings, you identified three traps of the grants economy. One was the sacrifice trap, one was the dependency trap, and the third was the ignorance trap. My impression is that it's the ignorance trap that's the most dangerous to the grants economy—so much resources get misapplied and misdirected.

Boulding: I'm not sure. The sacrifice trap is very costly, too; you see it in war. The Vietnam war was a prize example of it. We were throwing live soldiers after dead, simply because we couldn't get out. Johnson couldn't admit to himself that he had been wrong. We see businessmen throwing good money after bad. A firm will get involved in something that clearly was a bad investment, but it takes a long time to get out of it because the personalities of the decision makers get involved and so on. If at first you don't succeed, at what point do you say to hell with it and try something else? On the other hand, you often try and try again until it's too late.

On the ignorance problem, one of the main issues is philanthropy. Private philanthropy receives extraordinarily little feedback.

Dowling: Although, as you pointed out, it is also a very small part of the total picture.

Boulding: Very small quantitatively, but qualitatively, much more important. The excuse for private philanthropy is that its sponsors do things that are unusual and imaginative—things government can't undertake. At least, the philanthropoids visualize themselves in this role. Certainly some of the foundations do. There are wide differences among foundations, however. The Russell Sage Foundation, for example, is known to be extraordinarily creative and imaginative.

Dowling: And it works with a relatively small amount of money.

Boulding: It's a very small foundation. But it has had much more impact than some of the larger ones. On the other hand, you've got some foundations that are stodgy from the word go, and they perform nothing but very conventional activities.

Dowling: Maybe you have to distinguish between two periods in the life of a foundation. The first when the founder is dispensing money for pet projects with very little regard for their utility and the second when they are being professionally administered.

Boulding: I've been arguing that we need an institution of philanthropy assessment. If assessment is good for technology, it's good for philanthropy too, particularly in view of the difficulty of obtaining valid feedback. I sometimes call this "Edsel's Law." When the Ford Motor Company produced the Edsel, the feedback was very rapid. It quickly knew what a lemon it had on its hands. If the Ford Foundation produced an Edsel, it might never know. Actually, it has produced one or two and it has found out, but I think it takes about ten years for a foundation to find out.

And it took the United States government ten years to find out that it had an Edsel in the Vietnam war. There the feedback was extraordinarily slow because of the sacrifice trap.

Dowling: Do you see much hope in an increased emphasis at the federal level on both cost-benefit analyses and cost-effectiveness analyses helping to improve valid feedback and thereby helping those in charge to circumvent the ignorance trap?

Boulding: Yes.

Dowling: This kind of cost-benefit analysis has been used, for instance, to prove that a change of the standards on coke-oven emissions, which will save 27 lives, will cost something like $250 million—the OSHA figure—or $1.3 billion—the industry figure.

Boulding: Cost-benefit analysis is potentially very valuable. But there are difficulties in using the technique, for the people who are making the decisions are making the evaluations and their judgments are apt to be colored by their dual roles. There's a lot to be said for independent estimates. This is true of the Bureau of Reclamation's analyses, for instance, which tend to be justifications for what they want to do.

We had a very interesting seminar yesterday with Professor Howe of our department on these water projects and the cost-benefit problems involved. A particularly interesting case is the Narrows Project on the South Platte. It seems totally unjustifiable, certainly from a national point of view.

Dowling: What is it?

Boulding: It's a dam, an irrigation project, that will provide water for about 15 large farms, and that's all.

Dowling: At what cost?

Boulding: At a subsidy of $60 an acre. The distributional impacts are horrifying: it displaces a lot of small farmers; the recreational advantages are practically nil; the environmental advantages are nil, probably negative. Even the regular economic cost-benefit analysis only shows returns at an absurdly low rate of interest. But our governor, who is an environmentalist, is supporting it. The state cost-benefit analysis comes out fine because the federal government pays all the bills. It's this kind of encouragement by the federal government that pushes the states into projects with enormous external diseconomies. The rest of us, as a result, are all worse off.

How one deals with this politically, I don't know, because politically everybody likes to grab something for himself at the cost of everyone else. Then these costs mount up. The great political problem is, if you have large individual benefits for the few and small individual costs for the many, the benefits tend to win, even if the aggregate costs are larger.

The benefits are obvious while the costs are very difficult to see. When I was a little boy, I used to have a pipe dream that if everyone in England gave me a penny, they wouldn't miss it, and I'd be terribly rich!

I could almost say political power is the power to persuade people to be irrational. It's extraordinarily difficult to have much faith in the rationality of political decisions.

I would have the cost-benefit analyses done by private agencies—farm them out. You build in two protections this way, protection against self-serving and protection against self-confirming prophecies. These could have some impact. An interesting example is the Office of Technology Assessment, which as you know has been under severe criticism. Because it is an agency of Congress and breathes down the neck of the executive, it possesses a degree of independence. It has had a certain impact on the energy agencies simply because it represents the anxious money of congressmen who want to do a good job. They always have a fear of being fooled by the executive. A congressional agency adds to the system of checks and balances, in which I am a great believer.

Dowling: You talk about the grants economy, and one of its valuable functions as providing certain kinds of aid and encouragement to economic development that would not occur if we left it up to the mixed exchange economy. How does the grants economy, in general, aid economic development?

Boulding: The stock answer to this is that wherever there is market failure, there is a place for the grants economy to allocate resources for activities that are socially beneficial. Knowledge, of course, is a classic example of this, particularly when it is generalized knowledge. But you can't really appropriate scientific knowledge. This is the case for the National Science Foundation. The scientific community is producing a public good. On the other hand, many things that are subsidized actually might be done better privately. That might be true for higher education, especially at the undergraduate level. I'm in favor of pushing everything into the market that you can, simply because grants economy resources are scarce.

Dowling: And very difficult to monitor.

Boulding: Very difficult to monitor. The case for looking at the grants economy as a whole is that the scarcity element is not often realized. If I get a grant from NSF, somebody else doesn't. He doesn't know who received the grant or why, which is just as well. But there is this kind of generalized scarcity of the grants economy, which makes it really quite hard to administer effectively. In the market, someone gets something, and the somebody who doesn't get it usually knows that he doesn't and why; there is more information and more feedback. In the grants economy, however, feedback is difficult. It has to be organized better than it is.

On the other hand, there are some public goods that have to be provided through some sort of grants economy—whether public or private—because there is no way by which the market can provide the goods. So, on the whole—I've argued this with my friend Mancur Olsen, for instance, who insists that the grants economy involves public goods and not much else—I argue that the grants economy involves public goods and something else, which is primarily the redistributional aspects of it. In a certain sense, this public redistribution is also a public good. There are some distributions that we feel uneasy with. If we have a society in which some people are outrageously poor and some people are outrageously rich, people feel uncomfortable about it. It isn't a society you're proud to belong to, and pride has a lot to do with redistributions, along with some sense of humanity.

Dowling: You make the point in a number of your writings that the answer to the problem of distribution of resources is not to take away from the rich and give to the poor but to engage in the kind of economic development that makes everyone richer.

Boulding: That depends on the potentialities for development For instance, in this country in the last generation, we've done very well. We've had a growing economy for 40 to 50 years. Everybody got twice as rich—the per capita income about doubled since World War II—but the proportional distribution of income has hardly changed at all. So the poor have gotten twice as rich, the middle class has gotten twice as rich, and the rich have gotten twice as rich. On the other hand, in the next generation, this may not happen—what with energy shortages, the increasing difficulty of getting materials, and a certain slowdown in technology. We don't know. It's quite plausible that per capita incomes are not going to rise very much over the next 30 years. Now, under those circumstances, the only way you can reduce poverty is to redistribute income or property in some way. It's a pretty fair objective for a society to halve the amount of poverty every generation.

Dowling: You're saying that we're getting a scenario in which it's plausible that what you call the "Duchess's Law" will take over. You derived the law, as I recall, from something the Duchess said in *Alice in Wonderland:* "The more there is of yours, the less there is of mine." In other words, we may be facing a society with zero growth.

Boulding: I'm not saying this is necessarily so, because there is always the factor of the unexpected. I'm extremely dubious of any projections of the future because of the enormous technological uncertainties. Still, one has to be prepared for the worst as well as for the best. There's a plausible no-growth or very slow-growth scenario for the rich countries in the next 30 years. The real price of energy is likely to rise, and we are going to have to put much more into it. We may find ourselves with higher rates of investment rather than lower rates to find a substitute for the extraordinarily cheap energy we've had from oil and gas. It's hard to visualize anything as cheap as digging a hole in the ground and having high-quality and very convenient energy come out of it.

Dowling: The bill is bound to go up, no matter what the circumstances.

Boulding: I think so. Even though it isn't fatal, it's bound to be a drag. The increase in per capita income over the past 50 years has been due to two major factors. One is the cheapening of energy—energy is actually as cheap today as it was in the thirties, in real terms. And the other is the extraordinary developments in agriculture, which have liberated 30 million people from agricultural work to make our color TV sets and all sorts of other goods.

That was a one-shot operation. Now ask yourself: Where are the occupations that will have a high increase in productivity? They're not easy to identify. Increasingly, we're moving into occupations like education and medicine and government where an increase in productivity is extraordinarily difficult to achieve. How do you increase the productivity of a string quartet? Do they play Beethoven twice as fast?

The so-called service industries, in particular, which are actually often capital intensive, tend to be industries in which increases in productivity are very difficult to achieve. One suspects that we are tailing off in economic growth.

Dowling: You're fond of talking about traps. When you wrote your book on the twentieth century, roughly 25 years ago, you talked about a kind of conflict between evolution and en5ropy, and you expressed qualified optimism as to the outcome of the conflict. You looked at technology and saw antientropic forces at work. As I recall, you talked about it in terms of a technology that would concentrate diffused material rather than diffuse concentrated material. It's 25 years later. How do you look at what you call the entropy trap now?

Boulding: I was farsighted in the sense of getting into this business before most people did. Let me give you an example. You could have written a beautiful Club of Rome report in the United States in 1858 (you know, the Club of Rome predicts catastrophe and disaster and so on) pointing out that 75 or 80 percent of our energy was derived from wood, that we were cutting down our forests at an enormous rate, and that by 1920 or thereabouts it would all be gone. We also could have predicted that New York City would be under 50 feet of horse manure by about that same date.

And it could have happened, you see, because other societies have run out of wood. The Greeks did; the Romans did; even the British did about 1600, and then they found coal.

Dowling: You chose your date carefully. The next year was Titusville and the discovery of oil.

Boulding: They discovered this enormous treasure chest in the basement. And what do you do when you discover a treasure chest in the basement? You live it up.

Dowling: We've been living it up ever since.

Boulding: While the Arabs put in a false bottom, there's a real bottom underneath it. We know perfectly well that in 50 years, as most people expect, or in 100 years, if we're incredibly lucky, all the oil will be gone. Then what?

Of course, there's another treasure chest, which is uranium and thorium, but all treasure chests are Pandora's boxes. You open the treasure chest, and you open the door to all sorts of evil. This was true of Prometheus. You know what happened to him. Fire, after all, expanded the human niche and the range of human artifacts enormously. It has also led to people being burned to death. It led to metallurgy; it was used in war. Oil and gas led to automobile accidents. The devil came to us about 1890, after we found the oil and gas, and said, "I've got something really wonderful for you. It's a suit of armor with 200 horses inside and it will take you anywhere you want to go." But he also said, "Wait a minute, I've got a price for this—about 50,000 rather unpleasant deaths a year and a certain amount of human injury and suffering."

Dowling: There was certainly no unwillingness to strike the bargain.

Boulding: No. And nuclear energy faces the same problem. It promises us the breeder reactor. We have a technology—at least the French have it—that will postpone the fuel crisis for perhaps two or three thousand years. We will be able to burn up all the uranium now—even without going to fusion. It's nice—we're going to have electricity for two thousand years, but we're also going to have nuclear proliferation and its potential for contributing to the destruction of the human race.

We've got these appalling choices. We look at this and say, let's stick to coal. We've got coal enough to last hundreds of years. We're lucky in this country—we've got alternatives.

Dowling: But inexpensive coal is something else.

Boulding: And nonpolluting coal is still much further away. And if we burn coal, this is going to increase the CO_2 in the atmosphere. This is going to produce incalculable but almost certainly very significant changes in the atmospheric system of the world, perhaps the melting of the ice caps.

Dowling: I read some figures recently that indicated we have a declining investment in research and development—in both the public and private sectors. In terms of the kind of continuing economic development and technological development that you feel is important, how significant is this? How negative is this? And what should we do about it?

Boulding: Organized research in universities has almost halved in the past ten years. As a percentage of total university expenditures, research budgets have gone from about 25 percent to 12 percent. As you know, it's very hard to estimate the quality of research, particularly organized research. It could be true that we are running into a period of declining productivity, that knowledge is reaching its limits, that the cost of research is constantly growing, and that we are getting less out of it. We just seem to be getting more and more conundrums; the more we spend on research, in a sense, the less we seem to know.

There are people like Gunther Stent who argue that science is coming to an end, that we will know all there is to know, and that will be that. People have said that before. I am a great believer in the re-creation of potential, but it is true that particular disciplines stagnate. Economics, for instance, has been in the doldrums, I would say, for 30 years. We have been in a period of what Kuhn calls normal science—adding sophistication—but with very little real advancement in the past 10 or 15 years.

On the other hand, it you look at geology, who would have thought 30 years ago that geology would become an exciting science? And then plate techtonics comes along and all of a sudden geology goes into a classical period. If you look at astronomy, it, too, was pretty dull 15 years ago, but it is now one of the most exciting of the sciences because of the new information from X-ray technology and radio astronomy. There are always these very unpredictable re-creations of potential. I have some hope even for economics. Of course, in the applied fields, certainly if you look at the energy problem, the need for research seems very great.

I'm on a committee of the National Academy of Sciences on nuclear and alternative energy systems, which will report in July. The big thing I've learned is how very little we know and the great variety of fields that are opening up before us. You look at energy from the biomass—

growing things to burn. This is an area that's hardly been touched; the Brazilians and the Japanese are doing some interesting things in this area, though.

Dowling: For instance?

Boulding: Well, they've made methanol out of sugar, and if they can make it out of casava, we're really in.

Dowling: What would you do with it?

Boulding: Burn it in tractors. You don't have to go back to the hay-burning horses. In fact, you might make methanol out of the hay. And, of course, you may breed things for energy—like water hyacinths. You see, there's a great variety in the biosphere in the degree to which plants absorb photosynthesis.

Dowling: What would the water hyacinths do?

Boulding: You make methanol out of water hyancinths. This might give us a more efficient means of utilizing solar energy. If you're looking at the whole solar energy problem, the answer could be in the biomass, not in mirrors.

Dowling: Friends of mine last year were thinking of building a house, and they investigated the solar energy route. They found that it would add, roughly, 50 percent to the cost of the house.

Boulding: The scuttlebutt suggests that solar hot-water heating is just waiting for a Henry Ford. This is highly practical because it's easy to store. The marvelous thing about gasoline is that it's storable. The trouble with the sun is that it absolutely refuses to shine at night; you have a storage problem. The same with wind, but in that case you have even more of a storage problem. Energy storage is a difficult problem and one that we really haven't solved. It isn't much better today than it was in 1900, at least with large-scale storage.

Dowling: What do you think of the ideas of Martin Felstein at Harvard, who believes that we need more economic development and better capital formation? Specifically, what do you think of his idea that we should substitute a consumption tax for the income tax? People would pay taxes only on what they consume, the idea being that their income surplus is going to be reinvested in ways that will ultimately constitute a contribution to society. You take care of the problem of inequities this tax approach creates by jiggling your inheritance tax structure at the other end to be sure that no one gets too rich from saving too much. Do you find this idea attractive? Practical?

Boulding: It all depends on the numbers, on the quantitative functions, on the motivation for saving, and on the uncertainties of the future. Mind you, the idea of a consumption tax is a very old one. Fisher and Kaldor had it before. There is something attractive about it, particularly if you combine it with what would be a system of inheritance outside the family—a system of social inheritance. The cumulative inequality comes because inheritance almost entirely goes to the family.

Dowling: Our inheritance tax structure does accomplish a considerable amount of redistribution.

Boulding: It's pretty feeble at the middle levels. It only hits the very large estates. And it doesn't hit the problem of people who inherit nothing. That's one of our major problems, self-perpetuating poverty, poverty subcultures, and so on, or negative inheritance—parents who neglect children and so on.

I don't know whether we will need to expand the proportion of GNP going into investment.

Dowling: What I was thinking of is that we have a declining percentage of GNP currently going into research. Is one possible answer to try to reverse this trend by making surplus capital available by increasing it through changes in the way we tax?

Boulding: The investors supply the savings in response to their perceptions of the rate of return and also of the uncertainties. This is a very difficult problem in advanced economics—what the overall tax structure does to the rate of return on capital. I suspect that, overall, it may not have much impact. In fact, in looking at particular cases, I suspect what this comes down to is, if private savings will not provide the needed investment funds, they will have to come from public savings. It isn't so much how you pay taxes, but how much is collected and the budget surplus involved. You could have public savings that would be privately invested. This would involve public ownership of private securities.

Dowling: I suppose we've done it with the partial government ownership of the Communication Satellite Corporation.

Boulding: Yes, we've done a little of it. Of course, you had it in the atomic energy field too. The picture is so confusing that I confess I've never straightened it out. The other place we've done this is in housing, and this is the Fannie Mae and the new one, Ginnie Mae, the Government National Mortgage Association. This, in a sense, is a case of the government holding mortgages, rather indirectly, on private houses. We certainly don't do this with industrial securities.

But, on the other hand, if the general consensus is that private savings are not going to be sufficient—as they may not be, no matter what the tax structure is—subsidizing private savings through the tax system may not affect savings enough to do much good.

Dowling: You mean it may not affect the private savings available for economic development.

Boulding: Or in terms of getting consumption below production. After all, if you're going to have real savings, you have to produce more in real terms than you consume. Inflation is partly a symptom of an inadequacy of private savings, of an unwillingness of people to restrict consumption. Of course, it's complicated by government fiscal policy and budget deficits that amount to a kind of self-generating inflation.

Dowling: I was intrigued in one of your earlier books by the marvelously simple mechanism that you devised for curing inflation. As I recall, when inflation starts, you automatically increase taxes.

Boulding: Precisely.

Dowling: The mechanism consisted essentially of two pieces: the relatively new withholding tax and the fact that you had available pretty reliable and current data on how the economy was doing. Contrariwise, if deflation appeared to be starting, then you simply turned the mechanism in reverse and reduced taxes.

Boulding: I'm a little entranced by automatic machinery.

Dowling: Do you still think it would work?

Boulding: I don't see why it wouldn't, that is, technically. The political problems are different. One reason why it might not work is that it would not control an autonomous rise in the price-wage level.

If you have a rise in the price-wage level, it's simply a result of a kind of epidemiology of prices and wages rising. I raise my prices because I see that somebody down the street raised his. Because I raise mine, somebody else will raise his. The real difficulty is that the monetary checks will then produce unemployment rather than deflation. We have put ourselves in a position where a decline in money prices and wages is extraordinarily difficult to achieve because of collective bargaining contracts and a price policy that is quite unresponsive to deflationary movements in the monetary system. The effect of the collective bargaining contracts that contain automatic cost-of-living adjustments is to insulate some groups in society from the impact of inflation. This means that the political incentive to avoid inflation is correspondingly weakened; it also means that the impact of inflation works all the more hardships on the unprotected groups.

Then there are the rigidities in our pricing policy. I remember once asking Fred Maytag what constituted a crisis in the washing machine industry, and he said, "Three days' accumulation of washing machines." I said, "Well, what do you do? Do you have a sale? Do you cut the price?" He said, "Oh no, the price policy is decided a year in advance. We just cut back the output in the factory."

This is a prize example, you see, of how a deflationary move can produce unwanted inventory. You don't cut prices, you cut the inventory. That has cumulative effects. So the unemployment-inflation dilemma is a very real one. I've been thinking about this a lot. The real difficulty is that we find it extremely hard to intervene in particular markets, especially in the labor market. Government policy almost has to be wholesale, large-scale, like President Carter's original $50 refund. That's an example of a wholesale policy. It was almost certain to be inflationary, and probably wouldn't have done very much for unemployment. And yet all the problems are at the retail level; how to translate the wholesale policy into the retail reality is extraordinarily difficult. I think this is particularly true with the labor market, especially in a society where we have an extraordinarily heterogeneous labor force. It's not too difficult to get to the end of the unemployed "queue" of the middle-aged, blue collar, white workers, but this still leaves many of the young, the blacks, the women, the Chicanos, and the other heterogeneous participants in the labor market out in the cold. I think that's why Sweden has a much easier time with unemployment. For all practical purposes, in Sweden there's nobody there but Swedes.

Dowling: An exception is your automobile factories, in which Swedes don't want to work. I've been to Volvo and Saab-Scania, and the majority of employees are non-Swedes. If they don't like the working conditions, there's an abundance of alternatives.

There's another factor that you pointed out that affects the unemployment-inflation dilemma—the built-in inflationary impact of cost-of-living increases in bargaining contracts. How widespread are these cost-of-living increases?

Boulding: There must be figures, but I haven't looked at them for a long time. Even if they aren't formalized, there's a very strong tendency in all labor markets to try to catch up with inflation. Some are less successful than others, like universities, and the declining industries would be less successful than others. But actual reductions in money wages, of money salary, are extraordinarily hard to achieve. It was very hard to do even in the Great Depression. If you can't reduce prices and wages, the only way to get an adjustment of relative prices and wages is to raise some and not raise others. That means that relative adjustments increase the overall level, and then the monetary system and the fiscal system come along and justify this.

Dowling: How do they do that?

Boulding: An elastic money supply many times justifies an increased price level. So you have a system—it's like a balloon with no string if there's nothing to stop it. The only thing that stops it, and it's unacceptable, is unemployment.

Dowling: In recent years, the ugly word is "stagflation." We have been combining the worst of both possible worlds, relatively high unemployment and a relatively high rate of inflation.

Boulding: That's right. And it's happened because the relation between unemployment and inflation has been moving adversely in the sense that if we wanted to reduce unemployment, we'd have still higher rates of inflation. And, of course, you get into the very tricky question of whether the fact of inflation isn't partly a result of it being unanticipated. It that's the case, then you might find yourself accelerating inflation, which is a real no-no. A constant rate of inflation is something that's fairly easy to live with and only amounts to a tax on money after everyone has adjusted to it. In the early days of inflation, interest rates were very low; real interest rates were, in fact, almost zero in this country. Interest constituted an extraordinarily small proportion of the national income. Now, of course, normal interest rates have risen to compensate for about 5 percent inflation. This means that the burden of interest is rising in real terms. And this raises the possibility of accelerating inflation.

Dowling: Isn't Germany just about the only country in which the rate of inflation is significantly lower than ours? Is there anything we could learn, should learn, from Germany about controlling inflation?

Boulding: Maybe we just don't have enough Germans!

Dowling: I guess you mean that we don't have as many hardworking Protestants. It's no accident, I suppose, that the Protestants are mainly middle class. The traditional Protestant with his character structure, his work ethic, is almost certain to end up at least not being poor.

Boulding: It's called Wesley's Law. You were saved, and then you saved and got rich.

Dowling: You were suggesting that some of these elements are characteristic of German behavior patterns.

Boulding: I think there's something in it. Ours is a much more heterogeneous society; also we've been richer for a longer time. When you've been rich for as long as we have, you begin to get the culture of the rich. On the whole, what's happened to us may be the aristocratization of the middle class and a decline in thrift and the work ethic generally. It's easy to exaggerate this because there are an awful lot of hardworking, thrifty people in this country, students who have sacrificed to go to college and so on. Certainly, this student generation is a great deal more sober and hardworking than that of the sixties. There's been an extraordinary change.

Dowling: How do you explain the change?

Boulding: Part of it is the combination of the removal of the pressure of the draft, of the Vietnam war, plus a little depression. Maybe people are more worried about where the jobs are coming from. But these changes in cultural fashion are very hard to predict or explain. It was very dramatic in the universities in 1970. Nineteen-seventy was the turning point. Partly that may be because this is a very plentiful student generation.

Dowling: Your postwar babies.

Boulding: This is the boom. I suspect that when the drought comes at the universities, we're going to have all sorts of fun and games again. Students of that generation are going to have it easier, in a sense, because they're going to be scarcer. This is a plentiful generation. Unemployment is very heavily concentrated in the young, and this is a result of the population bulge.

Dowling: To cite an extreme case, you have a 30 percent rate of unemployment among young urban blacks.

Boulding: The only way to deal with this is through some sort of direct intervention in the labor market. But how do you do it? Any system of wage subsidy, and so on, gets to be an administrative nightmare. We had an interesting meeting in Atlantic City last fall on wage incentive contracts. One idea advanced was that you should have wage incentive contracts, which would constitute, as it were, subsidies for additional employment, and you set up a market in which people bid for these contracts. You may have a $500 contract, you see, in terms of payment from the government—the government promises to pay an employer for hiring an additional worker—and an employer might bid $100 for this.

Dowling: There are elements in some of Carter's proposal for making tax credits for business dependent on hiring additional workers, but the details were different.

Boulding: There is a principle here that is quite sensible, but it seems to be extraordinarily hard to develop the administrative structure to make it practical. I have a feeling that there's some terribly simple trick here that we just haven't thought of, and after we think of it, we'll be terribly surprised that we hadn't thought of it before. But so far we haven't determined how you intervene at the retail level in the labor market without mucking up the whole thing.

Dowling: You mean without causing all kinds of resentment among people who are going to be made relatively less well off as a consequence of the intervention?

Boulding: Yes. Of course, one of the difficulties is that a lot of the unemployment problem revolves around the problem of uncertainty. When you hire somebody, you give up real money for what may be a slightly uncertain hope. The greater the uncertainty, the less likely you are to give up the money. Government policies that vacillate and create uncertainty can often do more harm than good. What you have to do is establish a policy and stick with it. Almost everybody greatly underestimates the impact of uncertainty on economic behavior and on the economy as a whole. I've argued, for instance, that the extraordinary technical growth in agriculture was a quite unexpected by-product of price supports. From the point of view of redistribution, the improvements are horrifying because it just made the rich farmers richer. Government policy had a tremendous impact on diminishing the market uncertainties in agriculture and encouraging investment. So, if you want to get back to talking about encouraging investment, one way to encourage investment is to diminish uncertainties. This does not necessarily mean investment insurance, which is a very tricky problem since it often ends up subsidizing the undeserving or corrupting the decision-making process.

Dowling: To get back to the subject of inflation, if you were sitting in Mr. Carter's chair, what would you do?

Boulding: I don't know. The sort of Nixon stop-and-go price control you can get away with once, but you can't get away with it more than a few times. And price control is an administrative nightmare. You can control prices only under conditions of extreme emergency.

Dowling: You can do it in wartime. In his energy speech, Carter used the phrase the moral equivalent of war. It seems to me very clever, a recognition of the fact that the only way to get people to accept stringent controls is to convince them of the fact that they are facing the moral equivalent of war.

Boulding: That really requires a remarkable degree of persuasiveness. He could almost have used the phrase the cultural revolution. I thought his energy speech was a beauty. It's the best presidential speech I've heard since Roosevelt's first fireside chat. It created, I think, a certain sense of emergency, although it's terribly hard to sustain in a long-run crisis. That's the real trouble on the energy side. It's a 100-year crisis, and how do you sustain feelings of urgency over that long a period?

On inflation, well, there are some ideas on the tax side. Gardner Means has a very interesting view. He proposed putting a surtax on income derived from a price or wage rise.

Dowling: Isn't this another one of your administrative nightmares, putting a surtax on extra income as a result of inflation, either on the wage side or the price side?

Boulding: It means you have to keep two sets of books. I don't think it's administratively feasible because the tax system is difficult enough now, and I think you would have a wholesale political revolt.

Dowling: And you'd have endless challenges as to what prices would do.

Boulding: I think we can forget it. Here again, it's the retail/wholesale problem. The price level is a statistical myth. In reality, it's the price of a certain kind of cheese in the supermarket. . . .

Dowling: Maybe the only way an idea like Means's would work is to apply it in a few bellwether industries. The question is, would it spread?

Boulding: That's right. And then you'd find that the wether had lost its bell. The plain truth is that we don't really understand the formation of actual money prices and wages very much. Economics has concentrated on the theory of relative prices so it doesn't tell you very much about the formation of absolute prices. There are enormously complex decision-making processes here. I've argued that we should have something like an epidemiological theory, the dynamics of price rises being a kind of epidemic. Look at it this way: Nobody raises his prices unless he thinks he can get away with it. Why does he think he can get away with it today when he didn't think he could get away with it last week? Usually because he heard of somebody else getting away with it.

Dowling: You used the illustration about deflation rather than inflation, but it works equally well in the other direction. You have a vicious spiral operating. If people think prices are going to increase, then everyone will increase his prices and the anticipation constitutes a self-fulfilling prophecy.

Boulding: The dilemma is that we have inflation because we can't stand unemployment beyond a certain level. The other approach to this is how do you increase the efficiency of the labor market and how do you intervene in an effective way? Here again, some ideas are floating around. There really isn't any good theory about it, particularly in terms of the complexity of the labor market. There has been the work of Professor Thurow on the two-part labor market.

The thing that worries us is that the unemployment problem is concentrated in a segment of the society that is troublesome anyway. It is related to crime and it's related to urban deterioration and race and all these factors, and we find it extraordinarily hard to deal with all these things at once. Hence, if it is a choice between one percent rise in inflation and one percent rise in unemployment rate, I would have to choose the one percent inflation. Thirty percent would be a different story.

I've had all sorts of crazy ideas on the subject. I thought, for instance, perhaps we could pay wages and salaries in yellow money, and then you would have to turn this in at the bank for green money to spend in the stores. You would establish rates of exchange between yellow money and green money. If wages and salaries are rising too much, you lower the rate of exchange to allow all sorts of inflation in the labor market that doesn't get translated into the commodity market.

Dowling: It's an interesting idea, but I think it would run up against the same kind of resistance I felt in reading your earlier article about automatic adjustments to combat inflation, that is, it runs contrary to what might be called—it's a fancy word—the "genius" of the system. In other words, as you said yourself, social democracy is government by talk, by discussion, and these forms of automatic machinery are something that we as a people tend instinctively to resist and reject.

Conversation with
FRITZ J. ROETHLISBERGER

Fritz Roethlisberger and Elton Mayo are generally regarded as the founders of the human relations movement in industry. The Hawthorne experiment, with which their names are permanently associated, remains after 40 years the most extensive, the most significant, and the most influential behavioral science study ever conducted in a business enterprise.

The study attempted to determine what made employees productive. At the core of the study was the study of the relay assembly girls. To use Roethlisberger's own words:

> The idea was very simple: A group of five girls were placed in a room where their conditions of work (assembly of a telephone relay) could be carefully controlled, where their output could be measured, and where they could be closely observed. It was decided to produce at specified intervals different changes in working conditions and to see what effect these innovations had on output. Also records were kept such as the temperature and humidity of the room, the number of hours each girl slept at night, the kind and amount of food she ate for breakfast, lunch and dinner.

Over the years Mayo, Roethlisberger, and their colleagues collected tons of material. What did it prove? There are almost as many interpretations of Hawthorne as there are interpreters, but few would deny the importance of the central finding of the relay assembly experiment that with the introduction of each variable production kept rising or question that the answers to the puzzle lay somehow in the changing social environment.

Reprinted from Organizational Dynamics, *Autumn 1972*

From an ordinary group of workers performing routine jobs with little or no recognition from management they had been transformed into important people.

The lessons and insights that Roethlisberger himself derived from Hawthorne have by now, through his writings and teachings, become part of the intellectual folklore of the current generation of behavioral scientists. By the time he died in 1974, Roethlisberger was a living classic.

Still, some fruits of the Hawthorne experiment were sour. The more responsible practitioners of the human relations movement have advocated, with variations, Roethlisberger's approach; alas, the naive and the greedy have assembled a plethora of canned programs and panaceas under the banner of human relations and invoked the imprimatur of Hawthorne.

In talking with Roethlisberger, we sought to answer several questions: What are the enduring lessons of the human relations movement and the Hawthorne experiment? What alleged lessons would he disavow? What has the human relations movement accomplished—in what way has it changed the industrial climate? Lastly, what legitimate tasks of the human relations movement remain to be completed?

Dowling: Why don't we begin with the Hawthorne studies? After four decades, Hawthorne is still the most exhaustive as well as the most influential behavioral science study conducted in a business setting. In the light of all the years that have passed since Hawthorne, all the writings about Hawthorne, and all the research at least partially inspired by Hawthorne, what do you feel are its most important lessons?

Roethlisberger: I suppose that what has come to be called "the Hawthorne effect," from a scientific point of view, is the most important result of these experiments—that is, the big difference that the little difference of listening to and paying attention to the employees made to them. The crucial point came when we took away all the advantages we had given the employees—or so we thought—and still output remained at a high level. What we hadn't realized was how completely we had changed shop practices and how substantial the effects of these changes were. We had consulted operators about any changes in advance, and in some cases modified our ideas to meet their criticisms. Their opinions, hopes, and fears had been objects of concern throughout. And in the process, we had revolutionized the attitudes of the girls toward their boss and their jobs.

I also think the concept of the work group as a social system is an important way of investigating industrial situations. It encloses all the major dimensions with which the manager's job deals, and contains them within an area that's small enough for the researcher to handle. Other researches of a similar kind since Hawthorne have had lasting effects. But I don't go along with many of the particular conclusions reached by others from the Hawthorne researches.

For example, we were accused of being ideologically tainted, of holding to the belief that all in-plant difficulties were caused by social or personal problems outside the plant, that the dissatisfied worker was a maladjusted personality. We never took that viewpoint; this evaluation didn't make sense to me then—and it doesn't now.

Dowling: I'm reminded that Landsberger, when he wrote *Hawthorne Revisited,* drew a distinction between *Management and the Worker* and some of the more extreme statements he found in some of Mayo's books. He gave you a clean bill of health, whereas he accuses Mayo of being a prophet of doom and of romanticizing the security the worker found in the plant society as a cure for his ills.

Roethlisberger: Landsberger did a great service by collecting and evaluating all the criticism made of the "Mayo group" in his book *Hawthorne Revisited* (1958). And he did distinguish between Mayo (1933) and Mayo (1945) and *Management and the Worker* (1939). Still, I wonder now—as he wondered then—why I never answered these criticisms about the "Mayo group"—some of which I will try to answer in my autobiography, which I'm currently writing. At the time, however, I remember Mayo saying, "Let the heathen rage," which he followed up with, "The cobbler sticks to his last," and which Henderson followed up with "Never dispute about words," and which my mother reinforced by "Sticks and stones will break your bones but names will never hurt you."

As I look at it now, I was making a set of assumptions about the nature of knowledge and about the relation of knowledge to action and knowledge to skill that were quite different from the assumptions being made about these matters by social scientists at the time. And this is the ball park I want to walk around in in my autobiography. What were these different ways of slicing the cake? Why were we drawing our lines so differently about these things? There was no question but that I was drawing my lines around the group and what was external to the group and what was inside it in quite different ways. Also, I had a concept about the relation of theory to skill that was quite different from the orthodox version.

Dowling: Do you think it's fair to say that a good many of the applications that stemmed from the Hawthorne researches represented a perfectly sincere misinterpretation of the lessons of Hawthorne, but nevertheless a misinterpretation? I guess what I'm thinking about is the tremendous amount of effort, energy, and money spent on developing and instilling human relations techniques, most of which can be traced back to Hawthorne.

Roethlisberger: As a result of the Hawthorne researches, the Western Electric Company introduced its counseling program in 1936, which lasted twenty years until 1956, and which Bill Dickson and I made a reevaluation of in our book, *Counseling in an Organization*. And then here at the Harvard Business School, we used a great deal of it in training for administration. Then there was a tremendous emphasis later on in training for human relations—first at the lower levels of supervision and then more and more into the upper management levels.

Dowling: You're talking about the results that quite legitimately flowed from Hawthorne. I'm thinking of the distinction between human relations as a technique, which you said it wasn't, and human relations as a skill. I'm reminded of Marx commenting on the misinterpretations of his ideas: "Thank God I, at least, am not a Marxist." Well, from one point of view it seems to me you might say, "Thank God I, at least, am not a human relationist." A tremendous amount of human relations training was done that had no right to claim Hawthorne as its parent—but did anyway.

Roethlisberger: There's no question about that. For me it got to be a nightmare—the way in which people picked up "human relations" and made of it something gimmicky and gadgety. I wasn't preaching any model of the way an organization should be. The conceptual scheme of a social system was primarily an investigatory, diagnostic tool. And this aspect, I think, was missed by many programs in training for human relations that advocated one particular style of leadership as the right approach to human relations. It was so distorted by all the do-gooders and preachers of sweetness and light that I made many talks in which I tried to disclaim the parentage of the Hawthorne researches for the ball of wax that had come to be known as "human relations."

It was always difficult to draw a distinction between the descriptive clinical research in human relations as opposed to its normative action aspects. When I taught human relations here at the Business School, it was to people who were going to be administrators in positions of responsibility, and I tried to tell them something about human beings and their relationships to each other that would help them. But it was never an attempt to preach one kind of administrative or leadership style. We took a case, analyzed the situation, the ins and outs of the relationships in that particular situation, and tried to understand them. And after that, we tried to act as sensibly as we could in relation to the diagnosis that we had made.

Dowling: I recall in *Management and Morale* you talked about the fact that the day would come when no one would think any more of asking "What's the morale like in your department?" than a physician would go in and say "What's the health of the patients in our hospital?" The latter, obviously, strikes everyone as absurd. The former, unfortunately, is still the subject of a good deal of writing and discussion.

Roethlisberger: Human relations research, it seems to me, should start as a diagnostic and investigatory tool. I had a clinical-medical model in mind, whereby you would try not only to diagnose and deal better with particular human relationships, but also in time to get the beginning of more systematic knowledge about human behavior in organizations from them—that is, from the clinical uniformities you had found in looking from case to case.

Years ago, I quoted Dr. L. J. Henderson on what the physician needed in order to gain a knowledge about human ills: "First, intimate, habitual familiarity with things; secondly, systematic knowledge of things; and thirdly, an effective way of thinking about things." I said that knowledge about human relations problems required a parallel development. You begin, in other words, not with a theory or a gimmick or a technique of influencing other people, but with the slow, laborious task of observing how workers actually behave in the shop. And this includes, of course, observing yourself and your relations to others. Human relations skills, in other words, exist within a particular organizational setting in which the manager, by patient observation of himself and others, gradually becomes proficient at promoting cooperation and participation in a common task. Only after the Toms, Dicks, and Harrys in management have done this, can they begin the search for the simple uniformities that reside in human situations and finally obtain a theory of explaining the behavior of people in an organizational setting.

Dowling: In the very last essay of your latest book *Man-In-Organization*, you take a very pessimistic view of the progress in management theory over the past thirty years. I think you used some phrase like, "All this huffing and puffing and we have nothing to show for it." The implication one gets is that you don't feel we've gotten any place, that we're just putting new tags on old concepts.

Roethlisberger: I do feel this. I think there's been a great deal of over-claiming. Too many people have entered the field and tried to develop it too fast. In addition, they tended to discredit the direction of the Hawthorne research, which was, I think, on the right track. It's ironic when you think of it, what we expected to accomplish by changing the name of our area here at the Business School from "human relations," which had become a dirty word, to "organizational behavior." The concepts and the approach had not changed that much. The same is true with much of the work and writing that's gone on over the past 35 years—we keep restating the same things in new words. The semantic problem here is a difficult one. We talk about breakthroughs when we are really only using new words or new metaphors for saying the same old things we said before. I don't mean to be too pessimistic.

Dowling: You were in a more constructive vein when you wrote the essay, "Toward a General Theory of Management," in the book I mentioned earlier. You make a statement there that what we need to do is to begin to compile an inventory of simple descriptive findings and then seek for some more general propositions that would explain them. Do you have any simple descriptive findings about organizational behavior that you think hold up on the basis of time?

Roethlisberger: It's difficult for me to put these findings in any elegant propositional form. Most of them are of a clinical nature; more like syndromes. One such finding was the "restriction of output syndrome"—that is, the reaction of workers to a so-called "scientific standard" of what output should be, which resulted in a concept of a day's work that was not too high or too low to get them into trouble.

Also another finding was the "man-in-the-middle syndrome": The first-level supervisor has to find ways to resolve the conflict between trying to get the cooperation of his employees and trying to get them to do what higher management expects of them—at the proper place and amount and using the proper methods. This presents frequently a real dilemma to the first-level supervisor; time and again he has to do things that are disloyal to management—or at least management would feel they were if they knew about them—in order to get the work out on time.

Then there's what I call the "vicious circle syndrome"—that is, the breakdown of rules, such as the breakdown of close supervision, begets more rules to take care of their breakdowns, and this vicious circle leads to a continuous search for new control systems to correct the limitations of previous ones.

Another finding, which George Homans has stated much more elegantly in propositional form than I was able to do, is "the distributive justice syndrome." This syndrome says that when status factors get out of line—that is, when people feel that what they're getting is not proportional to what they should be getting in terms of their age, skill, education, seniority, and so on—they feel that this is unfair or unjust, and this leads to trouble. That's the one I found earlier in the Hawthorne researches, and which I tried to state in my chapter on "Complaints and Social Equilibrium" in *Management and the Worker*.

Dowling: Yes. I recall one application in the salary area. The interviews showed that people were just as much concerned with how much they earned in relation to other people as they were with the absolute money involved. In fact, they were probably more excited about what they considered to be an unjust wage from a status point of view than they were about one that wasn't sufficiently large.

Roethlisberger: In the paper you referred to earlier, "Toward a General Theory of Management," I stated some other findings that I think can be also expressed in terms of uniformities, syndromes, propositions, or what have you, from which a more general theory about management in time could develop. I think that's the right direction to go in for those who are interested in theory. I agree with George Homans that organizational behavior is just human behavior in the context of the organization and under those constraints.

Of late, however, I have become more concerned with what I call intrinsic relationships. Science tends to deal with essentially extrinsic types of relations, where the scientific way of explaining things works very well. But when you get involved in intrinsic relationships, such as love, trust, loyalty, and relations of this sort, perhaps a different notion of science is needed. I think the humanistic psychologists, such as Adler, Maslow, and Carl Rogers, are pointing in this direction. There's a world of difference between the intrinsic growth of individuals that the humanistic psychologists speak of and the extrinsic knowledge about human behavior that social scientists speak of. There seems to be a kind of antithesis between the two.

I'd like to keep the intrinsic and extrinsic together. It is true that I have been always interested in intrinsic ties that developed within groups that made them cohesive, and I was also interested in counseling, as a way of thinking that looked at things from the client's point of view and his internal frame of reference. But I was also concerned with the purposive aspect of an organization, which can be expressed in extrinsic terms—for example, in terms of logical means-end relationships. Technology and technological space, it seems to me, are extrinsic wholes or systems composed of extrinsic relations. But the minute you become involved with social space—man's relation to his fellow man, his interpersonal relationships, and his life space—you are in the world of the intrinsic. This is what I want to go around in my autobiography.

Dowling: What do you mean by "go around"?

Roethlisberger: I want to see if I can express this problem of the relation of the extrinsic to the intrinsic better than I'm expressing it now. In this area, I think there's a real confusion about the nature of science. In other words, if science to be science always requires that the intrinsic has to be translated into extrinsic terms, then I think a whole aspect of human life is going to be left out of the picture.

To go back to the question you asked earlier, about why I was pessimistic about management theory and practice—it's because we have underestimated the importance of this problem and not only the importance of it, but some of the difficulties of this problem for human relations and management training. Man's behavior is mostly nonlogical. But we won't face up to it. The new rationalism of looking at organizations from the point of view of rational decision-making and of using the computer as one's model it seems to me is just another way of escaping the problem. It works beautifully until you have to deal with the interactions, emotions, and such aspects of human behavior. The computer's internal environment is not like man's internal environment or a social system's internal environment. Yet Herbert Simon talks about the internal environment of a computer, which can be reduced to a set of linear equations under a set of given constraints and parameters, as being very much like man's internal environment.

Dowling: I've talked to a good many people who have been concerned with the introduction of computer systems into corporations. In many cases there are enormous problems involved; the computer seldom realizes the expectations that were mapped out for it in advance, and it's the human problems that arise in the introduction that really cause the difficulty.

I don't mean to cut you off, but let's go back for a moment to one of the descriptive findings you talked about—the restriction of output in a work group. Is it safe to say that this is one norm that you will find in any work group worthy of the name? When I say restriction of output, I don't mean necessarily low output; it might be medium or even high.

Roethlisberger: In any work group I imagine there is an output norm. But this norm varies under different conditions. I probably didn't state too clearly the constraints under which the kind of norm I called "restriction of output" would appear. But in the standard shop, that is, where you have strict management standards, I would expect to find a norm about what constitutes a fair day's work that does not quite coincide with management's expectations.

Dowling: I remember in the bank-wiring-room experiment at Hawthorne, the standard set was not significantly below what management considered reasonable. As I recall, it was six thousand to sixty-six hundred parts per hour—a figure management was quite willing to live with.

Roethlisberger: Yes, for a while.

Dowling: The thing that fascinates me is that in areas where employees set standards, they can vary greatly, even within the same plant between different work units. Some standards can be relatively high; others can be relatively low.

Roethlisberger: Obviously, human behavior varies under different conditions. The limitations in applying the findings of the Hawthorne researches are demonstrated by this fact. The given conditions under which we found certain uniformities were not spelled out too well. So if you try to apply them generally, you're going to get into trouble. In fact, the direction today of much research in organizational behavior is to correct for this possible misapplication. Many of the things that I treated as givens—technology, formal organization, and culture—are being studied to determine the effects of different cultures and different conditions of technology on formal and informal organizations. I pretty much assumed a more closed system model of organization drawn from classical economic theory. A more open system model is being assumed today.

Two men here at Harvard, Paul Lawrence and Jay Lorsch, are going very heavily in their researches in the direction of studying the impact of technology on organization. I would say that's the big push today.

Dowling: Joan Woodward, in her book *Industrial Organization*, talks about a work group that in terms of the technology of the factory has management in a bind when a change is introduced. This group quite consciously sits down and asks, what can we make out of the change? What concessions can we exact as our reward for going along with it?

In other words, the functional power possessed by the work group in the organization, which in turn is determined by the state of technology, has a good deal to do with its cohesiveness and its attitude toward management. In short, your tool and die men or your pattern-makers don't look at the supervisor or management in the same way that the shipping clerks do.

Roethlisberger: It's an important difference, and one that requires much more study. Many of the old statements I made need to be corrected, because I was assuming a mass-production assembly line type of operation.

Dowling: What advice would you give to the supervisor who has a group with low output norms and who wants to turn them into a high-producing group?

Roethlisberger: He should begin by trying to see how much he's contributing to the low production—how much is his own behavior contributing to it. In talking to employees, he should keep this in mind. But I can't give him any rules except to diagnose the situation and the factors underlying the problem, particularly his behavior in relation to it. He should use interviewing and direct observation and listening as key tools. He could interview the workers individually, but it might be better if he discussed the problem with them in a group. If this were a new supervisor, talking to each member of the group singly might arouse a lot of apprehension and suspicion, whereas if it was done more openly, they could hear what each said to him.

Twenty years ago, I would have interviewed each man singly, because in the single interview I could have gone into the problem at a much greater depth than I would have been able to do in a group. But today I tend to favor more group discussions. I like to keep things aboveboard. The advantages of the single interviewing approach by a supervisor, at least in this type of situation, it seems to me, are far outweighed by the suspicion and distrust it would create among his subordinates. I would be apprehensive about fostering those feelings by having single interviews. And I think an open confrontation, saying frankly to the men that management is dissatisfied with the way things are happening out here, and I'd like to improve them but I need your help, might work. There's no guarantee.

Dowling: No. I wasn't expecting any formula or philosopher's stone for how to turn a low-producing group into a high-producing group. And if I had gotten one, I would have been highly skeptical.

To jump back a bit, you've made remarks about sensitivity training that have sounded somewhat negative.

Roethlisberger: I think T-groups and sensitivity training are the modern versions of human relations training. However, I think they have some of the same problems that we had with counseling in the older version of human relations training. Many people who have picked it up are not too competent. In my opinion, you need a great amount of skill to lead a T-group. I attended a group at Bethel, Maine, in 1953 I think it was, and then the T in T-group stood for *training* in group development and not for *therapy*. Most fortunately, I had Lee Bradford as my T-group leader; he was then head of the National Training Laboratories. And I learned a good deal from him. You see, I had been trained more in the two-person relationship, the counseling relationship, listening to the feelings and so on. And I hadn't been trained in looking at group processes—that is, in observing the different roles people play in groups and the effect of these roles on the satisfaction of its members or on reaching the objectives of the group. What had me bothered was the absence of *task* in T-groups. We were looking too much at our interpersonal relationships, and too little at what we were trying to accomplish. I had been used to looking at work groups in which the task was emphasized. And although I had a lot of fun in my T-group and learned a lot, still I felt that many things we were learning and practicing would not work successfully in a group that had really a task to accomplish. For example, we would make up our minds whether we should have tea or coffee for the coffee break. That kind of stuff I couldn't take too seriously.

Dowling: Wasn't that part of breaking the ice? You tackle something simple that is not emotionally charged, like coffee breaks, and then you build to more significant interaction?

Roethlisberger: I suppose so. As you know, the T-group is a kind of cultural island where all your status symbols are taken away. We called each other by our first names; our professional backgrounds and so on were supposed to make no difference. And then there was much talk at that time about behaving democratically. Not that I'm against behaving democratically, but the discussion was often emotionally located around this issue, and people who vied for leadership were accused of being undemocratic. It seemed to me that there was an awful lot of, to use a bad word, of "cultural brainwashing" going on, as well as training for inter-personal competence. It seemed to me that they underestimated the time it took to train for interpersonal competence. But also, it was the norma-tive elements in T-groups—incidentally, something they had in common with the old human relations movement—that bothered me.

At first I couldn't believe it, but management became very in-terested in T-groups. And now the National Training Laboratories is a huge operation. But this development hasn't stopped there. Bob Tannen-baum and the people at UCLA practice T-groups, only for them T stands for *therapy*, and at Essalen T stands for *touch*. In fact, the human potentials movement, of which T-groups are just one expression, is spreading all over the country.

What does this mean? It's all part of man's search for the intrinsic, for his identity and self-knowledge, a human potentials de-velopment that goes far beyond what the Hawthorne researches ever dreamed of accomplishing. Some of it's great, and some of it I wonder about.

Dowling: What about the fact that before the supervisor can understand group relationships and how to deal with subordinates, self-knowledge is paramount? In one sense, the T-group is a logical development of one side of Hawthorne, the side that emphasized self-knowledge and interviewing in depth. You do get out of T-groups insight into yourself and your impact on other people and how you react to them, and you get it in a concentrated way.

Roethlisberger: Yes, but in an artificial setting, not in a social system within which the manager actually functions. Looking at the executive apart from his customary social setting isn't very helpful; not if you're trying to help him function more effectively in his job. Quite the reverse. When the manager goes back and tries to apply what he thinks he's learned, he only causes trouble for himself and for other people. This has happened again and again.

Dowling: One answer might be to have so-called family T-groups restricted to managers at several levels from the same company.

Roethlisberger: At TRW they're trying the family T-groups, whereas back in 1953 you'd never, at least in industry, have had supervisors of different levels from the same organization in one group. Certainly it meets one of my reservations; actually, it would be a good idea whenever industry uses T-groups to have executives at the very top of the organization take part.

Dowling: How would you summarize your attitude toward T-groups and sensitivity training?

Roethlisberger: In a word, *ambivalent.* I'm fascinated, but I'm afraid we've gone overboard. We're going to be disappointed by expecting more than we can get. The people in charge make a lot of difference to this type of operation. I'll take T-groups with Lee Bradford. I'll take Bob Blake and his management grid with Bob Blake. Or I'll buy the Scanlon Plan with Joe Scanlon. But if you put these things in the hands of other people, I'm afraid they can be horribly misused. Again, I think we underestimate the difficulty of the problem of training people, and especially the difficulty of changing people.

Dowling: You talk about the difficulty of training people and the difficulty of getting them to change their behavior. Maybe there's a clue here to the failure so far of efforts at participative management. In any meaningful sense, it is restricted to a handful of companies—fewer than sixty or seventy at most.

Roethlisberger: Participative management has become a slogan, blown up as if it were a cure-all for whatever ails the organization. Joan Woodward and her group are finding that where the technological environment is fairly simple and certain, participative management doesn't work nearly as well as it does when the technological environment is more complex and uncertain. Their findings are, of course, only a beginning, but they *do* suggest that technology and probably other factors in the environment help to determine the success or failure of participative management.

Dowling: You're probably familiar with Non-Linear Systems on the West Coast, one of the best advertised instances of participative management. I remember talking to Andrew Kay, the president of Non-Linear Systems. He mentioned that when he gave the women control over assembling a complete product instead of working on a tiny fraction of it, along with more discretion as to how the assembling should be done—it didn't work. He found that there was a great difference among the individual women in how big a job, how much responsibility, and how much discretion they wanted. Some were pleased, but not the majority.

Roethlisberger: They got more prerogatives and more responsibility than they felt they could cope with. I also heard that although Kay's relations with his lower-level subordinates improved, his relationships with his higher-level managers got worse. But this is hearsay.

Dowling: Yes.

Roethlisberger: And then I heard that he went bankrupt. But again this is hearsay.

Dowling: Not when I talked to him, although he admitted he would never claim that his experiment in participation had resulted in bigger profits. Of course, this wasn't his objective.

Going back to Hawthorne, do you think that the counseling principles probably have had the widest application of anything that came out of Hawthorne? Certainly these principles can be used by any supervisor as a guide to diagnosing almost any situation.

Roethlisberger: What I liked about counseling was that you collected your data under conditions of responsibility. And it was clinically oriented. Also I think that if you begin to understand what's taking place in a two-person interaction, it has tremendous application under other conditions. In other words, many of the insights—there's a beautifully vague word—that you get from that relationship pay off in other relationships. When you try to understand a person from his internal frame of reference, you begin to understand human behavior from the right end up.

You learn something about how to introduce change from an internal point of view as opposed to an external or extrinsic point of view. And the difference between acting under conditions of responsibility and from an intrinsic point of view and acting from an extrinsic point of view are great and need to be understood by the human relations practitioner. I think he can learn this difference better through person-to-person reactions than in a T-group, where there is so much more complexity that it's difficult to separate the role relationships from the individual and his needs.

One gets through counseling, which is basically listening with understanding, not simply the meaning of the words a person uses but the meaning of those words in the total situation in which he finds himself. By total situation I refer to the employee in relation to the social system in his own department, the larger social system in the whole plant, and the social system in the community outside, of which he is also a part. The possibility of change, of control, of effective action begins once you understand the human situations to which the words refer.

In the two-person relationship, you can give full attention to the inner self; and I think very useful lessons can be learned from it, not only from the point of view of diagnosis, but also from the point of view of taking action. Many times you perceive through counseling what I like to call "the principle of the little-big difference"—that is, that what looks to the outside viewer like a little difference may make a big difference to the person from his inner point of view.

Dowling: Can you give a concrete example?

Roethlisberger: Well, I don't want to discuss the "Hawthorne effect" all over again, but I had a student in one of my advanced management program classes who was an engineer with a large firm in Milwaukee. He was very bright and very engineering-oriented, and he fought me all through class with the objection that "it"—meaning listening—wouldn't work. I thought he hadn't gotten anything from the course.

After he left, he went back to his job and was promoted to superintendent of the maintenance department. He hadn't been on the job more than a day when an angry voice over the phone said, "What the hell is going on in your department?" He was just about to say, "Who the hell are you?" when, as he later told me, "I remembered you, Fritz, and I counted up to ten and said, I don't know; why don't you come up here and tell me?" And the man came, and Hal listened to him—he was a shop steward reputed to be one of the most difficult stewards in the plant to work with. As a result of that interaction, Hal established a good relationship with him. Everyone asked, "How do you deal with this son of a bitch? What's your trick?" Hal was so impressed that he came all the way from Milwaukee to tell me—"Fritz, it works! It works!" In fact, "it" seldom works that simply. But his response wasn't gimmicky; Hal was telling the truth when he said he didn't know what was going on in his department, and listening was surely one way to find out.

Dowling: I suppose it worked in this setup because this guy had a reputation as being irascible and difficult. Obviously, all the other people had settled down into habitual patterns of reacting to him in a manner that was just as hostile and angry as his. It was one of those vicious circles.

Roethlisberger: That's what I mean by how a little difference in response can make a big difference in outcome. So many times when we're angry or disturbed, listening works—not listening as a gimmick, but listening for more insight and restating the problem to ourself as well as to the other person. Of course, listening doesn't always produce a solution to the problem.

Dowling: What it will do, in any case, is to deepen your understanding of the problem. Whether it will give you a clue to the solution or not is another question.

If you've got a subordinate, for example, with a severe authority problem toward a father figure, you may never be able to turn him into a cooperative person. But at least listening may help you to realize why he's so difficult to get along with. Mayo cited an episode he called The Case of the Six Destroyers, involving six anarchists who were all in prison when Mayo saw them. They all hated their fathers, and they had all transferred the hatred to authority figures in general. If you had such a man working for you, counseling would lead you to understand why you had to fire him.

Roethlisberger: Yes, I think counseling many times gives you the insight into the action you have to take—in the case you just mentioned, to fire the man. But I was also talking about the action that you can sometimes take right within the counseling situation itself. That's what I meant by the little difference that can make a big difference, even though it's not generally considered action.

Dowling: You were Mayo's friend and colleague for many years, even his disciple. Do you think that any of his insights are useful in diagnosing the unrest in our universities today or even in pointing the way to a solution?

Roethlisberger: I met Mayo when I was studying philosophy. I had gotten myself pretty balled up. For Mayo, much of what was being taught in philosophy was rubbish. He was anti-metaphysical. If he saw what was happening today, I think he might have said, "My God, I am not surprised by this accusation of irrelevance on the part of the students. From such a divorce between theory and practice, I could have predicted it."

I don't want to make a plea for the case method that we use here at the Business School, but I do think it could help to answer this question of relevance on the part of the students. In the more rigorous sciences, such as mathematics or physics, the case method might be a waste of time. But in the case of the social sciences and what I call life space problems, I think the case method is better than lecturing. We've got too many diagnostic labels for people in human and social situations. What we need is to get down more to the facts under particular conditions.

This raises the question, what is the subject matter of human relations? Or to ask really the same question—what's my subject matter? I've been searching for my subject matter all my life, and my identity and integrity is involved in this question.

The problem is what I referred to earlier—the difference between extrinsic and intrinsic knowledge. With extrinsic knowledge you have a real subject matter; you can state it, walk around it, quantify it, and so on. But intrinsic relationships are much more difficult to express in substantive terms and even harder to reduce to nice general propositions. Do you see what I mean?

Dowling: I think many people are engaged in the search for certitude—I think you might call it—and find it difficult to live with too much uncertainty. However, ultimately the search may be a will-of-the-wisp. I suspect it is.

Roethlisberger: I hope I am willing and capable of living with the uncertainty, ambiguity, and inconsistency of modern life. In fact, I think this is the direction in which human relations training should go—to help man to live with the ambiguity in today's situation and to help him to cope with it—not escape from it. We're expecting too many answers and asking for too much consistency, even too much perfection. You have uniformities in science, to be sure, but on the intrinsic side—in matters of human potential and the conditions for its realization—there are no certainties or first principles.

Conversation with
PETER F. DRUCKER

In a management publication no one needs an introduction less than Peter Drucker. Nothing is more evident about him than his sheer celebrity. He has written more words on management that have been read by more people than any other man—living or dead. A *Business Week* article cited the figure of three million copies of his books sold to date.

And the output continues. In 1974 the AMACOM division of the American Management Associations issued a cassette program, *Drucker on Management;* and in 1976 Harper & Row published his *The Unseen Revolution: How Pension Fund Socialism Came to America.*

Drucker's work shows a rare combination of qualities: inspired common sense; constant testing of the logical against the real, as he has personally experienced it in his capacity as consultant and clinician in hundreds of organizations in the United States and abroad; and last, the moral passion that illuminates and enriches his work—the conviction that salvation comes through self-development and the individual's commitment to excellence.

Drucker, by and large, eschews the word philosophy, because "it's much too big a word." In *Management: Tasks, Responsibilities, Practices*, however, he made it clear that he is preaching a philosophy of management, that of management by objectives and self-control.

Let him speak for himself: "It rests on an analysis of the specific needs of the management group it faces. It rests on a concept of human action, behavior, and motivation. Finally, it applies to every manager, whatever his level and function, and to any organization, whether large or

Reprinted from Organizational Dynamics, *Spring 1974*

small. It ensures performance by converting objective needs into personal goals. And this is genuine freedom."

Dowling: You mentioned in one of the cassettes you have just finished for the American Management Associations that you had anticipated Theory Y about 15 years before McGregor.

Drucker: Quite a long time ago, although I wasn't the only one. I first came up with what McGregor called Theory Y in *The Concept of the Corporation*, back in 1946, and I developed it further in 1950 in *The New Society*. I didn't present this as a theory of human nature, nor did Doug. I said that the manager has no choice but to act on the assumption that this is human nature, because otherwise he's licked before he starts. I was then and I still am terribly skeptical about any general theory of human nature; I think the way the modern psychologist is going makes no sense, because he starts out with the assumption that people are alike; if they were, then psychology would be totally uninteresting, as boring as can be. I think that what makes people interesting is that they're different. Most of those who read the book think that I believe that most people have Theory Y personalities. Not at all. I didn't think so and neither did McGregor. He was quite genuine in his assertion that both Theory X and Theory Y hypotheses were viable.

Dowling: Although he had a strong preference for Theory Y.

Drucker: No.

Dowling: No?

Drucker: That's what everybody thinks, but it isn't true. You read his articles in *The Professional Manager*. . . .

Dowling: The posthumous book that Bennis edited.

Drucker: Yes, and you will find that Doug was insistent that which theory works depends on the people and the situation. He had a preference for a Theory Y organization but he did not believe that it was possible in all circumstances, and he was damn sure that it was not in all circumstances preferable. When Doug said that he could not choose between his two hypotheses it may have been the result of his unhappy experience as president of Antioch. His conclusion was that if he had only treated the faculty like so many hogs and hit them on the snout—obviously, he didn't use those words—it would have worked. He treated them like human beings and they responded by kicking him in every place they could reach. He never really quite recovered from this experience.

Dowling: You also said that there are differences between you and McGregor, that you had to begin with the assumption that there were a considerable number of people in the workforce who wanted to achieve, but much more was needed to make them—I think your phrase was "even the strong and healthy"—assume the burden of responsibility. What more do you feel is needed?

Drucker: The one who pointed this out most clearly was the late Abe Maslow. Emotionally, he was completely on McGregor's side, until he came out to southern California and spent a year with a small company that was practicing—or thought it was practicing—Theory Y.

Dowling: You're referring to Non-Linear Systems?

Drucker: Yes. He became very upset, for he saw that the company was making extreme demands on its employees. Of course, Theory Y is not permissive—neither McGregor nor I ever made that mistake. We knew that it's far more demanding than Theory X, that it does not allow people to do their own thing, but demands self-discipline of them. It's a very harsh taskmaster, so it will only work if you start out with high performance goals and performance standards and don't tolerate anything else. Maslow's contribution was to point out that the demands may be too great, that people need the security of "I'm doing what I'm being told so that I know what I'm supposed to be doing; I'm not responsible for anything but what's assigned to me." He pointed out that both McGregor and I—but primarily his book *Eupsychian Management* was aimed at me—seemed to neglect the fact that the world does not consist of the strong and healthy ones, that there are lots of people who are weak and vulnerable, impaired and handicapped, lame and blind, and so on who can't take the full exposure to demand and responsibility.

I had never thought otherwise, but that made a real impression on me. The question that McGregor never tackled and that I hadn't tackled until my newest book is what the manager has to do so that people can take responsibility, can accept performance goals and performance standards. I don't know what proportion of humanity, of the labor force, wants to perform well. I won't talk about motivation; there is no such thing. The good manager doesn't waste his time on mediocrity, though.

Dowling: I remember talking to Andy Kay, the president of Non-Linear Systems. He told me that he started with a bunch of ladies, each of whom assembled only a small portion of the electronic components that they manufactured; then he suddenly had them assembling the whole component and they resented it. Their job was being enlarged far more than they wanted; they were being given far more responsibility than they were willing to tolerate.

Drucker: I can't talk about Andy Kay. I don't know enough about him. But if you came to me and told me you're going to do this, I would tell you not to. I would say, "Look, you're not only being cruel, you're abdicating your responsibility." First, *you* have to think through the work, and only then can the people who are going to do the job decide what is the optimal work pattern. There's no scientific method of determining that pattern, because we don't know what rhythms go together, what motions go together, or what speeds go together. We have to let the group work it out themselves. The Japanese have been doing it for 60 years; they work it out by trial and error very quickly.

Dowling: In the United States you cite I.B.M. as the company in which each worker—because he participated in engineering his work—did a better and a more productive job.

Drucker: I.B.M. probably does the most thorough industrial engineering on the nature of the job—the basic end result and how to get there—of any company I know, and they pass this information on to the work group. Once the work has been studied the responsibility for job design and work group design is left where it belongs—with the worker and the work group.

Dowling: If I understand you correctly, you're making two points: The worker is the expert on how to get the job done and, in response to what you call the "dynamics of working," the worker does a better and more productive job if he has a big, even a decisive, part in engineering his work.

Drucker: Yes, especially the first point about the worker being the expert on his job. We don't know and never will know what motions go together in the simplest physiological sense. For example, we don't know how many repetitions of the same operation are comfortable. Do you know what I mean? You watch a good tennis player serve and you see that he will use the same serve three or four or five times in a row, but then he'll vary it. Now, he may think he does this for strategic attack purposes, but I'm quite sure physiology is just as important. He senses that after five or six times of trying this kind of serve the arm becomes a little tired—there's a slight uneasiness in the muscles. The same is true of an engineer working on a design. He'll work for an hour very concentratedly, then he takes a break and draws. Economically speaking, a less-well-paid draftsman should do the drawing.

Dowling: Or a chemist will use an hour doing analytical work, then spend ten minutes washing test tubes.

Drucker: Even though he has a lab assistant. You need a break, a change in activities. So defining elements of the work has to be the manager's job; to expect untrained people to analyze their work is ludicrous. All history indicates that the proper structure of any work is not a matter of intuition—at this level creativity is hokum. You know the famous Taylor study of the sand shoveler. Shoveling sand has been done for several millennia, and most of the time the overseers were not greatly concerned with how people did it. They left it to the shovelers—there were a lot of them and they were expendable. Yet when Taylor, with a trained mind and instruments, looked at it, everything was done wrong, beginning with the design of the shovel—the length of it—and where the man stood and how he stood, and how he moved and how high he lifted the shovel. Taylor found that everything was simply wrong. That's an example of what creativity does.

Dowling: And Taylor showed what scientific management does. As I recall, there was a 627 percent increase in productivity.

Drucker: For perhaps a more precise analogy let's look at medical diagnosis. Here are highly trained men—of all our professions, physicians have had the longest period of organized training—highly educated men very much interested in their craft—they're not sand shovelers. Yet, when the first systematic look was taken at diagnosis, everything physicians had done and had taught turned out to be wrong and unproductive. They did not arrange the symptoms in a sequence; they did not establish a base line of normal; they did not arrive at a correct diagnosis by eliminating the probably wrong ones. Diagnosis is a process of elimination. Yet for 3,000 years every physician started out with a tentative diagnosis and then tried to verify it. Well, that way you come out with what you want to prove and nine times out of ten you are wrong.

You need a diagnosis to be synonymous with the patient's history and his symptoms; then you eliminate various possibilities until finally you have a manageable number of things it could be. Then you make your tentative conclusion and test it. It sounds so obvious, but it did not come out of creativity, it came through the logic of the work. This is the manager's job and no one else can do it. Thinking through what information is needed at what stage is management's job, although obviously, the worker himself has to be a key contributing resource.

Dowling: Which brings us back to I.B.M., where by accident, as I recall, production had to begin before engineering was finished, and so the foremen and the workers got the chance to work on the details. In consequence you had superior design and production engineering that was better, cheaper, and faster.

Drucker: An even better example is the Japanese. They got terribly excited about scientific management after World War I and adopted it wholesale—as only the Japanese can do—and found that they had a terrific shortage of industrial engineers. They had one where they needed 500. So out of sheer necessity the industrial engineers had to do the absolute minimum and had to use all the input they could get from workers and foremen. There developed, out of simple operational necessity, a system in which the industrial engineers—now, of course, they have probably more than they need—would spend a great deal of time very carefully analyzing the work itself. Of course, even in that phase the work group is a resource for the industrial engineer. At that point, when he understands the work flow, he turns over the actual design of the jobs to the workers themselves. Then the work group might ask him, "If we do it that way, what will it do downstream?" and so on. They ask him but they work it out; he acts as their adviser and resource. Maybe he says, "Boys, no, it won't work that way," or he says, "Have you realized that you are going back?" "Oh, yes," they reply, "but it's easier for us; it's easier to move the piece if we do that; if flows better." And he might say, "I don't think you are right; try it my way." So they say, "We will try it, but we think it's silly your way."

Dowling: Who wins?

Drucker: The workers—almost every time—because where their own work is concerned they have demonstrated that they are the experts. I.B.M., also by accident, as you mentioned, fell into a very similar understanding—that work is one thing and working is another and you have to mesh the two, the logic of work and the logic of working. It's idiotic and the height of management incompetence to ask the worker to take responsibility for his job when you haven't studied and set standards. To sum it up in an epigram: We undermanage work and overmanage workers.

Dowling: You made a brief reference in your most recent book to the fact that this team approach to defining what you call the logic of working is making some inroads into the automobile industry. So far, at least in the United States, I think the impact has been minor. Chrysler is experimenting.

Drucker: Chrysler is experimenting, the Swedes are experimenting, and the Germans have done better than anybody else for a simple reason: The Germans have not tried to change the assembly line. They simply have said, "How far can we automate? How far can we go replacing unskilled, repetitive human operations by machine work?" Where you cannot organize the flow of the work so that it fits the human nature—call it that—I think you may find it easier, more humane, more productive, to eliminate man as an operator and make him a controller, which is the essence of automation. And Volkswagen has gone quite far that way. Unfortunately, their direction stopped in midstream, because over the past ten years they were able to recruit enormous masses of foreigners who are still willing to work the traditional, assembly line way. But Volkswagen, until 1965, did a good job of truly automating operations. The automobile industry really has two alternatives: We know, for instance, that during World War II in airplane plants, work teams assembled an entire engine—a hell of a lot more complex product than any automobile.

Dowling: I visited Saab-Scania last summer and they're applying this team approach. What they've done sounds very similar to what you're saying. They have automated about seven-eighths of the job of putting together the engine of an automobile, but they've used the team approach for the remaining eighth of the final assembly of the engines. There the work teams themselves were separated into distinct areas and in each one the worker makes his basic decision—there are four on each team—as to whether each one is going to assemble an entire engine or the job will be broken into four distinct operations. The decision is theirs.

Drucker: It makes sense to have a team that works together. We know enough about the self-regulation of such production teams to know that they optimize output and optimize input both. Without really conscious decisions the team regulates its speed, its rhythm, its cohesion, and its relationships—both external and internal. The best work on this was done many years ago in the Forties by a Bennington student of mine who spent a two-month work period on the production line of a candy factory. Here were those long tables with girls filling . . . I think they were Fanny Farmer candy boxes. The workers were all on incentive pay for the teams and they worked so that everyone in the room got the most money possible—not at the top of the incentive rate but about the middle. In any one cycle—whether a cycle lasted one hour or two I've forgotten—one team rushed and broke its neck to reach an above-standard rate of production while the other teams slowed down but supported the lead team, going to get a carton for them and some paper and so on. Then the next team got its chance to excel. In consequence, every team was a high achiever within the standards set by the various work teams, but no one worked too hard as any reasonable man would define it. Actually, the whole plant got optimal production.

Dowling: These arrangements, I presume, weren't consciously arrived at.

Drucker: Not at all. That was the thing that puzzled the kid so much. She figured that with anything that complex there must be a master plan, but she couldn't put her finger on one.

Dowling: Or on a master planner.

Drucker: Yes. The women had worked it out: Here was Mary, and Mary was very good at certain things, but sometimes she got tired. She didn't see how tired she was, but the team would notice that there was slack and so someone else would take up the slack and Mary would do something else and get a break. Physiological fatigue would change her rhythm. Teams of six women each sitting around a table chattering about children and men and dresses would organize the work, but the work was completely engineered; there was never any doubt what candy went into what place, nor was there any doubt about quality standards. My student observed that on one line things were very much smoother than on the others. The difference was that the forelady on the one made sure her women had the information they needed to do their jobs. They knew, for example, that this week they were going to have a particularly heavy load of chocolate-covered cherries, so it was going to be a little sticky. She made damn sure that her people had the information they needed to organize their own jobs.

Dowling: And that they had it at the time they needed it.

Drucker: And in the right form—in operational form. The foreman typically gets information—good Lord, too much information—but he gets it in a generalized, statistical form that is operationally almost meaningless. That's one of the strengths of I.B.M. Have you been in an I.B.M. plant?

Dowling: Not, I think, for 14 years.

Drucker: Foremen spend a lot of their time at meetings in which they learn what's going on and in which management asks repeatedly how they can make this really meaningful to them—what they need to know so that they and their gangs can direct themselves. Nothing discourages people as much as managerial incompetence. They know damn well that they are paid to work and not paid to wait for tools and materials. If management doesn't make it possible for them to work, this is an indication not only of management incompetence but also of management contempt for its own work.

   The job of a manager essentially is to make sure the workers have the tools, the information, and the understanding they need to do the job. Another thing is that it's a criminal offense for a manager to create confusion—and it's very easy to do. That's why I advise every manager to ask the people he deals with what they need to know and in what form. This doesn't hold true just with assembly line workers; it is just as true with your engineers, your accountants, or your vice-presidents The failure to ask that question is one of the biggest reasons for the horrible failure of the computer. Let's be blunt; the computer has been a horrible flop so far.

Dowling: Aren't there some exceptions in individual companies?

Drucker: There are some exceptions, but not many. When it comes to the computer, the manager looks at the computer man and asks, "What can you do for me?" It's the wrong question. He should ask himself, "What do I need?" And he shouldn't care less how the computer specialist gets the information. It's the technicians' responsibility to find out what their customers need and also where their specific tool can help. Instead, they're doing the things they think the computer can do best, most of which are unnecessary. Maybe this is old age showing, but I can well remember a time when we all did payrolls without a computer and we never heard of anyone having payroll troubles. So that's the last thing I would have put on the computer, not the first thing, because the improvement was at best minimal. But it never occurs to the computer people to ask where they could be most useful and what is the need and in what form.

That's 50 percent of the reason why the computer is a failure; the other 50 percent is much more profound. In terms of the human resource, the computer is a monstrosity; it expects people to do totally routinized, moron's work and exercise judgment and imagination in doing it. On the one hand, the programmer is supposed to be a trained white rat pushing the right lever upon the right stimulus, but he or she is also expected to think and have imagination. On top of that, once a mistake is made in the computer you can't get at it; the computer is over-engineered, and as long as you have the human factor in the input, you're going to get mistakes. This is one of the basic problems of a tool that is getting worse and not better—as its use spreads the computer is becoming less productive and not more, no matter what I.B.M. says. It's really an impossible job. The computer programmer is semiskilled labor with a learning period almost identical to that of an assembly line operator.

Dowling: How about the systems man?

Drucker: I refuse to answer on grounds of First and Fifth Amendments. The computer people will say it takes eight months before a computer programmer is any good and it takes a year before he or she reaches, really, the learning plateau. It also takes about six to eight months before the fellow who puts bumpers on cars is really proficient in his job. And the programmer is doing routine, monotonous, repetitive operating work that is even less challenging than putting on bumpers. The bumpers you can at least see and feel, and you see the car moving down the line, but punching in data you feel nothing and you don't see anything. You don't know whether you're punching insurance premiums or geological fossil records or what—and it makes no difference. Then you expect the poor programmer to exercise judgment and realize where the data are not coherent; that's impossible. And so from the point of view of human engineering—engineering, not physiology—the computer is a monstrosity.

The most extreme cases are with medical records, where only a highly trained physician can understand those data and very often he cannot. On top of that the computer processing the data is usually hundreds of miles from the clinic or hospital that's generating the data, so a mistake is incredibly easy to make and impossible to correct. The data are processed not by names like Dowling or MacPherson, but by number, so if your data come back with my number, there's no way of correcting it. You see my point?

Dowling: Certainly I see the potential for error.

Drucker: These errors are not the result of human carelessness, although everyone says they are. There is a fundamental mistake in job design. If you want people for repetitive, moronic, unskilled work, don't expect them to be able to know when to exercise judgment. To recap, this is the other 50 percent of the reason why the computer is a failure. The remainder, as you recall, is that the people who run and the people who use computers both lack elementary discipline.

Dowling: You have pretty much demolished the computer. Let's explore another widely known area. You're the father of the concept of management by objectives. You first came out with the concept, as I recall, in *The Practice of Management*, back in 1954.

Drucker: It would be more accurate to say that I'm the popularizer of management by objectives and self-control.

Dowling: The last part, about self-control, gets at an important distinction you make in your new book. Management by objectives has become practically an industry—hundreds of companies practice it with endless seminars and meetings devoted to the subject, but very few companies practice management by objectives as you think it should be understood—in other words, self-control. They forgo what you see as the greatest advantage of the concept—that it makes it possible for the manager to control his own performance. What's gone wrong in applying the concept?

Drucker: One of the things that is wrong with it is that in many applications there is a fascination with the procedures for the sake of procedures. Another problem is a damaging emphasis on precision in areas in which you can't be precise. There is little Susy and you ask how old she is. The answer is, "Oh, she'll be four pretty soon." That's good enough; you don't want to hear that she's three years, eight months, 14 days, 12 hours, and 25 minutes old. Most objectives are like little Susy's age—about four years is close enough. Instead of which you get objectives worked out to the eleventh decimal. And you have batteries of procedures to ensure this needless precision. Recently, I got a letter from a company president who told me that they had thought through their company objectives and he was sending me a book-length statement of objectives. I can tell the good man he's not going to get much helpful response from his middle-management people.

Dowling: You would argue that the core of management by objectives consists of each man and his boss sitting down and determining the specific objectives for which the man is accountable and responsible.

Drucker: Yes, one starts with the man and his job. You ask Jim or Joe, "What should we hold you accountable for?" The boss doesn't start out with what he demands, not in the case of managers and professionals. You start out with the assumption that the man knows his job—although that may turn out to be a mistake—and that he wants to do a job well. It's his responsibility to think through what he should be paid for. If the man answers, "I get paid for the perfection of quality control," you might say, "Then maybe you belong on a university faculty." No. He needs to ask himself what purpose quality control serves. Is he the representative of the consumer? You can tell him, "Maybe you have to perfect quality control to accomplish some of the needed objectives; maybe you have to simplify. You have to tell us, though, and we're not going to let you off the hook." Second, if you don't enable a man to know how he performs against the objectives, the objectives become a threat and a menace.

Dowling: You mention that mutual understanding between boss and subordinates requires both the superior's willingness to listen and a tool especially designed to make lower managers heard, and you cite managers who have each of their subordinates write a "manager's letter" twice a year.

Drucker: Harold Smiddy at GE invented this device, and it was one of his most useful inventions. Twice a year, he got a letter from each of his men that ran like this: "This is what I had planned to do in the past six months and this is why. Within the overall company objectives, this was to have been my contribution. This is what actually has been accomplished, and this is my conclusion as to what went wrong and why. As you know, we're having real trouble with a certain policy, but in division X it works like a charm. Here's what I suspect are the reasons." The letter also spells out the man's goals for the next six months, the things he must do to attain them, the obstacles to attaining them within his own unit, and what his superior can do to help him. The letter also shows up whatever inconsistencies exist in what the boss and the company expect of a man.

I've used the manager's letter ever since Harold developed it, and it's been very useful. Now, like any such tool, it takes practice and it takes constant pressure—if you don't ask for it you won't get it. You also have to make damn sure that people can get the feedback from results, so that this becomes their tool and not another stick to get beaten with. In fact, it may be a good idea to make sure that in stating their objectives they think through and spell out the information they need.

Dowling: That would be crucial, because you can't assume that the boss knows what information is required.

Drucker: Two of the missing elements in most management procedures are first, that the manager hasn't been asked what information he needs to be able to do the job he has committed himself to, and second, he hasn't been asked what information he needs to be able to know how he's doing. Hence, people bitterly complain that they would like to manage themselves by objectives but, Goddamn it, they can't. Most of the time the answers to both questions could be written on the back of an envelope. There are very few answers in life that can't be written on the back of an envelope.

Dowling: You implied that one of the reasons management by objectives doesn't work is the fact that top management really doesn't have much faith in the ability of the younger, educated managers to contribute. In other words, they buy the concept on the surface but they don't believe in it.

Drucker: Yes, that's a partial answer. A great deal of fault lies with the "experts." We have had I don't know how many big management fads over the past 25 years. They all follow the same curve, beginning with a good idea, but a modest one, and then becoming fashionable. So the experts peddle them as panaceas guaranteed to cure cancer, menstrual pains, and prevent unwanted children. And every management has to have them—you can't be seen in polite society unless you sponsor operations research, or manager development, or what have you. Managements don't buy them because they believe in them; they buy them because they're told that without them they don't rate as managers—they're not part of the establishment, the elite. The idea that only teenagers are susceptible to peer pressure is a misunderstanding.

Dowling: There's no question about it.

Drucker: What we are learning is that the only ones who are not highly susceptible to peer pressure are small children. Becoming susceptible to peer pressure is a sign of growing up. So a certain management technique becomes fashion and everyone has to have it. Then, three years later, you get the disillusionment. You still have the menstrual pains; you still have unwanted pregnancies.

Dowling: Don't you think one of the reasons it hasn't worked is that you bought it but you didn't believe in it to start with?

Drucker: You just bought it because everyone's buying it. But then it seems not to work, so you go on to the next fashion, except for a fairly small number of people—make it one out of every five—who have found that it does something. So they develop the tool instead of dropping it, until it eventually comes back. It never attains the front page again, but it becomes another tool, and a useful one—not for every company, but for many. There tend to be ten-year cycles. For example, I first became exposed to the human relations binge in the late Forties; by the end of the Fifties there were quite a few businesses and institutions that were returning to human relations. Sure, they knew by then that it doesn't cure the problem of economic conflict or the problem of power conflict and a few others, but they knew that it was a good idea to accept the fact that human beings perversely insist on behaving like human beings, which is all human relations really means.

Operations research was next, and I'm one of the pioneers in it. One of our great difficulties was to convince top management that this was a tool and not an end, and a difficult tool, one that would take many years to make good. One major company in which I worked is now structured around its business research function, and the great resurgence of that company in the last five or eight years is directly traceable to this function, but it took ten years of work. One of the most difficult things was to convince the president and the chairman that they shouldn't brag about what their operations research was doing for the company, because up to that time we hadn't done a thing for them. And we wouldn't for a long time.

Dowling: The president had to have a lot of patience.

Drucker: He had no patience. We simply said we could do small things for him, but it would take a long time, partly because we had to learn what his needs were and partly because his operating managers had to become skilled in using the tool. Everywhere else people had huge O.R. staffs that nurtured great expectations—and then they collapsed. Now it's coming back, but as another tool, not as a panacea.

As for management by objectives, it's now past the fad stage. It's been oversold and overpromoted, so by now a good many people are saying it's no damn good. But in an amazingly large proportion of institutions they have found that it works, that it's a tremendous improvement over what they had before. In another five to eight years it will become another very important management tool. The other day I was in a management seminar of men from medium-size companies in which one man impressed me because he asked the right questions about management by objectives. After the break I asked him, "What kind of procedures do you have?" His answer—that impressed me even more—was, "We have none."

Dowling: When you say he asked the right sort of questions, what kind of questions do you mean?

Drucker: He said, "We have no problems with our managers and with our research and engineering supervisors, but with the individual professional it's very different." Now, this is a man who knows what he's doing. With the professional you are challenging a man who defines himself as a quality controller or a training man to think in terms of his contribution and not in terms of his discipline or knowledge area, and that goes against the grain of the man who sees himself purely as a professional. This is why the problem is so difficult and so important. I told him he was unlikely to get really good objectives out of the professional workers, but they need it the most.

Dowling: You had a suggestion in your latest book, as I recall, about how to handle the professional. You would have each member of top management sit down with a group of the younger professional people and say, "I have no agenda. I am here to listen. I want you to tell me what we need to know about your work and how you think we can make it most productive—as well as what we do to hamper you."

Drucker: I got that idea from Harold Smiddy, too. The manager is always going to have to interpret the organization for his professional employees. They will always see the world in terms of their speciality, say, metallurgy, and see the job in terms of metallurgy. They will look upon the company as a place where 8,000 people slave away so that they can practice metallurgy. It's the way most university faculties view the student body—there are 35,000 students at Berkeley, all so that one great scholar can decipher Chinese texts.

Dowling: I can remember standing on the steps of Littauer at Harvard with a distinguished professor on a beautiful June day. I commented on how perfect the day was and he responded, "There's only one thing wrong with it; it will be far more beautiful in a week—the students will have gone."

Drucker: No matter how much you love students, by the end of May you feel that way. And students, particularly in large numbers, are not good to look at. Don't kid yourself: Humanity in the mass at any age is repellent. It's not meant to run in herds. Gazelles look lovely in herds; human beings do not.

Dowling: Most of the time the setting of your writings is in large organizations, both profit-making and otherwise. How do they apply to managers in a quite different setting—the small or the medium-size organization?

Drucker: You're asking about the chief executive and subordinates in the small to medium-size company?

Dowling: Right.

Drucker: I would not start out with the subordinate, but with the chief executive. The central and crucial problem in a small or medium-size business is understanding the role of the chief executive. The small to medium-size companies I know, and I know a fair amount, suffer first from not thinking through the chief executive's job. Any business needs to think through objectively the key activities of the chief executive. One doesn't think personalities or people; one thinks about the few activities in the business on which success depends and that only top management can do. Then one asks, "How do we assign them so that each of the positions is covered?" Most medium-size or small businesses make one of two mistakes, both very serious. The chief executive is good in finance and good in analysis, so he—not even consciously—defines the chief executive's function as finance and analysis; the rest are neglected. Or he makes the opposite mistake. He knows that people and marketing and community relations are important, and here he's a finance and analysis man, so he forces himself to do things he is not good at. The intelligent thing is to make the analysis and then to perceive what are his strengths and weaknesses—then bring in someone to complement the weaknesses.

Dowling: As part of top management.

Drucker: Even in the small, and particularly the medium-size, business, top management is a team task. Every key activity has to be assigned to somebody and in that area he is top management, period. And if you have a top man—a chief executive—who is not at ease with people, does not know how to build a team, and likes to work by himself as an analyst, then the man in the group who is people-focused—maybe it's the manufacturing man—is top management in that area and he makes the decisions. Sure, the top man retains the authority and the duty to override him, but nine times out of ten he won't.

Dowling: If he overrides him too often his credibility is gone and the chief executive will have to get rid of him.

Drucker: If you have a people problem, you, as top man, talk it over with him and wind up saying, "Jim, you think it through and come up with a recommendation for our decision." He is top management. Incidentally, everyone in the business had better know that. It doesn't require a formal announcement, but the next time a district sales manager comes to the president for a personnel decision the president looks at him and says, "You know, Greg, if I were you I'd talk to Jim about it. He's really our best man for this sort of thing; you talk to him. Sure, you let me know what he says." You do that once or twice and the organization will understand how you work. But you also go back to the office and call Jim and say, "Jim, I just had Greg Brigham here from the Peoria office about some personnel matter; I don't know whether it was important—I couldn't figure out what he was talking about. But let me know if it's something we ought to pay attention to or whether he is just getting panicky."

Dowling: The sort of thing that Alfred Sloan did all the time.

Drucker: Sloan did a beautiful job. General Marshall did a superb job, too. There was never any doubt who the boss was; when anyone came to him with a logistics question—and Marshall was a good logistics man—he said, "Have you talked to General Somervell?" "No, sir." And if the same man came twice to Marshall with a logistics problem, Marshall would say, "Don't you know I'm a busy man?" Again and again, Marshall—and mind you, I'm only guessing now, I wasn't sitting in his office but I'm going on what I've heard—again and again Marshall would make a mental note and the next time he came in, he would say, "Andy," (or whoever it was) . . .

Dowling: . . . Brehon. A strange name—Brehon Somervell.

Drucker: It's an ordinary Welsh name. He would say, "Well, Brehon, that Third Corps winter uniform problem. You need any help with the War Production Board?" Brehon would say, "No, no problem at all," or, "That's only the beginning of a serious problem; I don't think I need any help, but if I do I'll come yelling." In the Army you had a formal announcement of who was boss in a given area. With Sloan there was no announcement, but the group had worked out the assignment of responsibilities very carefully.

Dowling: The top management group within themselves.

Drucker: Yes. And when there was a personnel change among the top team, these positions were restructured. When Albert Bradley succeeded Donaldson Brown as vice-chairman and head of finance under Sloan, there was quite a restructuring, because Bradley was a doer and Brown wasn't. Brown was a lonely man; Bradley was outgoing. Also, Bradley was a much better finance man than Brown, but he was just not interested in policy, which was Brown's primary interest. Actually, the main role Brown had taken, Bradley did not take over—the policy role was largely left to Bradley's subordinate. But on the other hand, Brown had not really been the top man on most financial matters—Meyer Prentice had been.

The next basic problem for the chief executive of medium-size and small companies is where he goes for advice and guidance and the information he needs. Most of them are terribly insulated. They have an accounting and auditing firm that audits and they have a lawyer, but let me say that neither auditors nor lawyers understand much about business, nor do they usually have any people sense or any strategic sense. Also, they're your employees or you retain them.

Dowling: So they're not free to be frank.

Drucker: They're not going to come in and say, "The trouble with this company is you." They may hint at it, but they're not going to say it.

Dowling: That would jeopardize their retainer, to put it mildly.

Drucker: If they are capable of rising above that consideration, they still see the president as their client. Therefore, the small and medium-size company needs an effective board of directors even more than the big one and usually has one that is even less effective. If I were chief executive officer of a medium-size company I would spend a fair amount of time thinking through what I want my board to do, what I need from a board—including, let me say, somebody who will look at my proposal and say flatly, "This is not good enough." One doesn't need a rubber stamp; one needs people on a board who can ask the right questions. You need people who can say, "Jim, you are moving into the toy business and you don't know a thing about it. Have you really thought it through? Or do you want to make this acquisition just because it's available at a good

P-E ratio? Well, usually if things are available at cheap P-E ratios, there's a damn good reason." Or you need a board member who says, "That's a very attractive youngster; you talk of him as your successor. What's his performance record? Oh, he's been your assistant for 18 years. What has he done?"

Dowling: He's asking for something you can really identify as his contribution.

Drucker: To put it bluntly, if he's been your assistant for 18 years, the chances that he can perform are poor, because people who want to perform don't stay 18 years as an assistant. They like to have their own command. The flag lieutenant in the Navy who stays with the admiral for more than three years has chosen to make his career on the admiral's coattails. He doesn't really want responsibility. So if you're the president of the medium-size company, you need people who can make objective criticisms. Instead, what you probably have on your board are six presidents of companies very much like your own.

Dowling: And you're on the boards of some of their companies—reciprocity.

Drucker: Yes, and each of these people is overextended, just as you are. You haven't taken a vacation in four years, because without you the business would sink immediately. When do you have the time to sit on their boards? What do you do? You study the figures on the plane ride from Pittsburgh to Detroit—55 minutes. All you have time for is to look at some bottom lines. And what goes on in their boards? Well, six months ago the question came up about a reliable contractor and you said, "We're using that engineering firm; we've been quite satisfied." That's your contribution for the last year. Other than that, you have listened to the results for the last quarter, have moved changes in the bylaws, have heard the treasurer report about the tax refund he's negotiating. If you hadn't attended the meeting, would the company be any different?

Dowling: All right, you need a strong board. But is it easy to find capable people willing to do the work required?

Drucker: No, it's very hard. I know one man who retired this past June at 62 after 15 years with one company. He's a very good finance man and he's taken on four directorships on condition that he give about 20 days a year to each. He's going to be a very uncomfortable board member—he's going to ask embarrassing questions. He's not going to vote against management; he'd go off the board first. But as long as he's around, he won't necessarily vote with management, either. He'll say things like, "I don't think you have thought this through; I don't think you are ready." Or he may say, "Very nice plan, but you know the two key ingredients are missing. You don't tell us where the money's going to come from and you don't tell us where the people are going to come from." He'll say it much more pleasantly than I have—but he'll say it. The companies will profit from his presence because they all need a conscience organ, even though the experience is going to uncomfortable. Well, a comfortable conscience is the wrong one to have.

Dowling: It's a contradiction in terms.

Drucker: Yes. And your lawyer doesn't belong on the board. No one who receives payments for any service except as a board member belongs on the board. Retired people don't belong there; if you want to retain them as consultants, fine.

Dowling: You mean people who have retired from your own organization.

Drucker: Yes. The Japanese have the useful device of the counselor. He gets paid a little and he has an office; he's available if people want to use him. But it is impossible for a man to move out of being an active member of the management group and on to the board and remember that he's no longer part of the top team. It can't be done. While he may be a tremendous source of knowledge and wisdom, he has no business being a director. He cannot keep the two roles apart; it is impossible. And so the really bright ones don't. Old man Sloan knew that when he stayed a director as chairman, he hadn't retired. I once asked the old gentleman, "Since you've retired, Mr. Sloan . . ." The old man went right through the roof and said, "Mister, look; if I retire I go off the board."

Dowling: He understood the distinction.

Drucker: Yes. He said, "I have not retired, and I'm not ready to. I'm no longer working every day, that's all." He also asked, "Do you want to see my work program?" I said, "Yes, sir." He opened the drawer and there it was, typed out: "Alfred P. Sloan, chairman of GM, assignments and work progam"—each with a deadline. It didn't amount to much, of course. He was in his eighties and was deeply interested in his foundation, but he attended every board meeting and he had done his assignments. He added, "I am not retired; I've just changed jobs." Then he grinned, as the old man always did when he got on his highest horse; he said, "I would not allow anyone else to do that. As a policy I think it is dead wrong."

So, the supplier of goods or of services has no place on the board.

Dowling: Including bankers.

Drucker: Above all. The bankers and consultants have no place on the board. The accountants have the right rule: You cannot be on the board of a company for which your firm is an auditor. I think it is high time that the lawyers adopted this policy.

Dowling: It's a common feature on almost every board to have the outside counsel on the board.

Drucker: Yes, and he has no business there. I don't understand why the Bar Association hasn't put it into the canon of ethics, because the big lawyers don't want to be on boards. You talk to them—the youngers ones, not the older ones—and you find that they clearly see that there is a conflict of interest there. But they say, "We are forced to do it because if we say no to a management, they consider that a rebuff and pick themselves another lawyer."

Dowling: They wish the Bar Association would get them off the hook by prohibiting it.

Drucker: Yes, they would like to say, "We would like to oblige you, but the Bar Association won't allow it."

Once you have your strong board you should think through what the main function of the board should be—discuss it with your board members and prepare a work plan for them. Most important, pay your board members and pay them well. Don't accept an unpaid board member, because you will always get what you pay for.

Dowling: And in this case, it would be little or no work.

Drucker: One gets what one pays for. Let me say that any doctor knows that one has charity patients not for the sake of the good one does them, because one doesn't do them any good, but for the sake of your own decency and immortal soul. Freud recognized this when he laid down the rule that psychoanalysts must not give free psychoanalysis.

Dowling: I was unaware of it.

Drucker: Freud said that unless the patient pays, it won't be worth anything to him and it won't help him. In part this was a result of Freud's own hangup, which, like that of his contemporary society, wasn't sex—it was money. Freud was greedy, and he suffered from the fear of being poor. You read in the biographies that he grew up a poor boy; that's nonsense—his was a very well-to-do family. He always made enormous amounts of money, but he suffered from the poorhouse syndrome.

Dowling: I've known people who are very rich who suffer from it.

Drucker: Yes. But aside from that, Freud had a point. In my time the medical profession in Vienna hated him, largely because it was an article of the faith that a successful practitioner spends more and more of his time on charity cases. However, some of them grudgingly admitted that from the point of view of contributing to people, the charity practice contributes very little, because the recipient does not appreciate it. It works in surgery, where the patient's role is passive, but with a cardiac patient, where the patient has to cooperate, paying makes a significant difference in the success of the treatment.

Dowling: Yes, it makes a lot of sense.

Drucker: And so most boards get no pay and therefore they don't try to contribute. Pay your board members on the basis that each one is a senior executive—so pay one-fifth of a senior executive's salary. Don't allow any of your board members to sit on more than five boards—that's all one man can really handle.

Dowling: You obviously need more than one of these people.

Drucker: You need four or five. Sometimes three will do—different people with different perspectives. If you're the chief executive officer, look at yourself: What kind of a person are you, what kind of people do you need, what kind of people do you listen to? And then work on building a board and be willing to pay them. If your executive committee is the equivalent of one full-time senior executive at 75,000 bucks, then that's $15,000 per member.

Dowling: If you have five of them.

Drucker: Yes. And the pay is cheap. You want diversity. You want the man who is primarily financially oriented and who shuts off when you talk people. You also want the man deeply interested in people, who can look you in the eye and can say, "That young sales vice-president of yours is not good enough; he may sell enough but he's basically only a corporal, and he's going to sell you down the road or corrupt people. Look out." Your good financial man won't ever see that. And you may need a technical man, not in your own field—you either know metallurgy or you don't—but a man who knows technology, who can ask, "Can you afford not to know about that? Do you know enough to say that it will never be a threat to our business? I don't know beans about plastics, but I know how one can find out—six telephone calls and you know the answer, if you know what people are talking about."

The best job on building a board I've seen was done by the late George Merck, when he invited Vannevar Bush, who had been chief scientific administrator in World War II, to become part-time chairman. And the two of them brought in John Connor, who's now chairman of Allied Chemical, to become first, general counsel, next, executive vice-president, and finally, the president. Those three built an effective board and a lot of the tremendous success of Merck was due to that board. Bush laid down the rule that he would not let anyone on the board whom they didn't pay and pay well. They only wanted first-rate people and they would pay first-rate sums for them. And they wouldn't bring anyone on the board to whom they couldn't say, "This is what we want you to do; this is the work for you."

Dowling: They identified the directors' contribution precisely.

Drucker: Precisely is the wrong word, because in many cases people could also come back to them and say, "Yes, but you also need me for this." At one of the early board meetings one member is said to have become so outraged by a proposal of Merck's that he said, "I think I should move that we fire you." And Merck retorted, "You can't; I own the company." The board member said, "But you won't have the votes until the next general meeting. Until then, we have them." This is the way an effective and responsible board member has to act. He's got to be willing to say, "Look, I'll quit your damn board before I'll go along with that harebrained idea." This is the kind of board member most medium-size businesses don't have, but badly need.

Conversation with
DANIEL BELL

Daniel Bell takes all society as his province. In a series of volumes, *Work and Its Discontents, The End of Ideology, The Coming of Post-Industrial Society* and, most recently, *The Cultural Contradictions of Capitalism*, Bell, a professor of sociology at Harvard University, has analyzed the current state of American society, described its problems, traced them back to their roots, and along the way offered some prescriptions for improvement. The combination of scholarship that ranges across many disciplines, of frequently exhaustive—and occasionally exhausting—research, of original insights, and magisterial formulations has earned him a front rank among our present-day gurus.

His basic formulation is that we can best understand our society by thinking of it as "an uneasy amalgam" of three realms based on three contradictory principles: first, the economic realm governed by the principle of efficiency; second, the polity or state governed by the principle of equality; third, the realm of culture governed by the principle of self-realization or self-gratification.

The contradictions exist even within a single realm. The corporation, for example, in its professions and practices epitomizes the principle of efficiency. Yet this same corporation in its products and advertisements promotes pleasure, instant joy, relaxing, and letting go. As Bell puts it, the corporation urges that "one is to be 'straight' by day and a 'swinger' by night."

Still, the corporation—or, to be more precise, its spokesmen—fail to recognize that life is not made up of watertight compartments. They

Reprinted from Organizational Dynamics, *Summer 1976*

register surprise, even indignation, when hedonism, subsidized and promoted by the corporation, undermines the work ethic.

Looking at the overall picture, Bell sees a society in which the claims of the polity, what he calls "the public household," are in a clear position of primacy over the claims of the economic realm (for *economic realm*, substitute *corporation*). Whence the primacy of the public household?

To quote Charles Lindblom: "One of the great puzzles of the twentieth century is that masses of voters in essentially free democratic societies do not use their votes to achieve a significantly more equal distribution of income and wealth as well as of many of the other values to which men aspire."

Bell's position is that such an effort, what he calls "the revolution of entitlements," is now under way—and the end is not in sight. "In the last generation of the twentieth century we now move to state-managed societies. And these emerge because of the increase in large-scale social demands (health, education, welfare, social services) which have become entitlements for the population." To put it another way—again using Bell's words—"where workers once feared losing a job, they now expect a job and a rising standard of living."

Does Bell celebrate his vision of the future? Not altogether. His embrace is selective, not promiscuous. He approves of the commitment of the public household to redress the impact of economic and social inequalities, a commitment that responds to the demands for more and more social services as entitlements. What he fears are the possibilities of coercion and the loss of liberty that could accompany the predominance of the public household and the decline of the economic or corporate realm.

To Bell, liberty and pluralism are indivisible. The subordination of the corporation to the public household is both necessary and desirable; its subservience is something else again—equally unnecessary and undesirable. His consummate concern is to somehow achieve the proper balance between the public and private spheres "of public care for private needs—which enhances liberty and equity."

Dowling: You quote Schumpeter that stationary capitalism is historically a contradiction in terms. And you agree with Schumpeter that capitalism can't exist without growth. We face the problem in our society not of how much growth, but of what kinds of growth are desirable.

Bell: Schumpeter was a good Marxist. One of his strengths was that he absorbed the best of Marx into his thinking. What made Marx's theory central to capitalism was his insight that the capitalist system, by its very nature, had to keep accumulating profits, reinvest, expand—and come into crisis. He didn't believe (this is Marx) that you could have a stationary state. Nor did Schumpeter. But Schumpeter did believe that capitalism could lose its élan. He said at one point that the Stock Exchange is a poor substitute for the Holy Grail—that it is incapable of the kind of emotional charge that men often seek and need. Still, Schumpeter's basic notion was that capitalism could live only by expanding the standard of living of a society.

Asking what kinds of growth is the question, though, because some kinds of growth become unproductive. I suppose the Egyptians were a high-growth society. But I doubt that the pyramids benefited anyone, least of all those who lay inside them.

Dowling: I was thinking more of your observation about the necessity of striking a balance between growth and redistribution of income. You pointed out that redistribution of income is one method of increasing consumption; on the other hand, it also decreases the amount available for investment.

Bell: In high-rentier societies in which the rich merely inherit money and spend it sumptuously, there is no real investment. There, a tax on capital wealth is more feasible. In fact, when Schumpeter was finance minister of Austria in 1919, he advocated a capital levy. But in *this* kind of society, where most people feel, and I think quite rightly, that they've earned their income, redistribution is more difficult. In the 1960s you could finance a social program out of a rising government surplus. But when the absence of a goverment surplus doesn't permit this kind of financing, the problem of redistribution becomes more complex.

Two things have taken place: One is that the redistribution of income presumably has not benefited those whom it is intended to benefit—namely, disadvantaged groups. In the process, some of what was to be redistributed was consumed by the growth of bureaucracy. Second, we have had an inflation that has limited government monies for social expenditures and wreaked havoc with the fiscal structure of local governments.

We are sophisticated enough to know that there is no single cause of inflation. Inflation has so many different causes; some go back to the Vietnam war and the unwillingness of the government to increase taxes to meet the increased expenditures. There were the pressures of a worldwide boom in demand and the temporary shortages of primary processing capacity. And there was the politically manipulated increase in the price of oil that added $20 billion just this last year to the American economy. No one of these things was decisive by itself, but they all contributed to the problem.

Dowling: You pointed out the inherent difference between the increase of productivity in the goods sector versus the services sector. As the services sector becomes more and more important, because of what you call the revolution of entitlements, this tends to aggravate the relationship between growth and inflation.

Bell: One has to distinguish between kinds of services sectors. After my book *The Post-Industrial Society* came out, my colleague Ted Levitt said to me that a large-scale effort was under way to increase productivity in the private services sector. Obviously, advances in data-processing technology constitute such an improvement because ours is such a high-transaction society that the substitution of electronic media for the physical distribution of pieces of paper is a way of increasing productivity. And logically, this would apply just as easily in the public sector. But for a whole variety of reasons, it is much more difficult to achieve substantial productivity increases in a public sector than in the private services sector.

Dowling: In *The Post-Industrial Society*, when you talked about the halcyon days of R&D, you mentioned—I think the year cited was 1966—that the Europeans were spending 30 percent more in the civilian sector on R&D than we were in the United States. Have you kept track of the trend? Has this continued? I have an impression that R&D expenditures overall in the United States have declined.

Bell: For many years, people thought we spent much more on R&D in America than in England or Europe. But if you subtracted a large portion of *military* R&D here, then it was clear that the civilian R&D in Europe was much higher than here.

Once that is said, there are still two necessary qualifications. First, even though a high proportion of R&D has been in the military, there are spillover effects that are difficult to calculate. Second, a large part of the ostensible military R&D in this country *was* intended for the civilian sector. It was voted in the military budget simply because it was easier to do it that way. After the student riots in 1968, Senator Mansfield proposed an amendment limiting Defense Department research monies strictly to mission-oriented research. On the surface that sounds fine. But in practice, the military had been very active and successful in sponsoring *basic* research. An old example is that of Emmanuel Piore and the Office of Naval Research, which financed a large part of the basic research in this country. At the recent hearings of the Senate committee on economic growth, under Senator Lloyd Bentsen, Jerry Wiesner of M.I.T testified that the Mansfield Amendment was really harmful because the Defense Department had had a number of very good science administrators, and this capacity has been dismantled or is being lost.

Dowling: My thinking was that one way to achieve growth without inflation is to have a large extent of the growth accounted for by the end effects of effective R&D.

Bell: Most economists I know—this is by now received wisdom—argue that you can't have growth without *some* inflation.

Dowling: The problem is "how much" inflation.

Bell: That, of course, is a tricky problem. There is always a tendency during expansion to build up inventories and compete for capital, so the normal elements of a business cycle come into play—all of which tends to expand the aspects of demand and therefore leads to a moderately inflationary situation. There may also be a structural factor—roughly 3 to 4 percent inflation—built into the economy simply by the disproportion between the productivity of the services and the industrial sectors. In addition, there is 2 to 3 percent inflation built in by normal pressures for full employment, so that 5 or 6 percent inflation is a norm. I have always felt that the problem is not inflation per se, but rather its yo-yo effects. If inflation is fairly steady and consistent, the effects can be discounted.

Dowling: Even the effects of rampant inflation?

Bell: Up to a point. I'm talking about your 6 to 7 percent inflation—if you know it's steady, you can discount it and pay for it as part of the price of an expanding economy. It's only when inflation goes down to 2 percent, jumps up to 12 percent, down to 3, and up to 15 that you begin to get high uncertainties. Rampant inflation, which I would define as above 10 percent a year, is not a problem that this country faces—not, at least, in the foreseeable future. The big problem, of course, is the increasing inability to *insulate* oneself from the much more uncontrollable inflation abroad.

Dowling: You had an interesting chapter heading in *The Post-Industrial Society:* "The Subordination of the Corporation." Could you expand on what you had in mind?

Bell: It's a subordination to a different mode of responsibility, the tension between the "economizing" and the "sociologizing" mode. I set up two prototypes—what I call the economizing mode and the sociologizing mode. The economizing mode in many respects is the conventional one. Take Alfred P. Sloan's *My Years at General Motors* as the textbook of what I call the economizing mode. It is the effort to create complete efficiency, to maximize the rate of return, to mandate the installment of tight budgetary controls. When Sloan came to General Motors, he didn't know whether a unit was making money or not. It was all piled into general accounts. By breaking down each of the units into profit centers and cost centers, he was able to know at what point he made or lost money. (Henry Ford I, partly because he was suspicious of outside controls, never knew whether it was more efficient for him to buy steel or to make it. Ford used to say, "I buy for one dollar and I sell for two dollars. I'm satisfied with my two percent profit.")

We need to remember that the modern corporation is a social invention; it doesn't come out of the blue. It was really created by three or four people: Theodore Vail at AT&T, Walter Teagle at Standard Oil, and Sloan at G.M. It is a highly flexible organizational device to coordinate men, materials, and markets for the mass production of goods or for the efficient delivery of services. Within that context, to use the vernacular, the bottom line is what counts. If you have a better bottom line, the managerial group gets a higher bonus—or, more important, the company can attract more capital, the price of its stock goes up, and the shares the managers have appreciate as well. But everything gets subordinated to that one end—I'm being extreme for a moment—to maximum efficiency and the rate of return on capital.

In recent years, a whole series of pressures have modified the role of the corporation. Tom Clausen of the Bank of America states, for example, that there are other aspects of the social environment and the physical environment that one has to take into account. More money is increasingly being diverted from the capital available for investment and spent instead on communal purposes and on people. Corporations increasingly recognize that they have long-term obligations other than simply maximizing immediate returns on investment. Are you obligated to employ certain proportions of minorities? Are you obligated to provide child-care centers? Theoretically, in a free market you should be able to locate a plant wherever you want in order to make the greatest use of your resources in terms of waterways, natural gas outlets, and so on. Yet someone may say, "Look, this will have a negative effect upon our residential community; we don't want you." These are a set of alternative claims that are communal claims. They may not necessarily equal the claims of the managerial group, but they need to be taken into account.

The economizing mode goes back to a nineteenth and early twentieth century "fiction" of a corporation—that of ownership. But what is a corporation? I don't believe the corporation comprises economic owners, because owners are a legal fiction. There are a few situations in which the owners are still those who built the corporation, but these cases are exceptional. The owners of most firms—not in the sense of the legal fiction, but in the psychological sense—are those who have given their lives to a firm. Some of them spend 20, 30, 40 years with a firm—and because they invested their entire lives and their emotions in the firm, they have a sense of identity with it. In that context, people shouldn't be allowed to take over a firm and wreck it—eviscerate its earnings and then simply walk away from it, as you would pluck a nice ripe chicken.

Dowling: It certainly happens, all too frequently.

Bell: Of course it does. My point is that we're looking for the grounds of a new morality, or a new sociology, for a corporation. The corporation is not an instrument with the sole purpose of turning out goods for a given rate of return. The bottom line is an effective discipline—a *necessary constraint*—but to be looked at only in those terms. A corporation is a social institution that encompasses the lives of its members. Who, for example, owns Harvard? It's a huge enterprise with a billion-and-a-half-dollar endowment and a budget of $700 million, as big as many of the large corporations in the country. A lot of people spend their lives there. And one has a sense of obligation to them. Who owns Harvard? No one owns Harvard. It's owned by those who have a stake in its history and continuity.

Keynes once said with a degree of truth that people who are investors should be considered rentiers and simply earn a fixed return on their investments. In other words, you reduce the equity components held by the people who technically own the corporation. This is already true of certain kinds of utilities with a very high debt to equity ratio where, in effect, the bondholders are getting a return of 8 to 10 percent and don't worry about capital appreciation. For that, however, one needs a high degree of political and economic stability.

Dowling: You pointed out that it was the corporation more than anything else that killed the Puritan ethic—killed it with installment and instant-credit plans and all the advertising that fuels feelings, as it were, of self-gratification or self-realization. On the other hand, it seems to me that if you relate these feelings of self-realization and self-gratification to one of your axial principles, that of equity in the polity, the corporation has contributed a great deal to this revolution of entitlements, with its increased demand for services. The corporation is being forced to pay the bill for those services—the demands for which were largely of its own creation.

Bell: You've put together two arguments in a complicated way. It's not the corporation that has killed the Protestant ethic. It was the mode of mass production and mass consumption. And the promotion of mass consumption through new marketing devices, particularly through installment and credit plans, led to hedonism rather than a sense of vocation as the major motivational factor. In that sense, you have an ineluctable historical contradiction. Capitalism built upon what Weber used to call "this worldly asceticism"—in which you reinvest and don't live in a sumptuous way—is being undercut by a new system in which you are constantly promoting goods.

That leads within the corporation to a second contradiction. Namely, the corporation wants people to be devoted to the corporation, spend their careers inside the corporation and work hard, move around readily in terms of the needs of the corporation, and therefore to delay their gratification. Yet at the same time it is promoting hedonism in terms of products and savings. So I said—perhaps too blithely, but there's some acid truth in it—that the corporation wants its people to be "squares" by day and "swingers" by night.

The second point is somewhat different. In my way of thinking about society, I separate the *technical-economic order*, which is oriented toward efficiency, the *political system*, which is oriented toward equality and participation, and the *cultural realm*, which is oriented toward self-gratification.

Now it's quite clear that the organizational form of an economic system (no matter how much you've prettied it up with committee systems and other cosmetics) is still basically a top-down, hierarchically organized system—perhaps necessarily so. At the same time, it has produced large amounts of goods—but many more people are quite often, for various reasons, excluded from these goods and therefore make political demands for them in the name of entitlement.

What has happened in the past ten years is that equality of opportunity, the older definition of *equality*, now has been transformed—because many people can't make it even when they're given equal opportunity—into equality of results. The consequence of this phenomenon is that more and more demands are being made upon the society *for direct allocations of resources through the political system rather than through the economic system*. Now, that's a separate problem from the first, the *internal* contradiction of an economic system that grew out of a Protestant ethic and converted itself to hedonism. The second contradiction is one in which the political system becomes a mechanism for the allocation of goods that are no longer being allocated through the market mechanism.

So my book really deals with a number of *different* kinds of contradictions within the capitalist system.

Dowling: But the corporation collectively is paying its share of an increased bill for these kinds of services, which it helped to stimulate in the first place by firing the fuel of self-gratification. In other words, a fair percentage of the taxes that a corporation pays can be attributed to this increased demand for the provision of services by the public sector.

Bell: It's not that the *corporation* pays; it's simply that the incomes generated get taxed. In this particular case, the place where the tax is collected is the corporation. If you didn't have corporation taxes, you'd have taxes on higher incomes elsewhere. Presumably the corporation would pay out larger proportions of its monies in dividends and salaries, and the government would take it back through taxes on salaries. The whole system is an anomaly. Many corporations, because of taxes, *reinvest* the company's money. But that is against a "pure" theory of capitalism. Theoretically, all profits should go out as dividends and the "owners" should decide whether *they* want to reinvest or not to get the best return. Why should the managers have that power of decision if there is a "pure capitalism"?

It's not the tax on corporations that is the crucial matter, but rather at what point the tax structure as a whole becomes dysfunctional because it militates against the creation of more capital. It's a mistake to say, as corporations sometimes do in their advertisements, "After all, we're paying a large part of the taxes of this country." That's not always true—often they're passing them through in the form of increased prices. However, we have a real problem with a tax system set up so as to discourage effective capital formation.

Dowling: You anticipated that the public sector was going to play a larger role in the provision of capital, that the scope of the private corporation in the management of capital was going to increasingly diminish. You have a footnote, for example, in which you mentioned Felix Rohatyn and his suggestion that the situation has gotten to the point where another reconstruction finance corporation (RFC) is needed.

Bell: There are two or three different sides to the problem. One is that we're getting more and more into the multiplication of public goods. Defense is the obvious example. No one brings his musket into the army. In 1776, people brought their own muskets into the army and today some people take muskets out of the army; but by and large a musket is not a private good. More and more you find the government purchasing goods that are necessarily public goods. So it's generating employment and generating capital because most of the production is not being done by government; it's being done by private industry. The second are transfer payments that are essentially pass-through arrangements with Medicare, Medicaid, and so on. And the third, which is the Rohatyn proposal, is simply the direct loan of monies by governmental units to private units that are incapable of getting money from capital markets. Now we do that already. We call it investment credits. I suppose when Rohatyn was writing in *The New York Times* a year and a half ago he had something larger in mind, like the old Jessie Jones RFC. That's simply a faster and more direct way of getting monies to particular firms than we do it right now via investment tax credits. I think businessmen would do much better to stop using a double standard with government—"Stay out of our affairs, but give us more investment tax credits." I don't begrudge the investment tax credits—I'm not antibusiness in the least.

Dowling: Do you think that the tax system has already reached the point of being dysfunctional in terms of the formation of capital?

Bell: I'm not a public finance expert, but I try to keep abreast of such trends because, as I say in *The Cultural Contradictions of Capitalism*, in a post-industrial society the old issues of labor and capital are being subordinated to struggles that essentially revolve around the allocation of resources by governmental budgets. After all, if one looks ahead 20 or 30 years, the major decisions that will affect us more than anything else are the ones concerning allocation made by the state budget. In Britain, 60 percent of the GNP goes first through government accounts. We're up to 35 percent. That's the new class struggle in the post-industrial society, not the struggle between labor and capital. All this is what I call, following Schumpeter, "fiscal sociology." In that context, taxes and capital formation are central.

     I'm persuaded of the scheme of my colleague Martin Feldstein. He wants to abolish the income tax and substitute a straight *consumption* tax—not a sales tax, because that's levied at the source of sale. A sales tax or value added tax is usually a flat tax, which is not necessarily a good idea—because it's not progressive. There is a good socioeconomic logic in having progressive taxes.

     What he wants people to do on April 15 is simply to calculate how much they have *spent* and to pay a tax on that amount. And if they *haven't spent* their income, *it is not taxed;* it's used for investment purposes. *It's only when you spend your money that you pay your tax.* The key is that it doesn't penalize those who might use the money for savings and for investment. Currently we make no distinction on April 15 between those who save their money and those who spend it. At the same time, we may need to enact a wealth tax—especially on large, unearned, inherited incomes.

Dowling: Would it be similar to the wealth tax that Great Britain has recently enacted—an annual levy on capital?

Bell: No, it would be more similar to the estate tax that we have now in the United States. The principal point is that 85 percent of all people today are wage-and-salary employees, and it's difficult with this income alone to build up sizable amounts of savings. We're far from the situation where in 1940 25 percent of the males were self-employed—independent farmers, businessmen, lawyers, doctors, and so on. Anyone who lives entirely on income is unable to build much of a stake relative to those who live on capital gains. Now I'm not even saying that we ought to tax capital gains, because there is a certain virtue in using capital for other purposes. We need something such as death duties above certain levels—but more important, we neeα to shift the burden of taxation from income to wealth. What I'd like to do is to combine Feldstein's idea with this idea. If you have an income during the year of $30,000, and you've spent only $15,000, you pay a tax only on that $15,000. If you have saved the other $15,000 and invested it, fine. Then you pay a tax on the money only when you spend it. At the same time, in terms of death duties you increase the amount of taxes above a certain level—say, a million dollars.

I'm trying to establish the principle that the people who are most unfairly-taxed in this country are the middle managerial groups. In relation to their responsibilities, the time they put in, and the income that they get, they are taxed more heavily than any other group in society. And that makes no sense because they are the people who have the responsibility for production and services. It seems to me better logic to enhance their income and, at the same time, allow them to save larger portions of their income. If you abolish income tax, substitute consumption tax, and at the same time have a tax that prevents the extreme forms of accumulation, you'd do better from the standpoint of justice, equity, and efficiency.

Dowling: This wealth tax would be collected as an estate tax is collected?

Bell: In a country like England, where so much of the wealth is essentially land, it may well be that the wealth (land) tax might be dysfunctional, because you're forcing people to break up large areas of land and ruining the countryside by forcing development. In some ways the same thing is true here in such areas as New Hampshire or Vermont, where agricultural land is reassessed as recreational land. In consequence, people with equities have to cut up the land and sell it off in small lots—and some lovely vistas are absolutely destroyed.

Dowling: There's also President Ford's proposal to increase the estate-tax exemption on farms.

Bell: I accept it. It makes sense because it means we want to maintain the family farm by counteracting inflation—because higher assessments push people into the market and force them to break with their farms.

Dowling: In *The Post-Industrial Society*, you pointed out that because of the decline of the family, the decline of the church, and the decline of the small community, the corporation is an important mechanism for providing social support and a sense of security—in general making life more meaningful.

You added that the corporation's margin for social experiment was declining. I am wondering whether you feel that the corporation is less able to respond to such new demands as the thrust for job enrichment or other efforts to improve the quality of working life.

Bell: I'm not so sure that the margin is declining. Having been the director of a small company, I know what you can do through LIFO or FIFO with profit margins. They are pretty elastic. But let's agree in principle that margins are declining. Let me make two points. First, I don't think that the real issue is essentially things like job enrichment or job enlargement. They may or may not work and I think in many cases they don't for a whole lot of reasons—one of the important ones being that workers don't like them because they are imposed on the workers. I think there is a broader principle at stake here—the degree of autonomy you give people to do things they have to do on their jobs. Giving such autonomy is much more difficult, of course, at the production level and correspondingly easier at the managerial level.

Second, I was enormously impressed many years ago by a book by the British industrial psychoanalyst Elliot Jaques, called *Equitable Pay-Payments*. He worked with Glacier Metal, a rather extraordinary firm in England, and he came up with the principle that what a man earns should be based on the time that elapses before his decisions are reviewed. I think if we look ahead to the future, one of the major issues—and not only within the corporation—is going to be the whole question of pay differentials. It's more and more difficult to apply market principles—that is, to differentiate among jobs on the basis of individual differences—to jobs that are fundamentally coordinating jobs or jobs that depend on interrelationships. One can say that Barbara Walters may or may not be worth a million dollars a year for five years. That's a market principle based upon her scarcity and upon the fact that she may run out of steam in five years. That's a special situation. But with jobs that are customarily found in a big corporation, the real issue can be one of differentials. If we take an industrial corporation and look at the spread between the common labor rate and what the top man makes, what would it be, roughly? In U.S. Steel, would it be roughly 40 to 1?

Dowling: I was going to guess 25 to 1.

Bell: Well, I'm assuming $5,000 as the common labor rate.

Dowling: In this day and age, that strikes me as low.

Bell: All right, let's say $200,000 to $8,000—25 to 1. In a hospital, the rate between a doctor and an attendant is not 25 to 1. In a government bureau it's not 25 to 1. In a university it's not 25 to 1. What is the rationale for 25 to 1 in a corporation? Well, it might be responsibility in terms of the volume of money handled. But that's not a very satisfactory way of measuring responsibility. It's not clear, really, that you have a direct relationship between the fiduciary responsibility and the amount of money handled. Let's forget such people as Mr. Murphy at G.M., who may get a $500,000 bonus. But take a vice-president at roughly $100,000 to $150,000 a year. Compare this figure with the common labor rate, and there is a real problem in justifying this exact differential. The market principle, more and more, doesn't apply. These are differences that have arisen because of vague historical circumstances that have become more or less formalized and that are more and more coming into question. Any personnel-manager knows that the rate between workers doing similar jobs can be the thorniest problem in a plant. The most serious complaint in the workers' vocabulary is, "That's unfair."

Dowling: The worker's sense of equity is offended.

Bell: The real problem of the future is to come up with generally accepted standards of fairness. What is fairness? What I'm suggesting is something like an equitable payment that deals with the elapsed time in which you have to do a job before you have to report to somebody. . . .

Dowling: Or before what you've done is reviewed.

Bell: This gives you a measure of differential responsibility. And it seems a better, fairer, more imaginative base for establishing pay differentials. Now, that's what I mean by the socializing of the corporation: not job enrichment or job enlargement, but a sense among people within the corporation that they're being treated fairly, that their pay situation is fair and equitable. And I'm not thinking primarily of the trade union constituency, but of the management group as a whole and what they feel about the equity of payments to the people at the top.

Dowling: In *The Post-Industrial Society*, you seem to be saying that within the public sector, controls are going to be increasingly centralized. In *The Cultural Contradictions of Capitalism*, on the other hand, you seem to say that it is necessary and important to avoid, I think you used the phrase, "bureaucratic overload." You also pointed out that we had thousands of governmental units at the bottom level and that most of them could not cope with their problems. On the other hand, many of these problems are not best handled at the federal level, either.

Bell: It is true that *The Cultural Contradictions of Capitalism* came out two and a half years after the first one. But they were written simultaneously, only not published at the same time. What is common to both books is an emphasis on the fact that in a complex, interdependent society, you're going to have more and more communal regulation. And the problem is how to control it. You have federal regulation for one fundamental reason. It has nothing to do with socialism or capitalism, which is why I get irritated by people who convert these issues into ideological tags. You get more regulation at the federal level simply because problems of a national scale require correspondingly broader control. If you look back historically at the New Deal, the New Deal was not, by introducing federal regulations, eroding capitalism or increasing socialism. There were national markets and national corporations, but until then economic policies were in the hands of the states. What we had was a redefinition of federal power to match the broader-scale problems of a more complex society.

In the same way, we now have a national society because of revolutions in communications and transportation, so that questions of welfare, health, and education have to be met on a national scale. The question is, how do you do it? Here, my argument is twofold. First, you inevitably need national standards and national funding. Otherwise, you face the situation you have in New York City today—where New York City pays something like $159.00 per capita on welfare, in comparison with Chicago's $34.00 per capita. It's true that New York was mismanaged in many respects. I don't apologize for the contracts with some of the unions—with the boondoggling, low productivity, and so on. But after admitting all that, the fact remains that New York is bearing a large part of the fiscal burdens of the rest of society—and that's immoral. These things need national funding, and they need national standards. You need national standards so that the whole country doesn't tip itself and flow into New York, so that New York doesn't get an overflow of people from, say, Mississippi.

The real question, then, is how do we combine national spending and national funding with *decentralized* administration? Here, it seems to me, there are two different problems. One of the things I have said—and this goes back to the Commission on the Year 2,000, the enterprise in which we predicted the blight of the cities (you'd have to be blind not to have foreseen it)—was that any society had to maintain simple services: collect garbage, deliver mail, provide security. These are questions of *administration*. Administration is a dull subject, but it is a necessary component of understanding how society operates.

In the United States today, we have a dynamic economy, flexible and responsive at least to private wants in the marketplace. But we also have what my colleague Sam Huntington calls a Tudor Polity. We have thousands of sheriffs (though not Sherwood Forest). We have 3,000 counties in the Midwest so laid out that anyone can go from any part of the county to the county seat in one day by horse and buggy—that is the limit of the county size. We have in the New York metropolitan area 1,400 local governments, water districts, parks districts, health districts, and so on; incorporated townships, unincorporated townships, and so on. This isn't decentralization—this is disarray, chaos.

What I'm saying is that we need some effective principle of the necessary unit of government to be responsive to what people want. I would, in principle, try to do as much as possible at the local level of government. But, in a curious way, you have to centralize policy in order to decentralize administration. Any large firm does that. You can't tell me that ITT is run on the basis of decentralized policy.

Dowling: No, nor General Motors or any other successful large corporation, for that matter.

Bell: It's run on highly centralized policies and decentralized operations. The same principle operates in government. I don't see how you can escape a degree of national standards and national funding, and still hope for effective decentralized operations.

There is one more point to this long litany. I think business does itself a disservice, as do we liberals, in looking at a problem in terms of government versus the market. If liberals see something wrong, they say,

"Let the government step in and run it and regulate it." Or, if something goes awry, businessmen say, "Let the market take care of it." I do believe that the market is the most efficient mechanism we have for dealing with most problems: The market is impersonal, and individuals have to discipline themselves in the face of impersonal rules. But as a mechanism, the market can be used just as effectively for social purposes as it can for purposes of individual enterprises—so that if you have pollution, you can have effluent charges determined on market principles. If you need to have rationing, you can do it through market principles and have rebates to compensate for any sizable injustices rather than through coupons and a heavy-handed regulation system. This is government determining social purposes, but using marketing mechanisms to do the job.

Dowling: Another distinction that I thought occurred between the two books was in your discussion of leadership. I got the impression in reading *The Post-Industrial Society* that you were anticipating a meritocracy dominated by technocrats. You had a statement to the effect that the decisions were so interrelated that they were necessarily technical in nature. To reverse Walter Lippman, the expert was going to be on top rather than on tap. But I didn't get the same impression in *The Cultural Contradictions of Capitalism*. There, I felt you were saying that moral issues were crucial to the future survival of society, and therefore our prime need was for leaders who embodied moral standards, who could help to forge a moral consensus.

Bell: There are two elements in my position. When it comes to positions of authority, it's ridiculous to have positions based either on rotation or on quotas. Those who have earned their authority through their competence deserve to be on top. If a society doesn't have its best people on top, woe to that society. Therefore, meritocracy is a principle that applies to all positions—not just to technical positions, but to political positions, artistic positions, and so on.

About the key role of *technical* expertise. Technical components make a problem more and more complicated, but this doesn't mean that the technical person will make the decision. I say quite explicitly in a chapter called "Who Will Rule?" that a technical person can *initiate* decisions, but only the politicians can say "Yes" or "No." In other words, there is a new relationship in which pointing to a problem, defining a problem, and bringing it up for attention become more and more the province of the economist, the engineer, and so on.

Dowling: In other words, the experts define the premises of the situation.

Bell: The expert defines it, or spells out some of the implications. But by the very nature of things, since he has no constituency, he can't say "Yes" or "No." He has influence, but not power. I would be a fool to assume that an expert would ever rule in any society. The political systems clearly control, because the political system, in effect, deals with people who have interests and try to express them in and through their representatives. A politician, you see, is something a technocrat is not. A politician is a manager of discontent. And therefore, he's got to satisfy—even when it may mean modifying what would be a technically useful decision.

Dowling: Can you think of an example?

Bell: The decision to build nuclear power plants or not will not be made primarily on the basis of technical considerations but on the basis of mitigating the fears of environmental groups and others who raise problems about nuclear power. Or one can say that, in efficient terms, if you want to build a road between points A and B in terms of the least cost, you draw a straight line. But for political reasons, because there is a very powerful constituency either in the ghetto or among the very rich, the road won't follow that route. Political factors are going to be overriding considerations in the final decision.

Dowling: The other point you make in both books equally strongly is that our society suffers from a lack of, or having no normative commitment to, a moral consensus—or, as you put it at one point, there is no public philosophy that would mediate private conflicts.

Bell: There are contradictions between an economy geared to efficiency, a culture geared to self-gratification, and a polity geared to equality. These are structural incongruities that are very difficult to override. But I would make a further distinction. To some extent, there *is* a moral consensus because this country, more than any other country, still has a sense of the "rules of the game." We have a Constitution and we abide by it. And that is a moral consensus. You may say, "Well, is this really very much?" My answer is "Yes." I don't predict—but in 1960, when I was doing forecasting studies, somebody said to me, "Give me a prediction." My reply was that in 1964, we'll have an election for president of the United States, and in 1968 and 1972 and 1976 and 1980, there will be elections for presidents of the United States. Now, if you look at 150 countries in the world, in about how many of them can you make that prediction? Can you take Portugal, Spain, Italy, or even France?

Dowling: I was going to cite France as an exception.

Bell: But look at France. Less than a decade and a half ago, you had a French army in Algeria threatening to send paratroopers on to Paris and overthrow the French government until De Gaulle stepped in and stopped them. So France could have been ripped apart. In this country there is a deep stability, which is part of any moral consensus.

Yet there is still something much more difficult and more diffuse about the moral problems in America. There is a lack of transcendental conception—of any sets of purposes outside ourselves or our immediate lives that would allow us to make sacrifices. Is there anything that we regard as basic in our society that serves to give our people a sense of relatedness or a sense of something sacred? Many years ago, you may recall, there was a movie with Carole Lombard entitled "Nothing Sacred." And if there is nothing sacred, anything goes. That's pretty much our moral state.

Dowling: Do you see any hope for future improvement?

Bell: For the economic and political process—in the near future—yes. There we can design and manage different programs. But culture is something different. These are long-range processes and cultural processes not subject to social engineering. You can't simply design a program that by spending money builds cultural institutions. All that may be necessary, but a cultural revivification is derived from the sense that your leaders are acting in a trustful way and that there is a moral purpose to what they do. That comes strongly from a leadership that has that sense of transcendence. And I don't see any among our leaders today.

Conversation with
WARREN BENNIS

Warren Bennis has lived two professional lives as a distinguished thinker and writer on behavorial science, with his professional base at M.I.T. and, from 1967 on, as an academic administrator, first at the University of Buffalo and later for six years as president of the University of Cincinnati.

As a theorist, he achieved fame as the father of what he dubbed "organic populism," a view of organized society in which the key words were smallness, temporariness, and participation. He wrote about rapidly changing organizations that were made up of temporary groups, temporary authority systems, temporary leadership and role assignments, and democratic access to the goals of the firm. If rapidly changing technologies and unstable, turbulent environments were to characterize corporate organizations, so Bennis argued, then the structure of firms should be temporary and decentralized.

Participation in the decision-making process he viewed as a functional necessity. In a time of complexity and chronic change, society could not afford to lose the contribution of anyone with competence to participate in the decision-making process.

But all this was before Bennis left the security of his M.I.T. professorship to go where the action is and test out his theories of organizational change and growth. As he wrote in *The Leaning Ivory Tower:* "All of my academic life and long before that, I have been intellectually preoccupied, virtually obsessed, with this dilemma, with the problem of practical intelligence, with the theory of practice, with the relationship between men who make history and the men who write it." It was inevita-

Reprinted from Organizational Dynamics, *Winter 1974*

ble that he himself should become one of the men who embody and reconcile this dualism.

What impact have his years as an administrator had on Bennis's thinking? Clearly, he is no longer a member in good standing of what Charles Perrow calls the "Buck Rogers school of organizational theory." In his efforts to match theory to practice, to play "a tune upon the blue guitar of things exactly as they are," his ideas have undergone a heap of changing.

Exactly how they have changed we will leave to Bennis, except for one brief observation. As we talked with him we were reminded of what Joseph Conrad said to H. G. Wells: "The difference between us, Wells, is fundamental. You don't care for humanity but think they are to be improved. I love humanity but know they are not." Bennis began with the love of Conrad and the optimism of Wells. We suspect that he retains the love but has shed most of the optimism.

Dowling: Dr. Bennis, several years ago you wrote frequently about the fact that bureaucracy was on the way out, that democracy was inevitable, and that over a period of time—the time scale wasn't too clear—bureaucracy was going to wither away, to be replaced by temporary systems made up of diverse teams of specialists. Now, if I read you correctly, you've undergone a complete change of heart. You feel that bureaucracy is the inevitable form of organization in a large-scale enterprise, be it public or private.

Bennis: Yes, I think that's true. I began changing my mind about the democratic tendencies because the original hypothesis was so sweeping that it wouldn't have validity for every kind of situation. In fact, when I first wrote about the demise of bureaucracy I did talk about certain conditions that had to obtain if bureaucracy was to disappear, although critics never understood them fully, because they were easy to overlook. Actually, it's very difficult to do too much damage to the hypothesis for one reason: The time scale was between 25 to 50 years, which is kind of laughable, because it doesn't leave too many people around to see whether it's going to be true or not.

Dowling: I came across a speech that you delivered in India in which you hedged on the time factor. You talked about the tremendous intellectual commitment to democratic ideas but you didn't spell out how long it would take for those ideas to predominate in practice. You avoided suggesting that the future was around the corner.

Bennis: There's another, more important thing than just the hedging on the time because of my own uncertainty. I first presented the temporary-systems paper in 1964 at the annual meeting of the American Psychological Association. Five years later, in another invited address before the same association entitled "A Funny Thing Happened on the Way to the Future," I did start criticizing and reevaluating that original temporary-systems, democracy-is-inevitable hypothesis. The important thing to recognize is that there are two broad views of how the future is going to look.

If you take, let's say, Daniel Bell's hypothesis about the postindustrial society dominated by a technocratic structure of people with advanced degrees in science, engineering, and management—a world view that implies that the capitalistic, production-oriented society simply gets bigger, but with more and more of a science basis to it—if you take everything that existed in 1965 and simply extrapolate it exponentially or however one does to the year 2000, I think that my original notions are still correct. There are two things, however, that blocked the view, that I couldn't see at the time and that I think Daniel Bell and most of the futurists with the technocratic, depression-based mentality don't see today. I would put Bell, Herman Kahn, De Jouvenel in France, Alvin Toffler, and Ken Boulding all in the same boat as futurists whose cosmology and perspectives were born out of the Keynesian economics of the Roosevelt era.

What was wrong with that view—which I shared with them—was two phenomena that it overlooked. One was the then-recessive but very visible and disruptive antitechnological bias of the young that was partly demonstrated in the free-speech movement starting in Berkeley and spreading out through all the campuses—the cry that people ought to have decision-making power over the pace of their lives, the idea of participating individualism, of a kind of return to nature. None of these currents that are now classified as a counter-culture, as liberation movements and so on, were ever taken into account, and they still have not been taken into account in the postindustrial society. To give you one example, there is an enormous tension between the technocratic, Galbraithian, "expert" idea of progress and the "new populism" as expressed by, say, McGovern. It is now being exemplified in Cincinnati, in a charter amendment to the city government to give over control of our general hospital, which is now managed by the physicians and medical hierarchy of the University of Cincinnati, to a 15-person board, nine of whom would be elected by the people. Here you have a beautiful demonstration of what I'm saying.

Dowling: Are there similar moves under way to establish popular control over hospitals in other cities?

Bennis: I think that in your own city of New York there's a board selected by the mayor to represent a variety of constituent groups, so that the board is not exclusively an *expert* board, but a *political* board. The point I'm making is that the postindustrial society assumes rather wistfully and wishfully something all of us would like—that philosophers should be kings, that scientists, technologists, management experts—the so-called technostructure—will take over the world because of their brains.

The fact is that there were two very big considerations that none of us took into account seriously enough back in 1964, when I wrote that paper. One was the emergence of the so-called counter-culture, with its emphasis on self-realization rather than achievement, on instant gratification rather than the work ethic. The other, and more important, factor that was almost entirely overlooked, at least in the original essays by Bell, Kahn, and the rest, was the meaning and importance of the public sector, the nonproductive part of our society.

Dowling: Would it be accurate to refer to it as the service sector?

Bennis: No, service is a broad word—service could mean McDonald's or Midas Muffler shops, both of which are highly productive. It's important to put this as precisely as we can. There are two kinds of institutions. On the one hand, there are institutions that have a reasonable chance of raising their productivity on a regular basis, say annually. They can produce *more* for less expenditures, or sell more than they did before by effecting economies or by applying inventions. Most of our large corporations—GM, Union Carbide, and the rest—operate that way. Then there are a host of other institutions that have been ignored by most of the economic game plans we've seen in the last several years, institutions that are incapable of having any significant rise in productivity. I would include such organizations as universities, hospitals, welfare agencies, local and state government, some service areas, and all cultural activities—museums, symphony orchestras, ballet companies, and so on.

These public-sector institutions are for the most part very badly managed. I'm making no excuse for them except that I don't think it's been sufficiently recognized that they are not productive and cannot be run exactly like large and efficient productive industries.

Dowling: That's true, but still it should be possible to improve their operations by adapting some of the techniques used in the large business-for-profit organization.

Bennis: One of the big psuedo-solutions is that you can make these institutions more businesslike. Of course, that's not a new conception. Peter Drucker and others have been talking about this for some time. And back in Louis XIV's France, Colbert, who, I guess, is the first villain that we know of along these lines, kept attacking the French bureaucracies—the nonbusiness side—for not being businesslike enough. He instituted a set of practices to rationalize and train civil servants to be efficient and to run those places in a businesslike way. That probably explains why the French bureaucracy is one of the worst in the world and has been the most tormented, difficult, and stodgy—full of dry rot. Ours aren't much better.

There are a lot of principles of management that one can use in a public bureaucracy but you can never effect large-scale economies given the conditions there. Of course, you can cut costs, but not enough to keep up with the inflationary spiral, which is higher in these public-sector areas because the annual rate of inflation is higher there—it's 13 percent in libraries, for example, and 12½ percent in universities.

To get back to the original question, the most important consideration that I didn't take into account is the fact that our greatest employment growth area would be in the public sector and these organizations don't lend themselves to democracy—to management by consensus—first, because of their size, and second, because of the divergent interests of the individuals who make up the organizations. I was visiting Haverford College yesterday, which has 720 students, and there's an enormously important conflict going on at this marvelous Quaker college about whether it should expand to a thousand students. The people there still, in fact, pretty much govern that campus on the principle of consensus through Quaker-style meetings. However, in a place the size of the University of Cincinnati, with 37,000 students, consensus is totally impossible given the mosaic of individuals who come there, the diversity, the balkanization of interests. In fact, in almost all institutions we're at the end of the consensus period—if we were ever in one at all.

Maybe consensus is a kind of folk dream. We're witnessing the finale of the kind of liberal leader—liberal in a broad, nonpolitical sense—who could negotiate differences and arrange compromises. If you look at some of the great liberal university presidents of the past and their methods, you realize that they just could not cope with today's problems. You cannot shave an inch off the hair of a black person's Afro and hope to make the basketball coach under whom he plays be nicer to him or less racist. We no longer have communal values, which are what make consensus and negotiation possible in the first place.

Dowling: I remember a quote from Lord Balfour explaining the success of the British Commonwealth—"We can afford to disagree because fundamentally we're at one." He was talking about consensus and, of course, the statement no longer holds.

Bennis: Yes, and that's what we're very wistful and nostalgic for. Look at the English constitution—there is none, at least in a formal sense, because there was no need for one in a communal setting. The conditions under which I specified the end of bureaucracy and the democracy-as-inevitable thesis were those of the postindustrial society in which you had intelligent people working on solvable problems through technical solutions. One of the interesting things about postindustrial society is that it assumes that the problems society faces have an elegant, or if not elegant, at least a sound technical solution. By contrast, the problems we're dealing with now that cause us the greatest concern, even though they may have in part a technical solution, are primarily political, economic, and cultural. You cannot, for example, do anything about cleaning up Lake Erie unless you get the city, state, metropolitan, and the Canadian governments to all cooperate in solving the problem. And so far they haven't been able to come together politically, for a lot of reasons.

Dowling: Certainly, the chances of getting the technically ideal solution adopted are severely restricted by political and cultural factors.

Bennis: The postindustrial society syndrome, paradigm, model, perspective—call it what you will—was heavily influenced by extraordinary achievements made in American science and technology—achievements that I think will continue. At this point, the only distinctive competence or comparative advantage of the American economy has to be its research and development. It can be outproduced by the Germans and

Japanese; the promotion, marketing, and advertising techniques now used in western Europe are almost up to ours; while in the design field the Japanese and the Italians are both superior. That's why I think it is serious that the Department of Defense has a reduced research budget—primarily due to the campus uprisings. People fail to recognize that much of that research money was spent for health purposes, for civil purposes, and for purposes of peace. Now it's being shortshrifted, and I think our R&D capacity may be winding down relative to that of other countries. That is a very unfortunate development.

Dowling: You're saying that your temporary-system model, or vision, of society is being achieved today in very limited sectors of our society— in the R&D labs and in industries with very advanced technology, such as aerospace.

Bennis: Yes, it was happening there when I wrote about it and it's happening there even more now. I'm not trying to hold on to a hypothesis that is demonstrably false. In all fairness—and I think I'm very critical— temporary systems exist even more intensely now in limited sectors of society. It's like that Chinese aphorism: "It's very difficult to prophesy, especially about the future." A lot of things happened that reasonable men would not have foreseen to restrict the application of temporary systems. Even so, temporary systems have their role, even in large bureaucracies like the one I head up. I recently set up a temporary system that accomplished something very significant. A team of eight people within six weeks increased the number of students by 1,320—this in a period of general shrinkage in college enrollments.

Dowling: What was the task?

Bennis: The task was to create—it sounds very simple but it's not—a promotional program to bring in part-time students to the university. It consisted of three elements. First, we had three rather extraordinary booths that could be transported by truck to various parts of the city. They moved practically every day—to the GE plant, to the Procter & Gamble plant, and to various shopping malls. One major location was in Fountain Square, a popular gathering place in the heart of the city. Second, there was one-stop registration—a place on campus with free parking and with counselors available. Third, we had a dial-a-class program so that, for most classes, you could simply phone in and get registered for a part-time class.

It sounds very easy—just set up four more phones. But what we had to do was train individuals in every one of our 19 collegiate units and 13 departments to deal with the kinds of questions that the people manning the switchboard couldn't handle. In the space of about a month—it took two weeks to set this up—we were able to bring in 1,320 students, 75 percent of whom had never taken a part-time course before. My guess is that we've also tapped wholly new populations, not just minority groups and the disadvantaged, but the very rich and the very well established, among them the women from Indian Hill, the fanciest suburb, graduates of Smith and Radcliffe, who never wanted to drive to the campus and wait in line. I was surprised to learn how intimidated people are, not by the lines, but by going back to school, even if they've been out just three or four years. They get very edgy about it and we made it very simple. So there's one illustration of a temporary system's working in a large bureaucracy.

Dowling: Is this the first time you've done something like this?

Bennis: No, I did it before in Buffalo, in a wholly different setting. So the temporary system has its place, but it's not going to occupy a paramount or pervasive position. There will always be a bureaucracy; the sun will never set on bureaucracies.

Dowling: You made a very interesting comment about how you felt that in a large, bureaucratic service organization like the University of Cincinnati, organization development really didn't work. As I recall, one of the reasons it didn't work was that most of the people you dealt with, with the exception of your key administrative staff, you dealt with as representatives of a subsystem; you didn't deal with them as persons. I wondered whether there isn't a corporate analogy. In other words, corporate top management, with the exception, again, of its immediate staff, deals with the director of R&D, the head of personnel, the head of manufacturing, the head of marketing not as persons but in their roles as representatives of a subsystem. I should think that the problem might be similar.

Bennis: Yes, but there's still another problem. Are you talking about the article in the *Journal of Higher Education*, "An O.D. Expert in the Cat Bird's Seat"?

Dowling: Yes, that's the piece I had in mind.

Bennis: You probably remember the epilogue. I'm trying OD anyway. The contradictions that flow from my behavior at Buffalo and Cincinnati work both ways. Sometimes I say something won't work and I'll try it; sometimes I say this is going to happen and I won't try it. Unfortunately, my need to clarify my own mind at various times is based really less on theory than on experience. So, in a way I'm at best a walking tester of hypotheses; at worst, someone who can be seen as not quite ever realizing what it is he writes about. I think I'll always be vunerable to that kind of criticism.

I think it is a criticism, incidentally, that I'm becoming proud of, because there's nothing more important than people in positions of leadership trying to make clear what it is they're up to in the way of leadership, or perspective about institutions. It is important to make clear that if experience changes, you get more data that show this isn't the way to go, that you can make adjustments. It's upsetting to some people who, at times, wonder why what you're doing now isn't like the article you wrote back in 1968, and they'll say you're being hypocritical or incongruent. I think, with a terrible trace of immodesty, that my ideas will always be ahead of my practice, partly because it's easier to have ideas than it is to change institutions. I have written articles in two or three days; their applications can take up to two or three years.

To get back to your question, yes, as president of a large institution you deal as much with a role as with a person. As an example, the student body president of my university this year is, I think, an outstanding leader and, in my view, will do something with the student body that I don't think has been done on many campuses. He's taking a political advocacy model, not an adversary model. When he and his vice-president see me, they're very much on guard, not because I'm not a nice guy— although if I weren't president I think they would have an easy time relating to me on an interpersonal level. But the fact that I am president creates a double referent. I like this young man, yet I don't try to show that too much, because I don't want to make him feel that I'm trying to co-opt him. So we deal with each other not in an overly formal way, but in a very businesslike way—not especially collaborative, but with just enough comity to preserve a working relationship. Because he and I, although we share a lot of educational goals and a lot of other kinds of goals, and though we may as our relationship matures even develop coalition of one kind or another, do not have a relationship of trust. Our relationship is not and perhaps should not resemble the kind of *Gemeinschaft*, the warm wine of community, that the OD team-building exercises develop. However, within my own top administrative team, yes, that is what I'm always striving for and what to a large extent has been achieved.

There are some who would argue with this; they would say, "For God's sake, why don't you do a team-building exercise with the head of the faculty senate, with the head of the university senate, with the head of the student senate, and really develop more trust, more collaboration?" Well, we could try, but I think that would be compromising their positions. The collaborative mode is very agreeable to me; however, this sentiment these days isn't widely shared. I think it would be a mistake to even attempt to approximate such a model with groups that have constituent interests to protect. We're living in a time of politics and roles and of subgroups within subsystems. This is the mistake that President Nixon makes. He claims that his *relationship* with Brezhnev is what has led to this détente. That's nonsense. It isn't true of him; it isn't true of Brezhnev.

Dowling: He's persuaded himself, irrespective of the evidence.

Bennis: Hell, no, it isn't true, because it will only be a détente based on a political model of advocacy that is, I think, much more à la mode than the Americans' wistful dream of community and collaboration. That shouldn't sound cynical, because I think there's a difference between realism and cynicism.

Dowling: Then you agree than an analogy exists between the difficulty of achieving the OD model in a public bureaucracy and a large corporation because of the fact that many of the people that the chief executive and his staff deal with really represent diverse interests in the organization, different perspectives, with different emphases, and different values.

Bennis: That's exactly right and I'm glad you said it. We are talking about the interests of groups within organizations. I talked about the balkanization of an institution. Even the notion of hierarchy is a little out of date when you think about a place like the University of Cincinnati, which is not that unusual. We have 63 or 64 important interest groups within that one university that have nothing to do with the hierarchy, but how do we handle this in organizational theory? I wish the word "caucusinization" were easier to pronounce; there ought to be a better word. At any rate, we have a whole set of new groups, some based on demographic factors such as ethnic origins, racial origins, religious origins, sex origins, and, on the other hand, some based on issue factors.

If you compare the faculty council on Jewish affairs with, say, the United Black Faculty Association, they're both interest groups but they're not in the same situation. The black faculty association pressures for more blacks on campus, while the council on Jewish affairs doesn't advocate more Jews, either as students or faculty. Ironically, 20 years ago there should have been such a council, because on some campuses there were restrictions and quotas. They're quite different subgroups, but where do we treat those systems within existing organizational theories? We still draw those neat boxes and talk about hierarchies. Good lord, we even have these new, what I call *arabissmo* groups. *Arabissmo* is a Peruvian word meaning the unbridled desire to rise—it applies to people who have felt out of it, not beyond the melting pot, but behind it. And they're trying to do not what I was brought up to do, that is, work hard, keep your mouth shut, and join the mainstream. These people are not going to keep their mouths shut; they may work hard, but they want to maintain their identity, not become part of some pabulum-like dream of whatever it was that we were all dreaming about in America.

Well, these groups are a terribly significant part of my life. And all public-sector institutions have similar groups. They're not bowling groups, and you can't think compromise and talk consensus in dealing with them.

Dowling: Just how do you relate to these groups and get the business of the university done when you can't think compromise and talk consensus? It would appear to be an uphill fight all the way.

Bennis: The greatest problem facing institutions right now is not so much the internal politics, bureaucracy, supervision, and so on. Instead, it's the concatenation of external forces that are impinging and imposing on the corporate or public-sector institution—that is, events outside the skin boundary of an organization. Fifty years ago this external environment was fairly placid, like an ocean on a calm day, forecastable, predictable, regular, not terribly eventful. Now that ocean is turbulent and highly interdependent and pivotal. So the key people in my institution right now—the key people for me to reckon with—are, for example, not only the vice-president, my own management group, the faculty, or the students, although God knows they're important. Many of the "key people" are external to the university: the city manager, city council members, the governor, the state legislature, the general assembly, the federal government (the Office of Education), alumni, and parents. There is an incessant community of voices out there. And because the university is a brilliant example of an institution that has blunted and diffused its main purposes, and through a proliferation of dependencies on external groups in terms of sources of financing, contracts, and everything else, its autonomy has declined to the point where our boundary system is like Swiss cheese. All of which means that if you're really going to do OD, many of the key players are *out there* and not within your own organization. I can build the greatest management team in the world, but our relationship with the city manager and the governor and the legislature may be far more important than whether or not I have a good team-building exercise going with my own subordinates. Relations with these outside forces take, I should say, about 80 percent of my time.

What I'm saying is that this environment is causal, turbulent, hard to predict; it interacts with the inside. And quite often what the external environment is pressuring us to do and what the internal audience or constituents want to do or feel right about doing are absolutely and totally divergent.

This last year, for example, we had about 8,000 candidates apply for medical school. We're allowed to take in about 120; that's all we can accommodate. In effect, we are making economic decisions for all 8,000, because we're telling those who can't get in—that's most of them—that they're not going to be assured of getting the M.D. that is going to make them secure economically, and we're telling 120 you're rich or will be. What happens when you start dealing with numbers of that magnitude? The state legislators get in the act, and they say, "Let's look at how many students U.C.'s medical school is taking. What percentage of them are Ohio residents?" We're not fully state supported, but we get some state support. "How many of them are Cincinnati residents?" asked a city councilman. "Why in the world should the city be paying the University of Cincinnati any money for its medical school if they just take in—what is the figure?—40 percent of the total from the city of Cincinnati?" Regents get into the act, too; then they start calling the shots for admission.

Dowling: Certainly, they'll try to exert pressure.

Bennis: It's more than pressure. It may be pressure, it may be legislation, or it may be the board of regents' handing down some policy. One effect, as I said before, is that my key figures may be out there, so whom am I doing OD with? Also, it makes the organization a great deal more hierarchical and centralized, because it is the president, and the president alone, whom the outsiders insist on dealing with. The overload is incredible. You may recall my *Saturday Review* piece where I talked about the leadership-management problem, about everybody's wanting to drop their wet babies on your desk and all that.

Dowling: Yes, and I remember that your solution was to attempt to have individual members of your staff develop expertise in specific areas so that they could handle the wet babies.

Bennis: Right, but it's hard for me to send a delegate or surrogate to talk to the mayor. So, just as in our national government top administration increases its size and power when it deals with international affairs, when the outside environment takes on that much salience and significance you get the same thing. We're now dealing with foreign affairs a lot at the university.

Dowling: There would appear to be similar processes going on in the larger corporations with the same tendencies toward centralization because of the increasing importance of outside relations.

Bennis: Of course, and more and more all the time. I think it will have some extraordinarily damaging effects in the long run. In the universities and colleges and in many business firms the powerlessness that so many top executives and people in leadership positions are feeling is a powerlessness caused by being caught in a buzz saw between internal constituencies and external constituencies that make it almost impossible to act intelligently at times. Your discretionary freedom is being progressively nibbled away. And in the process it's removing the entrepreneurial bite and zeal and a kind of capacity for self-determination. I may sound like a nineteenth century Whig talking. I sympathize with J. Z. De Lorean, a V.P. of General Motors who just quit. There's a piece about it in today's *Times*.

Dowling: Why did he quit? I haven't read the article.

Bennis: Because he felt he wasted time in too many staff meetings. He said the last real president that GM had was a man who was at GM for five years named Harlow Curtice.

Dowling: I remember him. He was called Red Curtice, and I remember a profile in *Time* that detailed his 85-hour workweek.

Bennis: He was the last real chief executive, and I wouldn't be surprised if he's right. But then, De Lorean does the thing that so many times people in institutions do—they start putting their fingers on people to blame rather than comprehending the constraints people tried to cope with. What he doesn't realize—or, if he does he never talks about—is that some of the initiative has been sapped and some of the entrepreneurial zeal has lagged because of these environmental forces and pressures. It isn't that the presidents or executive group are less virile or masculine. (He talks about how GM has lost its masculinity. That's really nonsense. They're every bit as tough and masculine as they ever were.) The fact is, they have far fewer discretionary powers, and that's something De Lorean had better understand. I understand he's going to open up a Cadillac agency. He will have an easier time of it. He will not have the same kind of pressures that he would as a vice-president of GM.

Dowling: No, he'll have more discretion within a much smaller area. He'll really be in charge of the agency.

Bennis: That's right. I was telling someone recently that the man I most envy at Cincinnati is the fellow a-perch the power lawn mower. I really envy him because he seems to have more freedom than I do; he moves where he wants to, he makes fancy turns, and he's also a kind of interesting fellow. Maybe he knows I'm looking at him; anyway, he makes figure eights on some days. It's like a Thurber cartoon; he's just full of abandon. Now, I really think there are more areas of discretion for him than for myself and for most of the top leadership in our country. I'm not wringing my hands; I'm just trying to analyze the problem and transcend it, because it's really tough to move.

Dowling: The man making figure eights in the grass reminds me of the glassblower who had been turning out glass rabbits for years with the ears standing up. One day he turned out a whole series of rabbits with ears that drooped. His superior asked him why and he said he just thought he would try something different for a change.

There's another level of management problem that concerns you deeply—essentially, resolving with your own key staff members the conflict between authority and authenticity. You had a great quote from Sam

Goldwyn: "I want you to tell me what's wrong with your operation even if it costs you your job." How can you resolve that problem?

Bennis: Well, again I'm thinking, as you can tell, more and more of political models. I will preface my response to your question by saying that what OD people interested in institutional behavior have not tried to conceptualize at all or deal with is power and constituencies.

If you think about the Victorian era, Freud and right through Bloomsbury, the liberated crowd in England, it was a period in which sex was a dominant issue expressed clearly either in its suppression or its celebration. By now it's easier for people to talk about sex on talk shows than to talk about finances. Finances are the next thing that will come into the open, as we become more of a public-sector society. Power is the last of the little dirty secrets. People who have it don't want to talk about it; people who don't have it don't want to talk about it. You know there are books called *The Sensual Woman, The Sensual Man, The Sensual Couple*. When we start seeing books on the powerful man, the powerful woman, the powerful couple, we'll know that this problem is no longer tucked away. There will be an occasional article called "Power: A Neglected Variable," and it will tell how we haven't discussed power—period.

Dowling: One person who has written about it recently—the neglect of the subject, the tacit suppression of the discussion—is Bertram Gross.

Bennis: Now, let me get to that question. I have not succeeded yet, even with the people who work most closely with me, in being open. One area in which OD can really be significant within a microstructure or within a team is that of trying to induce conditions where people can develop enough trust so that they can be open and "confrontative" about issues. I put trust first, because in order to be open you've got to trust; in order to trust you've got to be open. If I want to develop a trust relationship, I will have to take a risk—toward openness, at times almost deliberately so. I have to take the initiative, because I'm in the position of authority.

Dowling: As president you have to be the model.

Bennis: Yes. I think it's tilted that way. I haven't licked the problem. I've been here a little over two years and there have been some very significant changes made in terms of openness. Still, it isn't all there yet and never will be.

Another very general point: More and more, I'm convinced that the kind of institutions we work in (especially public-sector ones where there's no possibility for increase in productivity) are information-processing systems. That means that in such institutions power is going to be based on information, not on property, which turns Marx on his head. Marx thought that power is a function of property. Berle and Means really destroyed that thesis back in 1929 with their book, which was not entitled *Power Without Property* but should have been. It was called *The Modern Corporation*, and in it they showed the divergence between management and property.

Dowling: The divorce between property and management.

Bennis: Right, the divorce between power and property. Power is based more and more now on information. Notice, for example, how the Watergate scandal was a uniquely American one. What were they all going after? Information. All of them were after information, whether it was breaking into Ellsberg's psychiatrist's office or tapping telephone lines. Think about a nice, simple English scandal. It usually includes some frail, thin lord like Lambton chasing after some succulent young lady.

Dowling: Only, in his case, two succulent ladies at once.

Bennis: Two or more. The plumbers and the like weren't out for the succulent lady or for the buck. Amazing. It was information they were after.

The basic problem in the large institutions we're talking about is for the top executive staff and especially for the president to get the truth. There was one poignant moment when Mitchell was being questioned on Watergate and was asked by Mr. Dash by what right he had kept important data or information from the President. Mitchell gave a very feeble answer, and it should have been feeble, because he had no right to withhold information. The basic problem of any president is to get the truth.

Now, the truth, given the complexity and diversity of the systems, is complex. So what you have to do with your group of assistants is to develop a system, a multiple-advocacy system, a multiple-communications system that ensures the frank communication of divergent views. We'll never achieve complete openness. But you can make openness more probable, first, by rotation of assistants and keeping people in posts for shorter time periods, and second, by providing them with security.

Dowling: You stress the importance of the independent base.

Bennis: Right. That was the problem with Haldeman and Ehrlichman; they had no political base to return to, whereas Laird, or Harlow—I'm not commenting on whether they're good assistants—they have a base. Harlow, for example, could return to Procter & Gamble.

I hire as assistants only faculty members, and I want to hire as many of them as I can with tenure, so they return to the faculty after their two-year stint.

Dowling: Sometimes they're referred to as terminal appointees.

Bennis: That's right. These are the necessary conditions for staff assistants. They should have employment security. They should be from the constituencies you want represented. No matter how good your vice-presidents or deans are, they have to give you a skewed or distorted view of reality. I don't mean they're dishonest; they just have to *represent* their particular constituencies and causes—act as advocates.

Dowling: How do you achieve this sort of rotating, independent base in a corporation?

Bennis: Let's take planners. I think planners are among the people with a possibility of telling the president the truth because they have a detached perspective in the organization. But I think they should stay on their jobs only two or three years and return to something else.

Dowling: If you had, say, a planning staff of eight and rotated them every couple of years you'd still maintain continuity.

Bennis: Right. With vice-presidents you're in a tougher position, because usually they do have constituencies, and I'm saying that the president should have men and women around him who do not represent constituencies. That's one way of getting the truth. Of course, you can do what Lyndon Johnson did when he used George Ball and, to a lesser extent, Bill Moyers as devil's advocates. When Bill Moyers came into a staff meeting, Johnson would say, "Here comes Mr. Stop-the-Bombing." This is really interesting as a technique, but basically it doesn't work. What you've got to have are multiple advocates. You know what happens to devil's advocates. You bring George Ball in, and he gives his spiel. . . .

Dowling: . . . and is altogether overwhelmed. Two hours of Rusk, McNamara, and Bundy followed by ten minutes of Ball. . . .

Bennis: Your guilt is absolved because you're being so open. The devil's advocate feels good because he's made his point of view known. And you continue doing what you've done all along. This is the process of domesticating dissent. That's one person, when actually, George Ball was representing many, many people within State, within even DOD, and within many government agencies. If he had a system by which he could have tapped the thoughts, opinions, attitudes, knowledge, information of the people maybe three levels below on occasion, that would have been important.

When Clark Clifford took over the Department of Defense in March of 1968, the first thing he decided was to hold weekly meetings with representatives of the key departments within DOD, but he did not meet with their heads. He met with the second or third in command. He was amazed at what he heard. He was using a system of multiple advocacy, of multiple information, of getting information from more than the customary sources of information.

How else do you get the truth? By asking people who have nothing to lose by telling you the truth. Who are they? Sometimes they're people from outside the organization. Why do we hire consultants? Although some of them don't tell you the truth, there is a greater possibility of their telling the truth because of their greater objectivity. They're also found in personnel offices and in many other staff jobs, and usually a couple of levels from the top. At a university do you know what one of the major sources of truth is? The students. What do they have to lose? Many times they can be much more forthright than a faculty member. I'm not saying they're always wiser. But they certainly. . . .

Dowling: They try to give it to you straight.

Bennis: They do. So the tragedy of what you see happening is something I have done myself as a vice-president and as a department head—to allow the boss to make mistakes even when I knew he was wrong, because I'd rather do that, somehow, than tell him the truth. Allowing the company to fail or the university not to do the right thing was easier than telling the boss. That is the human tragedy.

Dowling: You remind me that one of the reasons you felt that many worthwhile changes made in Buffalo didn't last was the failure to sufficiently involve either the faculty or the student body in participating in the changes.

Bennis: That's true. You know there's a difference between participatory democracy and consultation. Let me put it differently, because I still have the problem. I don't think it's just the University of Buffalo or Martin Meyerson, the president, and his cohorts, including me. One problem that I haven't learned how to solve yet—there are many others—is how to develop enough ownership in the ideas that I initiate. They're still my ideas. When people say, let's see what Bennis does, this infuriates me. Yet my big mistake is not developing conditions under which people feel ownership, and take initiative.

Of course, the president's got to provide perspective, he's got to articulate goals. Who else if not the president? And my personal concern is that I do have a sense of coming things. But quite often the president—paradoxically—a person selected to provide leadership finds himself immersed in trivia and paper shuffling and not doing what he knows he should be doing.

Dowling: In what you call Bennis's First Law of Academic Pseudodynamics? There you observe that the routine will always attempt to drive out the nonroutine and the important. Yet you're making strides in negating the Law.

Bennis: I'm still forced to spend a lot of time dealing with representatives of outside constituencies—tasks that theoretically I should be able to delegate. How do I or does any top executive make the most effective use of his time? That's a problem that OD can't help to solve. You have to negotiate a trade-off between trust, group development, and the achievement of tasks.

Dowling: You have said that except for your own immediate subordinates, consensus is chimerical—as appropriate to today's organizations as buggy whips are to GM. And consensus is the end product of trust and group development. That leaves us with the achievement of tasks.

Bennis: True. And for the achievement of tasks you need three things. First, assistants who are free to be outspoken, because they don't have the vulnerability that comes from being dependent on one man, and who are objective, but who, because they come from a constituency—the faculty, for example, also know what is feasible and possible in dealing with its problems. Second, you must avoid confining, and often worthless, meetings that ultimately lead to shallow, bland decisions on the one hand and deplete both leaders and their effectiveness on the other. That, I might add, is one of the weaknesses of OD—it encourages bastardized forms of "participatory democracy" in our institutions.

Last, the president must lead, not manage, and create for his institution clear-cut and measurable goals based on advice from all elements of the community. Then he must be allowed to take risks, to embrace errors, and to use his creativity to the hilt. Like the man on the white horse, some might say, although I don't agree. I'll settle for a dray horse. All I want to do is to get one foot in the stirrup.

About the Author

William Dowling has been the editor of *Organizational Dynamics* since it began publication in the summer of 1972. A Ph.D. in political science from Harvard University, he has been an adjunct professor at New York University, the Columbia University School of Engineering, and the Columbia Business· School. Before starting *Organizational Dynamics,* he edited a number of management publications.

Currently Mr. Dowling is also associate director of The Research Center in Career Planning at the Columbia Business School. He is the coauthor with Professor Leonard R. Sayles of *How Managers Motivate,* published by McGraw-Hill.